SHAKESPEARE SURVEY

SHAKESPEARE SURVEY

AN ANNUAL SURVEY OF
SHAKESPEARIAN STUDY & PRODUCTION

12

EDITED BY
ALLARDYCE NICOLL

Issued under the Sponsorship of
THE UNIVERSITY OF BIRMINGHAM
THE UNIVERSITY OF MANCHESTER
THE SHAKESPEARE MEMORIAL THEATRE
THE SHAKESPEARE BIRTHPLACE TRUST

CAMBRIDGE
AT THE UNIVERSITY PRESS
1969

PUBLISHED BY

THE SYNDICS OF THE CAMBRIDGE UNIVERSITY PRESS

Bentley House, 200 Euston Road, London, N.W. 1.
American Branch: 32 East 57th Street, New York, N.Y. 10022

Standard Book Number: 521 06425 2

First published 1959
Reissued 1969

*First printed in Great Britain at the University Press, Cambridge
Reprinted in Great Britain by Stephen Austin & Sons Ltd., Hertford*

EDITOR'S NOTE

The present volume of *Shakespeare Survey* is largely concerned with the Elizabethan theatre—the topic which formed the basis for discussion at the Shakespeare Conference, Stratford-upon-Avon, in September 1957. Of the articles printed here those by C. Walter Hodges, Richard Southern, Richard Hosley, Rudolf Stamm, Nugent Monck and Richard David are based on lectures delivered on that occasion.

For the next, the thirteenth, volume, the central theme will be the tragedy of *King Lear*. The latest date for consideration of articles for Volume 14 is 1 January 1960. Contributions offered for publication should be addressed to: The Editor, *Shakespeare Survey*, The Shakespeare Institute (University of Birmingham), Stratford-upon-Avon.

CONTENTS

[Notes are placed at the end of each contribution. All line references are to the 'Globe' edition, and, unless for special reasons, quotations are from this text]

List of Plates . . . . *page* ix

The Open Stage: Elizabethan or Existentialist? *by* GEORGE R. KERNODLE . . 1

The Lantern of Taste *by* C. WALTER HODGES 8

Was there a Typical Elizabethan Stage? *by* W. F. ROTHWELL 15

On Reconstructing a Practicable Elizabethan Public Playhouse *by* RICHARD SOUTHERN 22

The Discovery-space in Shakespeare's Globe *by* RICHARD HOSLEY . . . 35

'Passing over the Stage' *by* ALLARDYCE NICOLL 47

The Actor at the Foot of Shakespeare's Platform *by* J. L. STYAN 56

Elizabethan Stage-Practice and the Transmutation of Source Material by the Dramatists *by* RUDOLF STAMM 64

The Maddermarket Theatre and the Playing of Shakespeare *by* NUGENT MONCK . 71

Actors and Scholars: A View of Shakespeare in the Modern Theatre *by* RICHARD DAVID 76

Cleopatra as Isis *by* MICHAEL LLOYD 88

Shakespeare's Friends: Hathaways and Burmans at Shottery *by* C. J. SISSON . . 95

Illustrations of Social Life II: A Butcher and some Social Pests *by* F. P. WILSON . 107

International Notes 109

Shakespeare productions in the United Kingdom: 1957 119

The Whirligig of Time, A Review of Recent Productions *by* ROY WALKER . . 122

The Year's Contributions to Shakespearian Study

   1. Critical Studies *reviewed by* CLIFFORD LEECH 131

   2. Shakespeare's Life, Times and Stage *reviewed by* R. A. FOAKES . . . 140

   3. Textual Studies *reviewed by* JAMES G. MCMANAWAY 146

Books Received 153

Index 155

LIST OF PLATES

PLS I–IV ARE BETWEEN PP. 32 AND 33

I.   *A.* Exterior view of a model reconstruction, made by Richard Southern for the British Council in 1954, of a 16-sided Elizabethan playhouse
(Photo: British Council)

    B. Detail from 'A Village Fête' (1632), attributed to Pieter Breughel the Younger. Reproduced by permission of the Syndics of the Fitzwilliam Museum, Cambridge
(Photo: Fitzwilliam Museum)

II.   General view of the model reconstruction
(Photo: British Council)

III.   *A.* View of the stage taken as nearly as possible from the viewpoint of the De Witt sketch
(Photo: British Council)

    B. A street scene erected in Brussels in 1594
(Photo: Royal Library, Brussels)

IV.   *A.* The interior of the model, showing the stage as if seen by a spectator in the lowest gallery
(Photo: *The Times*)

    B. Sketch by Richard Southern showing the audience at a performance

PLS V–VI ARE BETWEEN PP. 106 AND 107

V.   Unascribed painting at Drottningholm Theatre Museum, showing a booth stage. About 1660, probably Flemish

    A. The complete painting

    B. A detail
(Photos: Beata Bergström)

VI.   *A.* A Butcher (*The Ages of Sin, or Sinnes Birth & groweth*).

    B. A Cokes (*A Pake of Knaves*)

    C. The Damee (*A Pake of Knaves*)

    D. Sweetlipps (*A Pake of Knaves*)

PLS VII–VIII ARE BETWEEN PP. 128 AND 129

VII.   *A.* Katharine's Vision. Engraving by William Blake
(Photo: British Museum)

    B. Katharine's Vision. *Henry VIII*, the Old Vic, 1958. Produced by Michael Benthall, designed by Loudon Sainthill
(Photo: Angus McBean)

ix

C. Wolsey, Katharine and Patience
Old Vic production
(Photo: Angus McBean)

VIII. *Twelfth Night*, Shakespeare Memorial Theatre, 1958. Produced by Peter Hall, designed by Lila de Nobili
A. The figure of Feste
B. Sebastian and Viola
C. Olivia, Malvolio and Feste
(Photo: Angus McBean)

THE OPEN STAGE: ELIZABETHAN
OR EXISTENTIALIST?

BY

GEORGE R. KERNODLE

Stage scenery—the visible image of the solid fabric of the universe—seems to be going out of fashion. The existentialist *avant garde* no longer see the universe as solid. The lone barren tree in *Waiting for Godot*—the one reminder of an objective world—is not substantial enough for a man to hang himself on. Williams' hot tin roof is a platform projecting into the audience's lap, with Brick, Big Daddy, and the Cat caught up in the glaring searchlight of a criminal investigation, with no walls around them and only insubstantial suggestions of ceiling and light shutters. Their souls are bare, perforce; there is nowhere even their faces could hide. Anouilh's Joan of *The Lark*, and the characters of Berthold Brecht, are living in no more substantial a world than the characters of Saroyan—they are demonstrations of an idea pieced together of fragments taken from many places and times. Hence they need only fragments for their settings. The arena stage, where ordinary plays are stripped bare, is the latest fashion.

The new way to play old plays is to put them on a bare open stage, with little or no setting. Hamlet at Stratford, Molière's Don Juan in Paris, Wagner's men and gods at Bayreuth, stand alone in spotlights or surrounded by phantoms of the mind. Black cloth creates a great formless void out of which the characters suddenly appear from nowhere, play their moment, and disappear into nothingness again. Is this just bringing old plays up to date? Or is it a return to the great open platform of Shakespeare's theatre? Is this a rediscovery of the one true way that the great ages have always produced plays, free from the ornamental trappings of baroque scenery? Leslie Hotson declares that the Shakespearian stage was the same kind of open arena stage surrounded by audience on four sides that we know. Modern arena productions have merely opened our eyes to the fact that this is the only great way to play. Richard Southern is bringing out books on the open stage in medieval and modern times. Alfred Harbage insists that we are recovering the true Shakespearian stage when we put the actor before the audience without the distraction of scenery. When he saw Jean Vilar present Molière and Shakespeare in Paris on an open platform, backed by solid black, he felt that at last the true stage had been found. Yet, tempting as it is to identify the past with the present, the analogy will not hold. The Shakespearian stage was not a blank open platform, on which a lonely soul was spotlighted in an empty, insubstantial universe. We have not returned to the Shakespearian stage, but have invented a new form of stage. We use a new form of stage because we want to say something quite different.

Jean Vilar's platform stage in Paris for this Théâtre National Populaire is not at all a rediscovery of the simplicity of the Renaissance theatre. It makes a modern existentialist character out of the classic hero. Molière's Don Juan against this eternal, timeless black becomes a sceptical modern lone soul before an earth and a heaven he does not believe in, meeting disconnected fragments of his irresponsible past, seeing incredible reminders of the celestial world that like lightning pierce through his black shell. He lives only in his inner mind and only half believes what he sees. He grimly sits unmoved when his father, his wife, and the figure of the statue itself break through the outer void to upbraid him. Even at the end, hell has no scenic reality, but is only the pulsing, flashing spotlight of his own mind. Finally the Don, like all the other phantoms, plunges into the darkness from which they come. There is no scenery because they tread in no real world. As Harold Hobson said, reviewing the production in London, "Their little lives—our little lives—emerge out of no past, and they vanish into no future. It is a solemn thought, and strangely moving, even if we philosophically deny its validity." Molière created no such grim lonely modern soul. His Don brazenly and gaily tried to deny all earthly and heavenly claims, but the scenery gave a solidity and continuity to the father, the wife, and the commander, and just as brazenly showed that those claims had a reality that could not be denied.

The Stratford Hamlet of 1956 was an even more lonely existentialist hero—a desperate individual wandering in a disconnected universe, a universe with no meaning or continuity of its own. He moved on a free open platform with only a black velvet background. One isolated dark piece of cloth hung from an undefined point in mid-air, obviously a mere device for the eavesdropping scenes. Here was no Denmark, no Middle Age, no tangible world at all, but only the lost modern soul standing exposed under a strong spotlight. There was no question of the King's guilt—he was merely one of the many disconnected figures that floated in out of the darkness from many directions and disappeared again into the meaningless void. There was no political question at all, as none of the figures that impinged on Hamlet had any continuity. Only the inside of Hamlet's mind existed—all else was fragmentary, flowing, unfocused. When Fortinbras arrived there was nothing for him to take over, unless he came to expose his own naked soul. Even Hamlet's costume, until the critics' protest grew too loud, was an anonymous shapeless black felt that made him look like a pathetic bell-hop disconsolately looking for his space ship. He was as much a lost tramp under the empty milky way as the two tramps of *Waiting for Godot*.

Such a production makes of Hamlet a very exciting, even terrifying, modern figure. But the effect is very, very different from what Shakespeare's audience saw. When Shakespeare spoke of something rotten in the state of Denmark, there behind the actors, unchanging during the whole play, was a symbol of the realm. When he spoke of the dangers to a state if a king is killed, there on the stage was a large, three-story symbol of the throne. When Ophelia or the King prayed, there was a large symbol of an altar-tomb, with a heavenly throne and an angels' gallery above. When Tamburlaine and Romeo defied the stars, there were the stars, very visible to the audience in a canopy-heavens.

Shakespeare's background was not the bare machine for playing imagined by twentieth-century scholars, themselves brought up in an age of functionalism. It was a complex symbol, combined out of several age-old medieval symbols. For centuries kings had been presented to the public, whether real kings in public ceremonies or actor-kings in plays and pageants, in a throne backed by a symbol of the realm. That symbol combined elements from the pageant-castles, from the city gates, from triumphal arches, from the choir screen of the church. The throne was framed by columns supporting a canopy, a 'heavens'—exactly the same kind of pavilion-canopy used to frame an altar or a tomb. Heavenly singers proclaimed the divine praises of the king, and often a figure of God sat on a heavenly throne to endorse the earthly king below. The Elizabethan stage had absorbed all these medieval symbols. Its background structure resembled a castle, a throne, a city gate, a tomb, and an altar. It was a symbol of social order and of divine order—of the real ties between man and king, between heaven and earth.

The true historical prototype of the modern open stage is none of the larger Renaissance theatres but the mountebank theatre that dates from the Middle Ages. That stage was free and empty, uncluttered by symbols of social or cosmic order for the simple reason that the medieval mountebank, peddling his snake oil and entertaining on the streets, was the first completely isolated individual. He had no place in medieval society. He was an outcast, a vagabond. Everyone else had a place—a set place—and all the other stages of the time had elaborate scenic symbols of the temporal order. Noah spoke from his ark, Herod from his throne. God spoke from a heaven firmly planted on the top of a tower or castle or mountain. Saints and Virtues spoke from windows and galleries, directly above the earthly stage of men. The Gothic people believed in the reality and solid continuity of the cosmic order, the political order, and the world of virtues and values. Their stages were more than platforms for actors; they were visualizations of their basic philosophy.

The Renaissance saw the emergence of the great individual—not a lone existentialist individual trying to create his own subjective values in a meaningless and fragmented universe—not a homeless medieval vagabond intruding on a street corner—but a confident, princely individual. The stages of the Renaissance were platform stages, but they all had very solid, three-dimensional symbols of order at the back of the open platform.

Marlowe's Tamburlaine stepped out onto the new open stage of London a free man, proud and glorious. He defied the fates, and broke all the bounds and limitations of medieval order. Medieval men had felt they were subject to an inexorable Fortune. But Tamburlaine bragged that he held the fates bound fast in iron chains and himself turned Fortune's wheel. He was at home on an open free platform. But he did not despise the institution of monarchy. His freedom consisted in the ability to make himself king of city after city. The imagery of the play is filled with references to crowns. There, at the back of his free open platform, was a stage façade that symbolized a king's throne, backed by a city-castle and topped by a heavenly throne. The very 'heavens' or canopy over Tamburlaine's platform stage was no functional roof to keep off London's rain but a symbol of great antiquity of the sacred dignity of a throne. Tamburlaine's glorious freedom was asserted in a series of scenes of conquest and coronations. That background symbolized in turn the different cities that he conquered, and each city served as a background for a coronation, of himself, his attendant kings, and his Queen. Tamburlaine could assert his individuality to the fullest because on his open platform he was backed by a colourful, banner-decked symbol of monarchical order.

Simon Eyre, the hero of Dekker's *Shoemaker's Holiday*, one of the earliest heroes of capitalism, had broken away from the bonds and customs of medieval economy. He did not remain a master-shoemaker supervising his shop-home of apprentices and journeymen. Like many another Englishman of the sixteenth century, he ventured into speculative trade. He bought a shipload of merchandise and became a very rich trader. But he did not break completely with his shop. He was free to step out of line as an individual, but the old institutions supported him. He was made Lord Mayor and gave a banquet for his faithful men, and the king himself came and sat at his table. Dekker found the Elizabethan stage a perfect expression of his play. At the back of the free open platform was a symbol of home, city, and king. Simon's family and men, his city, and his king all fostered and supported him in his emergence as a new free-enterprising individual.

In the next decade, the decade of Shakespeare's great tragedies, that old assurance of order seemed to be breaking up. Lear is cut off from his throne, his house, his ancient dignity, and thrust out of doors, out onto the empty forestage, huddled with a few lonely outcasts and fools. In that pelting storm even the heavens seem his enemy. Lear and Gloucester have turned the world over to a new generation, come from outer space, of cold, calculating, inhuman monsters. The very basis of human and divine order is questioned. But there before the eyes of the audience, as always implied in the imagery of the dialogue, stood the columns, castle gates, parapet-balcony, canopy-heavens that for centuries had symbolized the social and cosmic order —man and realm, earth and heaven. The Elizabethans could face some of the anguished loneliness that turns the modern Existentialists back into the inner mind, but their stage was no blank vacancy. It put behind Hamlet and Lear symbols of the order from which they were displaced. It implied order and meaning in the universe, even when the hero measured his tragic individuality against the faults of the old order.

As a symbol of a castle and a whole realm, the Elizabethan stage would have given *Macbeth* a unity that is not visible in modern productions or in modern editions. Editors since Rowe have led the reader on a wild goose chase through many separate rooms of Macbeth's castle. Followers of Chambers and Adams suppose eleven separate places for the action between the first-act and fourth-act witches scenes. The Elizabethans probably saw one continuous action on the way to and at Macbeth's castle. Duncan greeted Macbeth on the unlocalized forestage, and they all started to the castle—"From hence to Inverness". Immediately Lady Macbeth established the façade as Macbeth's castle. Duncan and his retinue came on the forestage in sight of the castle— "This castle hath a pleasant seat"—and Lady Macbeth met them and took them in. Servants came to indicate the activity of the castle itself. The street pageants had long established the convention that any of the activities of a ruler could be shown in front of or in the openings of a complete scenic castle. Even the murder of Banquo took place nearby. The murderers started back to the palace—"hence to the palace gate". Then the banquet was prepared—a variation of the throne scene, which in the street theatres was regularly set in front of a symbol of the whole castle. In the latter part of the play the scene shifted to Macduff's castle, after Macbeth announced, "The castle of Macduff I will surprise". When Malcolm and Macduff, on the forestage, spoke of being in England, away from the castle, there was no reason for supposing the façade England. If special banners or shields had been hung on it to decorate it as Macduff's castle, there was no reason for removing them. With the sleepwalking scene, the action moved back to Macbeth's castle, and the rest of the play showed Macbeth pushed back against his castle, besieged, or the enemy crossing the forestage, getting nearer and nearer for the siege. At one point Macbeth had special battle banners hung on the façade behind him—"Hang up our banners on the outward walls". At the end Malcolm took over as king, standing, like Fortinbras in *Hamlet*, in the centre of an enormous throne-canopy, before a castle symbol of the realm, beneath the symbols of divine providence.

In the same way, all the other stages of the Renaissance were combinations of an open platform with some synthesis of medieval symbols of order. The new stage of the Low Countries is an interesting case in point, especially as it represented a transitional stage of a society only partly breaking free from the tight medieval forms. The merchants of Dutch and Flemish cities were gaining some independence from the Hapsburgs and showing some interest in the new ideas of the Reformation. They were deeply interested in the liberating ideas of the Greek and Roman classics. They organized new clubs, 'Chambers of Rhetoric', that cut across the old Guilds of the Middle Ages, as their trade was breaking free from the Guild economy. But they did not develop a completely free stage. They put on their plays at great annual festivals—a social form half-way between medieval ritual and modern free capitalism. The audience did not come as individuals, as in London, freely choosing an afternoon's entertainment among competing theatres. All the members of a club came ceremonially, as a group, making a processional entry to the festival. The festivals were competitive—competition was already important in civic life. But the competition was between the clubs of different cities and was governed by elaborate rules and regulations. The festivals were not produced for profit, as a free commercial enterprise, but were free to the audience as a great civic display. They did not depend on the same play each year, as the great medieval cycles did. Now there was keen competition with the writing of new plays. But all the plays of each year had to be in answer to a single given question, and all used the same general area of biblical and classical source material. As the clubs were often combined with the painters' guild, and the Dutch and Flemish peoples were deeply interested in art, the kind of play evolved was like a dialogue between a lecturer and a learner on the free forestage, and a series of tableaux disclosed in the façade at the rear. Hence the stage was very similar to the Elizabethan stage—a free platform backed by a combination of medieval symbols—symbols of castles, thrones, arbours, altars, tombs, and the frames of separate tableaux. The whole emphasis was on the old background, not on the lecturer on the forestage. That lecturer had no real development as a dramatic individual. He was constantly tied to the background structure. As his words gave much of the meaning, the background could be progressively simplified. The Ghent stage of 1539 still resembled the castles and towers and arcades and altars that it represented. The façade for the Antwerp festival of 1561 was little more than a Renaissance frame for six tableau openings and a throne of Lady Rhetoric at the top. But the Elizabethan stage was much more complex and used a far wider range of scenes. In England at the end of the century, capitalism had reached the stage where the mixed public was rich enough and interested enough to demand new plays—almost a new one each week. The theatre was an independent enterprise and new geniuses did appear to write their full visions of the interactions of the individual with the changing cosmic and social order.

To compare the Elizabethan stage with the Spanish stage of the same time is to see the importance of that symbolic background. The Spanish stage used a whole series of curtains which, most of the time, covered the back structure completely. Behind the curtains was exactly the same kind of composite façade as the Elizabethan, with formal doorways, inner stage, upper gallery, earthly and heavenly thrones, and choirs of angels. It was used to represent thrones, and castles, and arcades of honour as on the Elizabethan stages. But all was covered over with curtains, to be disclosed only in fragments, one part at a time. It would take a psychoanalyst to explain fully why the Spanish, even as early as the sixteenth century, concealed that symbol of unity of the cosmos—a symbol that tied together throne, castle, city, realm, heaven and earth, God and king, angel and man, poetry and reality—why they felt the cosmic order should be visible only in fragments. In the Spain of Philip II, the world had already lost its simple unity.

A veil of illusion, a theatrical curtain covered it. For most of his scenes, the actor appeared in front of that concealing curtain, or made his entrance through it. We remember that Spain in the seventeenth century, more than any other country, developed the favourite baroque theme, "Life is a Dream", the title of Calderón's most famous play.

But the baroque theatre, the theatre that was to drive out all the simple platform theatres and dominate our stages to the present day, had a quite different way of dealing with illusion. The baroque solution was to admit the breakdown of the old unitary symbols of order, to express fully the sense of shifting, passing illusions in a series of painted settings leading up to a glorious descent of heavenly figures in heavenly clouds. That solution was the changing painted settings of the baroque operas, first worked out in the court masque. Occasionally in sixteenth-century Italian courts, but especially in the courts of Paris and London at the beginning of the seventeenth century, an elaborate changing setting, at the rear of the dancing and acting area, dramatized the magic power of the royal person in dispelling grotesque dancers and replacing horrid caves and barren wastelands by charming gardens and splendid thrones. The setting presented first the homely or the dangerous, and after three or four transformations always led up to the disclosure of the royal personage and his noble attendants. Then the King (or the Queen if it was a Queen's ballet) would step out of the setting—a great, dominating individual. But of course the court occasion was not intended to celebrate an isolated individual. The royal masquers emerged from the dynamic sequence of cosmic symbols and stepped out onto a free platform or dancing area—but they immediately stepped into the patterned circle of court dancers. For the basic intention of the occasion was to celebrate the cohesion of the social order, under the leadership of the royal court. The disorder and confusion, indicated by the quick changes of settings before the eyes of the guests, was immediately rectified by the royal arrival. The circles and other closed patterns of the dances celebrated the sure, if complex, patterns of social order. In the French Ballet de Cour, that disorder was often under the control of a wicked magician who was defeated by the arrival of the King.

The baroque opera gave a still fuller expression to the sense of changing, vanishing illusion. A typical opera made a wicked magician or a jealous goddess responsible for a dozen sudden changes in setting. The audience was relieved of responsibility and worry in a world that had lost its old sense of unity and order. It was all the fault of the magician. Then Jupiter, or a choir of Christian saints and angels, came floating down from heaven to defeat the magician and trumpet the triumph of the good. The more realistic nineteenth and twentieth centuries have omitted the heavenly clouds and given more materialistic weight to the painted picture, and have devised extremely elaborate machinery, including the motion picture projector, to keep the heavier, more solid settings on the move.

The baroque theatre did substitute a unity, a meaningful sequence in unfolding time, for the older Elizabethan structural unity in space. Change did evolve into splendour at the end. But time is the special terror of the mid-twentieth century. Few people study history or find any meaningful continuity with either past or future. In theatre and cinema the flashback and dreams and subjective fantasies have broken up even the orderly time sequence of the realistic play. Few settings of either solid realism or painted delicacy give much reassurance that the world outside each person has any meaningful reality and continuity. Films still keep closely tied to the most solid of settings. But the camera sends them flying by our eyes at vertigo speed.

A series of sordid settings, however solid, is not calculated to lure the soul to attachment to the outside world. The delicate veils and traceries of Mielziner gave the stage production of *Death of a Salesman* and *Streetcar Named Desire* more poetry and delicate overtones than the sordid settings of the screen versions. There is a little something to hold on to in that poetic if indistinct treatment of reality.

The modern arena stage is the poor man's Existentialism. It gives the average person a bit of familiar everyday reality to hold on to in the merciless ring of lights. Few are the people who feel the cold modern plight to be as desperate as it is shown in *Waiting for Godot*. Most are satisfied with the traditional realistic scenery of scientific materialism, or the picturesque painted settings of romanticism. They really prefer the warm protection of an enclosing setting. But in the arena theatre they can have it both ways. There is enough furniture to suggest the material surroundings of an everyday home. The playgoer is not dragged off to the top of the universe with a cosmic tramp. Yet he sees the actors walking in a room with all the walls torn down. He does feel a little stripped and bare in the glare of the spotlight—if not quite like a criminal, at least like a prize fighter in the ring trying to keep upright until the end of the round. The environment exists only as the actors use it—a chair, a table, or a fragment of reality in a corner—perhaps several unrelated fragments in different corners. Often the actors appear out of darkness and at the end disappear into darkness again. If that is more loneliness than the spectator wants to contemplate, he has only to look across the open stage and there is the crowd, lonely but compact, staring back at him, reassuring him that even if there is no meaning or structure to the universe, at least there is a closed circle of daily faces.

The popularity of Shakespeare in an Elizabethan setting in so many schools and summer festivals suggests that many people have not lost the old sense that a unified structure can reinforce a unified vision of a meaningful universe. One dare not hope that Shakespeare alone can recover for us the sense that there is order in the world. It may be very useful fully to dramatize on our bare black platforms our lonely terror of an empty sky. But let us not forget that the open stage was once used as part of a vision of man's central place in a cosmos of dignity and order.

THE LANTERN OF TASTE

BY

C. WALTER HODGES

The study of the history of theatrical presentation is very largely a study of the general digestion of cultural tastes. One is faced with, let us say, the ornate scenic operas of the late seventeenth century, or the coarse bravura of Victorian melodrama, or the lean, structural vigour of the Russian theatre of the 1920's. All these represent schools of taste, now more clearly distinguishable than they were in their own time, exerting and reflecting the influences of social cultures. What is not always so clear is the way in which trends of thought in the field of scholarship or research are themselves affected by these prevailing cultural tastes. The objective facts of historical study lie as it were hidden in a dark place, where students go to search for them, each carrying his own lantern. But each of their lanterns has its own quality, brightness or dullness or particular colour, each illuminates the subject a little differently, and each will give occasion to a different version of the truth. Thus reports given at different periods, or against different backgrounds, will tend, even upon identical material, to vary, sometimes widely, in accordance with influences of taste of which the scholar concerned may not even have been aware. This is particularly the case in such a work as the reconstruction of Elizabethan playhouses, since, as is well known, the hard facts available are insufficient in themselves, and the subject by its very nature is particularly rich in appeal to the imagination. Reconstruction thus tends to become a work of artistic creation on its own, and the beams of the various Lanterns of Taste flash like will-o'-the-wisps in the happy dark.

In the first place it can be seen that it was owing to the sudden development of a certain new theatrical taste, more than by any action of a Puritan Government, that drove the Globe and the other public playhouses into dissolution; and it was not until there arose, a century later, a taste among learned people for antiquarianism that any further notice was taken of it at all, and then not a theatre but as an antiquity, to be mused upon in the same fashion as Dr Stukeley was then musing upon Stonehenge and inaugurating a somewhat fanciful interest in Druids. It was in concert with this antiquarian movement of taste that Garrick descended upon Stratford for the Shakespeare Jubilee of 1769; that the house in Henley Street, hitherto unremarkable, began to be a place of pilgrimage; and that the cultured Mrs Thrale suddenly rose to the occasion with a recollection of having once seen what she thought were the Historical Remains of the Globe. Thus, too, at this time Edmund Malone widened what for him at an earlier date would most likely have been a purely literary study, to include some antiquarian speculations about Shakespeare's theatre in his *History of the Stage*. In all these things an essential ingredient was the idea of ancestral quaintness, which looked so attractive from the drawing room windows of the Age of Reason; attractive, that is, as the Chinese Empire was attractive, mighty fine at a distance. Thus began the thatch-and-groundling approach to the Elizabethan Theatre, which has remained one of its chief enticements for many people ever since, and which in England (but not in certain other countries, Germany for example, as we shall see) has had a strong influence upon our particular way of reconstructing the phenomenon of the Elizabethan theatre. And it is important to realize how unconscious such an influence can be. The best example of this is the famous and not-yet-settled controversy over the Inner Stage. To some scholars it still seems that this disputed place could be put to valuable use for indicating changes of scene in a play, either by the installation of actual scenery or by a pre-arrangement of properties. It is not the purpose of this essay to dispute these arguments as such, but only to point out that the tradition of considering an inner stage in this form and capable of this sort of adjustment arose directly out of a prevailing theatrical mode (for painted scenery is, after all, only a mode and not an order of theatrical nature) which has been up to now so exclusive that until recent times not even the most patent evidence to the contrary has been able quite to detach the imagination of editors from the idea that some sort of visual changeability would in the very nature of things have helped Shakespeare's audience to remove their minds from one part of a forest to another. This arose in the first place because no other kind of theatrical experience had been for a long while available. Malone himself was not able to bend his imagination very far from the theatrical conventions of his own day, so that when seeking an explanation for some admittedly oblique textual references to what we now know as the Elizabethan stage Heavens, he could only suppose an arrangement of "pieces of drapery tinged with blue...suspended across the stage": similar in fact to the sky borders he was accustomed to see in Garrick's Drury Lane.

But the way in which the light of particular tastes has tinted the study of the Globe can be well seen if we compare English and German attitudes towards reconstructions of it during the past century. The English attitude, springing from antiquarianism and passing thence through the romantic history-world of Sir Walter Scott to the nostalgic idea of Merrie England, has grown up with a taste for picturesque old towns, crooked streets, overhanging gables, leaded windows and old oak beams. At an earlier time, in Malone's day for example, there had been no taste for this sort of thing at all, apart from its association with quaint antiquity. As dwellings, such buildings were then thought boorish and detestable. But towards the end of the nineteenth century there was a movement of taste in favour of barns, windmills and cottages, and during the first decade of the present one the tide for half-timbered houses was running strong. Enthusiasts up and down the land were busy peeling off cottage wallpapers to reveal the long-forgotten oak beams beneath, and blacking them up both indoors and out to make them show up well, which in many cases was the last thing their original builders had ever intended, who had been so careful to render them over with concealing plaster. And as the taste grew, so new houses started to be built in the half-timbered style, with great ceiling-beams and corbels and ingle-nooks, contrary to the best economics of modern building, but faithful to the Edwardian pastoral dream of Merrie England, to G. K. Chesterton's England of the rolling English drunkard, to the England of the Folk Dance and Song Society, to the half-timbered England of Stratford and Ludlow and to the coloured counties of the Shropshire Lad. It was with the rise and full spate of this tide of taste that Lawrence and Archer and Poel and Granville-Barker were at work on the study of the Elizabethan theatre, and it was in this prevailing mood that they were led to pay so much attention to the theatrical uses of old half-timbered, thatched and galleried Elizabethan inn-yards, as being the inspiration of the first public playhouses. It was an inspiration more inspiring to themselves than to the Elizabethans, and had they not been so obsessed with their rustic woodwork they might have been more alive to the implications contained in the de Witt letter and sketch. This indicates, and one would suppose conclusively, some measure of baroque

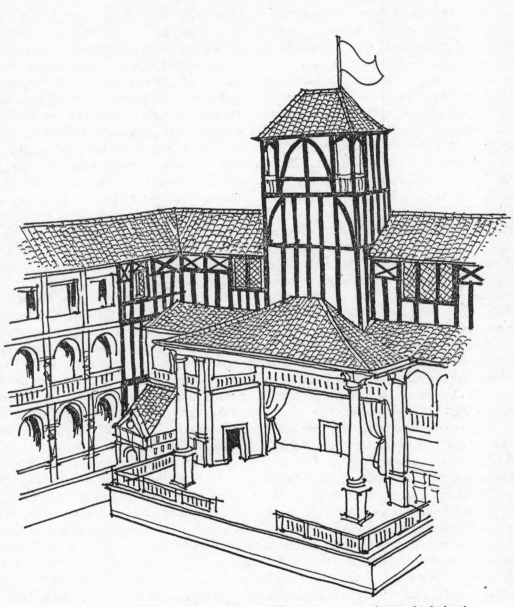

Fig. 1. Walter H. Godfrey's reconstruction of the Fortune, 1907. (Pen and ink sketch by the author, from the model.)

ornamentation; but Archer and Lawrence did not draw that conclusion. They were all for cakes and ale and mummers and nuts and hot codlins.

But in Germany the romantic taste was different. Half-timbered buildings, for example, are with them much more closely associated with farming or peasant life than with the atmosphere of an art movement. Also they have a much more lively tradition of popular baroque art and architecture than we have. They have therefore been much more easily inclined than we to think of Shakespeare as a baroque writer and his theatre as a baroque theatre. Is it only a coincidence that it was Karl Gaederz, a librarian from Berlin, who first drew attention to the de Witt letter with its strong baroque implications, and Wilhelm Creizenach, a Polish-German historian, who first pointed out the similarity of essential taste between the Elizabethan popular theatre and the baroque street theatres of the Netherlands at that time? And is it only a coincidence that these suggestions were disregarded in England at a time when English scholars were so surrounded by the flood tide of the half-timbered vogue that they could not see beyond it?

In this respect, then, we may compare two reconstructions, an English and a German one made from the study of the Fortune Theatre contract. Take first Walter H. Godfrey's reconstruction (Fig. 1), which was made at the height of the ingle-nook nostalgia in England. From a reading of the contract as well as from his wide knowledge of the architectural taste of the period, Godfrey seems to have derived a sense of baroque character, however modified, in the building, which he has delineated in the arched galleries, two pedimented doorways at the sides of the stage, and many details of panelling. Yet everywhere else, indeed wherever possible within and without, an abundance of black timbers proclaims the taste of 1907, the period of the reconstruction, and casts the strongest inn-yard atmosphere over the whole thing. Whether or not this was the most likely appearance of the theatre as it stood, it was for Walter Godfrey and William Archer, who had advised him on Elizabethan theatrical details for this reconstruction, evidently the then most satisfactory and heart-warming representation of it; and Granville-Barker selected it as the most suitable picture of such a theatre to publish in his *Companion to Shakespeare Studies* even as late as 1934.

But for an entirely different approach to the same subject take now Ludwig Tieck's rendering of the Fortune (Fig. 2) made as a drawing in concurrence with the architect Gottfried Semper in 1836. Some allowance must be made for the lapse of time between the two reconstructions, but even so the chief difference is that the instinctive approach here is from the direction of the baroque, as may be seen particularly from the dominant scroll work which crests the two flanking towers. This, be it noted, is a typical Elizabethan form, as at Montacute and Hardwick and Wollaton Hall and many other English places, but it took a German at that time to suggest it as an appropriate style for the Fortune. This by way of historical probability; but in so many other respects does this neat and logical design charm our imagination. It seems now to have everything that is necessary to a Shakespearian open stage, in a theatrically exciting and architecturally satisfying form. It is certainly a far cry from the original Fortune in some respects, but probably not more so than the Godfrey/Archer reconstruction, after all. Again, it is interesting to note that it has a certain resemblance in style to the Shakespeare Theatre built recently (1957) at Stratford, Ontario. And this may give us pause to reflect: for if in fact we do prefer this reconstruction to the other, it may only be because the wheel has come round again and this style of thing is now in accord with a special taste of our time. The lantern shines with our own light.

So far as the recent baroque interpretation of the Globe's style of decoration is concerned this may certainly be the case, since of recent years there has been a significant swing of taste in this

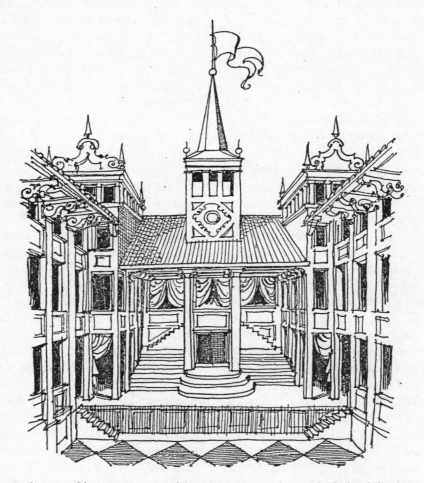

Fig. 2. Ludwig Tieck's reconstruction of the Fortune, 1836. (Pen and ink sketch by the author, from a reproduction of the original in the Munich Theater-museum.)

direction. In England this is marked in the designs of Rex Whistler and Oliver Messel; or in the flourish of parrots and pomegranates down the caryatid arcades where the Sitwell family have led the way; or even in the thorny protuberances of the paintings of Graham Sutherland. Elsewhere, as in the influence of Surrealism and in the later work of Picasso, the underlying style is still essentially baroque. All this may easily predispose us now to see certain adumbrations of a baroque character in Elizabethan theatrical documents which were always present though previously outside the reach of the prevailing vision. It may be that the pendulum will carry us too far in the other direction. In any case there is another factor that has to be observed, and it is one that will become very clear if ever a full-scale reconstruction of an Elizabethan theatre is built for performances. However much we may preach about the virtues of the open stage and the non-scenic theatre we are none-the-less, in fact, very dependent upon the stimulus of a satis-factory visual background, and it is unlikely that we should for very long be satisfied with one unchanging one, year after year the same. Commercial management would see its way to modify the style from time to time. Every now and again, instead of redesigning the scenery, it would be found appropriate to redesign the theatre. New developments in scholarship would doubtless give proper occasion for this. In the meantime, while reconstruction is still at the drawing stage, it must be confessed that a great deal of pleasure derives not from the single theatre but from the variety of ways in which it can be represented.

But the Lantern of Taste shines by fits and starts upon other things besides scenes and orna-ments. It guides the steps of actors and producers also, and their new movements in turn have effect upon the ideas we bring to the business of reconstruction. There is now no taste for a postured rhetoric in the speaking of verse. Actors today only at their peril work up towards the Big Speech, poise it and roll it forth, to be applauded at the end. This is ham. Neither are we content to wait between the scenes of a Shakespearian play while each set is got into position, beguiling the many intervals with pleasant anticipation. We have discovered how scene can follow scene like a pelt of peas, each coming so rapidly upon the heels of the one before that the corpse has hardly yet been dragged off on one side of the stage before the banquet has populated the other. This technique we have learned to like from the cinema. Combining the ideas of this new medium with the constructivist experiments of the early Russian revolutionary theatre, and taking a good hint from the medieval *décor simultané*, it has recently become popular in some quarters to describe the Elizabethan stage as a 'multiple stage', as Cranford Adams and his followers have done. To what extent this idea would be recognized or understood by an Elizabethan actor is debatable. Certainly it is partly, indeed typically, modern in its approach, as different in its own way from the happy-go-lucky conventions of the original Elizabethans as the folksy potted-shrub and inn-yard Art Nouveau ideas of 1910.

Thus we may review the trail of legacies that we have inherited to work from in recapturing the non-existent Elizabethan playhouse. First the antiquarian revival, dusting off the quaint old relic, bequeathing the idea of stiff homespun and bygone manners, an idea which recom-mended itself strongly to the later Victorians, and is indeed (as are all these ideas) partly true. Then the Timbered Cottage revival, during which a major part of the important groundwork of modern research was laid down, but which was predisposed by the light of its own prevailing taste to pay more attention than was useful or even justifiable to the notion that the Elizabethans were themselves so satisfied with their own picturesque timbers that they built their theatres to resemble the very inn-yards from which they were so glad to get away. Then the Cinema, the Experimental Theatre Movement and the Flow of Action, bringing the idea of the Eliza-bethan stage as a Machine for Acting. And now an ornamental baroque reaction against former primitivism, happily carrying into the Globe a lot of secondhand material from the supposedly nearby workshop of Inigo Jones. But which, if any, of these expressions of taste has the right to claim the centre of the picture, it is still for the unstable judgement of Taste itself to decide. And

13

if, as may be, all these ingredients are eventually amalgamated into a single reconstruction, the Shade of Shakespeare may be as surprised again as he was more than a hundred years ago on some other occasion, if the little sketch by George Cruikshank made at that time and reproduced below can be trusted as a salutory contribution to scholarship.

WAS THERE A
TYPICAL ELIZABETHAN STAGE?

BY

W. F. ROTHWELL

When Queen Elizabeth I visited Cambridge University in the year of Shakespeare's birth, 1564, Plautus' *Aulularia* was produced for her entertainment. The presentation of a Latin play before the Queen should not be, ordinarily, of particular interest; but the manner of production, in this instance, bears examination. Roman comedy, or an adaptation of it, generally calls for the representation of the houses of the characters on the stage; one might, therefore, expect the authorities at King's College, where *Aulularia* was given, to exert themselves in providing these houses for the actors. Such was common custom, if we are to judge from college account books and eyewitness reports of the period.[1] The producers at King's, however, did not act in the conventional way; instead of presenting the play, as tradition dictated, in the Hall (which proved to be inadequate for the occasion) they set it in the Chapel. A stage was built "in the body of the Church containing the breadth of the church from one side to the other, that the Chappeles might serve as houses. In the length it ran two of the lower Chapels full, with pillars on a side."[2] It may be noted that the houses were not on the stage itself, as we might think necessary and proper; they were off the stage right and left, and facing it. Moreover, there was obviously no attempt at providing 'Roman' or separate structures for the characters in the comedy. Perhaps from reasons of economy the college authorities acted as they did; but it does not seem to have crossed anyone's mind that the production was peculiar. The producers made use, after all, of whatever theatre and apparatus might be available. It is, therefore, perhaps likely that other producers of the period, especially the professional actors, may have been adaptable and flexible in a way that is difficult for us to understand. The belief, so widely held even today, that there was only one type of Elizabethan theatre, with its covered, raised stage, its 'inner stage' and balcony above, and its 'music room' above that, may have to be altered, as may also the belief that *all* of the plays were produced in the same way. A number of basic assumptions about the nature of the early Elizabethan stage, hitherto regarded as facts, have recently been questioned by some scholars.[3] A number of other assumptions may have to be re-examined before a clearer picture of Elizabethan staging conditions can emerge. Perhaps a view of the playhouses in which the actors performed before 1598, and the elements of setting with which they had to work, may throw more light on sixteenth-century theatrical practice.

It is evident that the dream of the Elizabethan player was to act before the Queen and her court; professionals had been doing so since the beginning of the century,[4] and would continue to do so for many decades to come. There was not only the anticipation of royal favour and, possibly, patronage, but also the prospect of comparatively superb theatrical working conditions. The actor would perform indoors, for one thing, and in one of the great halls of the royal palaces. Because of the size of the halls (Hampton Court, for example, measures 106 ft. by 40 ft., and is 60 ft. high)[5] there would not be much danger of a cramped acting area. Moreover, the delight of every actor, a raised stage, could be provided. The spectators, too, might be more perceptive than usual; though they might not applaud the broad strokes that appealed to the populace, they might respond to more delicate nuances of the actor's art. Lastly, the actors could expect a certain grandeur in the *décor*, provided by the Revels Office, a discussion of which will come later.

A number of actors, however, may never have reached the pinnacle of courtly success; and even those who did could not possibly hope to perform exclusively before the Queen. They had to act in public and, in London after 1576, they had at their disposition such theatres as the Theatre, the Curtain, the Rose, the Swan and, in 1599, the Globe.

Though the theatre at Hampton Court can be seen by anyone who takes the trouble to visit or look at photographs of it, such is not the case with the early public theatres. We have only one extant drawing of a theatre that existed in Shakespeare's lifetime, that of the Swan. It shows us a circular, galleried auditorium, a raised, roofed stage, two double doors in the back wall of the stage, and a gallery above them. Since the drawing does not fit in with the canonical view that *every* Elizabethan theatre possessed an 'inner stage' it has been often maligned. Moreover, Johannes de Witt described it as holding three thousand spectators, a number which seems to some scholars far too large. But the Arend van Buchell sketch is the only one we have of an Elizabethan playhouse *per se*, and unless it can be definitely proved that both De Witt and Van Buchell were lacking in probity, or given to fantastic flights of fancy, we must accept the accuracy of the drawing. Of the other theatres, built before 1598, we know little indeed. From the 'views' of London we gather that they were roughly circular or many-sided structures; we can guess that they, like the Swan, were not completely covered. Though Sir John Davies refers to the "thousand townesmen" who gathered about the theatre after the play was done,[6] we do not know exactly how large the playhouses were or how many spectators they accommodated. It is obvious that an acting area must have been provided, if possible in the form of a raised platform; and there must have been some means of getting onto and leaving the stage. As for the rest—silence. We cannot assume that every stage was covered, any more than we can assume that every theatre had an 'inner stage', a term that never occurs in the stage directions or texts of the plays of the period; nor can we assume the existence, always, of a gallery 'above', or of a third storey 'music room'. The references to music in plays produced before 1598 never refer to music 'above' but always to 'music' or 'music within'. I am aware that music within could also be above; but the writer or book-keeper or whoever wrote in the stage directions never places music 'above' even when he does place some of the action 'above'. Surely the fact that it was an age of experimentation tells us that the public theatres may have varied and that the actors, therefore, must have had to adapt themselves to whatever playhouses they found themselves in.

But the players could no more always act in the Swan or the Rose than they could at court. We know, of course, that they had recourse in London to the inns and, also, thanks to the recent research of C. T. Prouty, to certain guild halls, among which was Trinity Hall, hired from time to time during the years 1556–68. The hall itself measured 35 ft. by 15 ft. and was 17½ ft. high; there was a gallery at one end, beneath which were two entrances for the actors, who could have dressed in an area behind; and the gallery could have been employed as an upper or second-storey acting area.[7] The guild halls would often have made admirable theatres, depending upon size; how many were used, and whether they were available to the actors after 1576 is still unknown. They do not *seem* to have been as popular as the inns, if we can place reliance upon various official decrees issued in London during Elizabeth's reign;[8] and there are grounds for believing that the actors performed not just in the inn-yards, but indoors.[9] It was only after frequent recurrences of the plague, as the late T. S. Graves long ago noted,[10] that the actors were forced out into the yard; and despite the decrees, they sometimes risked trouble with the law and acted inside.[11]

When the players were obliged to perform outside they might find themselves in a temporary, rather crude theatre. We do not know that, in every case, they were provided with a raised platform; we do not know the size of the acting area which, of course, would depend upon the extent of the yard and the number of spectators present. But if, in many instances, the actors might be called upon to improvise a theatre, we do know that in one case they had a comparatively well-appointed playhouse provided for them. This was in the yard of the Boar's Head Inn.

In 1595 it was fitted out as a theatre. We know, as a result of subsequent litigation, that independent galleries for spectators were set up, having nothing to do with the ordinary galleries or verandahs running around the sides of the inn-yard. We also know that the Inn possessed a raised stage, with a covering over it, and two tiring rooms with a balcony above them.[12] But we cannot assume that all inn-yards were equally well fitted for the players, either in London or in the provinces. For the provinces were called upon to offer theatres for the actors, many of whom spent a good part of their lives upon the road.

Elizabethan touring conditions would no doubt stagger and appal the modern actor. Think of the bad roads, the possible infrequent meals of monotonous fare, the hostility of certain officials and clergymen, the crowding into often vermin-ridden beds, the general lack of cleanliness. Think also of the theatres the actors would encounter, and the ingenuity they would need to exercise in presenting their plays. One is reminded of Tucca's speech in *The Poetaster*, "If hee pen for thee once, thou shalt not need to travell, with thy pumps full of gravell, any more, after a blinde jade and a hamper: and stalke upon boords, and barrell heads, to an old crackt trumpet".

Possibly the best theatres would be found in the great halls, similar in type if not in grandeur to those of the royal palaces, the halls in the country houses of gentlemen and noblemen. If the hall possessed, as many did, a screen at one end, the actors would find a ready-made acting area, together with a place for changing their costumes (we must remember the doubling of roles and the resulting need for quick changes), and perhaps a gallery above the screen entrances. The guild hall, if the town had one, might offer like advantages; but the rooms would sometimes be small and hence would afford a very limited acting space. So with the inns themselves and, occasionally, the churches.[13] At least these were all indoor theatres; they might be stuffy, small, inadequate, the acoustics might be terrible, but they protected the actor (and his costumes) from the weather. They must have been infinitely preferable to the out-of-doors, in the inn-yard or perhaps at the market cross.[14]

If, from the foregoing summary, one is struck by the variety of theatres in which the actors had to perform, what of the perhaps equally varied ways of producing the plays?

Anyone who has ever glanced at the Revels Accounts must have conjured up all sorts of glamorous visions of plays presented before the Queen. Indeed, that the productions were elaborately mounted is evident. We do not, however, know exactly *how* the stage was set with the various 'houses' and 'cities' so often mentioned in the Accounts. There is the possibility, suggested by Leslie Hotson, of arena staging, in which the stage was placed in a central position and set with houses of a lattice-work type.[15] There is also the possibility that the stage was placed at one end of the hall, or at least against a wall, as was the custom in Italy and perhaps France,[16] and, occasionally, at those adjuncts of the court, the Inns of Court and certain colleges.[17] But exactly where the stage was placed (perhaps we should not assume it was always placed in the same spot) must remain a mystery for the time being, as must the type of house provided by the Revels Office. We do not know whether all of these houses were three-dimensional, as they were for the miracle and mystery plays, or two-dimensional perspective flats in the Italian manner. Certainly if one examines staging requirements of the court plays, together with the Revels Accounts, it is evident that some of the houses must have been acted in, while others need have been only façades—in other words, they were practicable or decorative. Perhaps a blending of the two was attempted and achieved. At any rate there was an effort at conveying a depiction of the locale that the action required. Think of such scenic pieces as "Orestioes howse Rome",[18] the "prison for Discord", the gibbets, rocks, arbors, pavilions, the trees for "A wildernesse in A playe",[19] and the battlements,[20] so useful for scenes of siege and assault. Moreover, there are the devices for the heavenly ascents and descents, such as the "coard & pullies to draw vpp the cloude"[21] and, at the other end of the cosmos, the survival of the medieval tradition is shown in the "hell, & hell mouth".[22] The actors must truly have revelled in such *décor*. But how would they adapt themselves when they departed for the Theatre, say, or the Swan or the Rose?

Surely the idea that Elizabethan public theatres presented a gloomy atmosphere and a barren stage has been exploded. Anyone familiar with the Elizabethan love of display and exuberance would agree that the theatres must have been as 'gorgeous' as their enemies described them. And in the matter of setting, Henslowe's papers provide us with a list of hand and scenic properties (belonging to the Admiral's Men) that closely corresponds to many of those noted in the Revels Accounts. Only the scenic properties are here listed: one rock, one cage, one tomb, one hell mouth, one tomb of Guido, one tomb of Dido, one bedstead, one pair of stairs, two steeples, one Tantalus tree, two coffins, one wheel and frame "in the Sege of London", one frame for a beheading, one bay tree, the City of Rome, one wooden canopy, one rainbow, one little altar, the cloth of the sun and the moon, two moss banks, "Belendon stable", one tree of golden apples, one "syne for Mother Readcap", and one cauldron.[23] Obviously the Admiral's Men had something to work with when it came to setting their stage at the Rose; and is it too much to suppose that other acting companies also possessed these, or similar, scenic properties and devices? The evidence supports such an assumption; it is known that the Revels Office borrowed a cloud device from an unidentified public theatre for the season of 1578–9,[24] and it may well be that a number of companies, or entrepreneurs, possessed a stock like that belonging to the Admiral's Men.

But it must be true that the public theatres could not match the display at court. When one considers the financial problems of the companies, what else can be expected? Moreover, whereas at court a number of houses might and could be provided for a play, the actors in the public theatres might have to do with one, perhaps a house or booth set up on the stage, the appearance or nature of which could be changed in accordance with the words of the actor or by the properties set within or about it. A neutral booth could be altered, by the addition of a tomb, into a mausoleum, by the addition of a bedstead into a bedchamber, by the addition of an altar into a chapel or temple, and by the addition of steeples, perhaps affixed to the exterior, into a church or even a city. In the same way although at court a forest of trees might make a wilderness, in the public theatres one tree might have to symbolize a wood.

Yet all the companies may not have had a large or even middling stock of properties. In some theatres, inns, and inn-yards the erection of a booth may have been difficult, if not impossible; and cramped acting areas may have made the use of scenic properties problematical. Economic difficulties may also have prevented elaboration of the stage in the London guild halls; and of course, so far as the provincial playhouses are concerned, there would often be a paucity of properties at hand or in the actors' luggage. Setting the scene, then, would depend almost entirely upon the ingenuity of the actor, with help from the descriptive passages of the playwright, from the costumes, from stage conventions, and from the imaginations of the spectators.

Let us imagine that the actors are performing a play that calls for an assault on the walls of a besieged city. At court, there are battlements provided, inspired perhaps by certain elements of *décor* for the masques, such as the "Pallys Marchallyn" (prepared in 1515, with timber reinforced by iron) which possessed towers "embattled, keystyd, inbouryd, and dormanddyd".[25] The court battlements for the plays would hardly be as large as the "Pallys", which measured 36 ft. by 28 ft. by 10 ft., but at least they may have been practicable and have looked like castle walls. At the public theatres, if the battlements exist they must perforce be of smaller size. But let us imagine that a particular company has no battlements at all; what does it do? If it acts at the Swan, it can assail the double doors or, better still, the gallery, supposing it to be comparatively free of spectators. But perhaps the actors perform in a theatre with no built-in gallery; there is, however, a booth erected for the performance, decorated for the occasion with steeples, and the actors can assault it. At Trinity Hall, and in halls possessing a gallery, the latter can serve for walls. But imagine the company to be in dire straits indeed: the performance is to be given in a small provincial inn. Here the actors must exercise all their ingenuity and imagination and, furthermore, the spectators must exercise theirs. The battlement can be improvised by placing a bench on top of another, for the scene is necessary to the action, and the play must go on; accordingly, the locale is simulated symbolically. If a company, on the other hand, has a play calling for the ascent into heaven of a divinity, what does it do? At court there is no problem; and some, at least, of the public theatres have devices for ascents—there is the throne in the 'heavens' which Henslowe installed at the Rose.[26] It is not too difficult, either, to rig up pulleys, even though they may creak, as Ben Jonson notes; and perhaps, in the provinces, the actors may go so far as to set up a device in the ceiling of a room in a guild hall—they may have done so in Barnstaple, where there is a record of money spent for "amendynge the seelynge in the Guildhall that the Enterlude players had broken doune".[27] But if no makeshift is possible, then the actors must simply let the 'divinity' walk off the stage. One should not forget the direction at the end of Greene's *Alphonsus King of Aragon*: "Exit Venus. Or if you can conueniently let a chaire come doune from the top of the stage and draw her vpp." And Greene was not the only playwright (or book-keeper) to have doubts about the theatres and scenic equipment available to the actors. We have such other directions as that in *John a Kent and John a Cumber*, to indicate the entrance of an Antic "out of a tree, if possible it may be"; and from

The Tragical Reign of Selimus there is the telling line, "Suppose the Temple of Mahomet". Moreover, there is help for the actors in the words of the author as he paints the scene, and especially in the convention of costume. So, if a rural landscape is to be the locale, it is indicated (in *Locrine*) by the stage direction "Enter Strumbo with a pitchfork"; a change of scene, indicating also a journey, is implied in the line (from *James the Fourth*) "Enter Sir Bartram with Eustas and others, booted"; and a tavern is noted (in *An Humourous Day's Mirth*) by the entrance of "Verone with his napkin vpon his arm". And so ingenuity, adaptability, imagination, and convention would all help to set the stage, depending upon the theatres available.

The theatres themselves may have been square, oblong, circular, or many-sided, small, middle-sized, or large, covered or uncovered, public, semi-public, or private, secular, clerical, or commercial. We cannot even assume that the public theatres were all similar in appearance, equipment, or size. So it is with the manner in which the plays were staged; at court, elaboration; at the public theatres and perhaps at the inns, adaptation, more or less elaborate, depending upon the *décor* available; in the other theatres, especially those of the remote countryside, a reliance upon ingenuity in the actor and imagination in and acceptance of conventions by the spectator.

Elizabethan England was, after all, a country in transition, politically, economically, socially, religiously; it was also an era of change and experimentation in matters dramatic and theatrical. Why, then, should one expect, before 1598, to find every public theatre equipped with a raised, roofed stage, and an 'inner stage' with gallery above, and a 'music room', any more than one would expect to find indentical methods of production throughout the length and breadth of the kingdom?

NOTES

1. See especially G. C. Moore Smith, *College Plays Performed in the University of Cambridge* (Cambridge, 1923), p. 28, for reference to houses at Queens' College, Cambridge, in 1522-3; Lawrence E. Tanner, *Westminster School* (1934), pp. 123-5; Richard Southern, 'The "Houses" of the Westminster Play', in *Theatre Notebook*, III (1949), 46-52; W. Y. Durand, '*Palaemon and Arcyte*...as Described by John Bereblock (1566)', in *PMLA*, xx (1905), 502-28; and the *Malone Society Collections*, ed. W. W. Greg (Oxford, 1923), vol. II, part II, p. 159.

2. See John Nichols, *The Progresses and Public Processions of Queen Elizabeth* (1823), I, 166.

3. The work of C. Walter Hodges, in *The Globe Restored* (1953), is of great value; and of particular interest is George R. Kernodle's *From Art to Theatre* (Chicago, 1944), and Leslie Hotson's *The First Night of Twelfth Night* (New York, 1954).

4. John S. Brewer, ed., *Letters and Papers, Foreign and Domestic, of the Reign of Henry VIII*, vol. II, part II, p. 149.

5. Edith M. Keate, *Hampton Court Palace* (1932), p. 170.

6. See *The Complete Poems of Sir John Davies*, ed. A. B. Grosart (1876), II, 18.

7. C. T. Prouty, 'An Early Elizabethan Playhouse', in *Shakespeare Survey*, 6 (1953), 65-71.

8. See, for example, the Decree of 12 May 1569, noted by Harrison in his *The Description of Britain*, and quoted by T. S. Graves, *The Court and the London Theatres during the Reign of Elizabeth* (Menasha, Wisconsin, 1913), p. 33.

9. Letters in 1582 between the Earl of Warwick and the Lord Mayor had to do with an application of one John David to play his prize at fencing in a room of the Bull Inn in Bishopsgate. The Mayor refused permission, sending him to perform in an "open place" in "the Leaden hall" (see Graves, *op. cit.* p. 36); there is no question of a play; but the Bull had been known for dramatic performances as early as 1578 (E. K. Chambers, *The Elizabethan Stage* (Oxford, 1923), II, 380-1) and David would have surely been allowed to perform in the yard there had it been fitted as a theatre. Obviously it was not; the actors perforce played inside.

10. Graves, *op. cit.* p. 40.

11. Chambers, *op. cit.*

12. See C. J. Sisson, 'Mr. and Mrs. Brown of the Boar's Head', in *Life and Letters Today*, xv (1936–7), 99–107.

13. See William Kelly, *Notices Illustrative of the Drama and Other Amusements at Leicester* (1865), p. 14, and E. N. S. Thompson, *The Controversy between the Puritans and the Stage* (New York, 1903), who notes a complaint of Cartwright to the effect that the clergy rattled through the service as quickly as possible, in order to see the afternoon sports or to make room in the church for an interlude.

14. John Bale tells us his plays were presented at the market cross in Kilkenny. See his *Writings*, ed. John S. Farmer (1905), p. 303.

15. See Leslie Hotson's *The First Night of Twelfth Night* for complete accounts.

16. I am thinking of the drawing of the performance of the *Ballet Comique de la Reine* in 1581. A reproduction of this may be found in Hodges' *The Globe Restored*, plate 39.

17. At Gray's Inn, in 1594, a stage was erected "at the side of the hall" for the performance, according to the account in Nichols' *Progresses*, III, 281. And Leslie Hotson notes in 'Shakespeare's Arena', in *The Sewanee Review*, LXI (1953), 354, that a stage was set up in the *parte superiore* of the hall of Christ Church, Oxford, in 1564.

18. Albert Feuillerat, ed., *Documents Relating to the Office of the Revels in the Time of Queen Elizabeth* (Louvain, 1908), p. 119.

19. *Ibid.* pp. 158, 200, 244, 200, 349, and 180.

20. *Ibid.* p. 320.

21. *Ibid.* p. 397.

22. *Ibid.* p. 140.

23. See *The Henslowe Papers*, ed. W. W. Greg (1907), pp. 116–18.

24. Feuillerat, *op. cit.* p. 308.

25. Brewer, *op. cit.* II, 1503–4.

26. *Henslowe's Diary*, ed. W. W. Greg (1904), part I, p. 4.

27. See John T. Murray, *English Dramatic Companies 1558–1642* (New York, 1910), II, 198–9.

ON RECONSTRUCTING A PRACTICABLE ELIZABETHAN PUBLIC PLAYHOUSE

BY

RICHARD SOUTHERN

The following is an attempt to estimate how far our present knowledge allows us to reconstruct a 'typical' Elizabethan public playhouse sufficiently authentic to permit practical study of production.

I. THE SHAPE AND SIZE

It is clear that all Elizabethan theatres were not built on the same-shaped plan, since the Fortune was square while to most others the adjective 'round' is applied. But what does 'round' mean? Both a circular building and a polygonal building may reasonably be said to be 'round'.

The problem is reviewed by I. A. Shapiro in *Shakespeare Survey*, 1 (1948), 25, and 2, 21 ff., and his final decision is in favour of a circular building. But there is a qualification, made by Shapiro himself, which must not be overlooked; he is perfectly ready to state on p. 22 of the second article "it does not follow that because the outer walls were circular the inner walls were necessarily circular also". Indeed a playhouse frame incorporating curved timbers so as to give a circular interior is something that an investigator may find himself regarding with increasing scepticism as he works on it, because there is so obviously a cheaper and more practical solution which (as it seems to me) meets the evidence all round. It is that straight timbers were used but that the frame was built with sixteen (or maybe more) sides (Pl. II).

Thus we produce an inner structure where the timbers are of convenient length (average 12 ft. long); where, though a polygonal character is present in the interior, yet the whole effect is such as to be quite legitimately called 'round'; and finally which presents us with an exterior that, even were it not a circular flint-stone wall but made up of, say, sixteen flat faces, would yet offer to a draughtsman (such as, for instance, Hollar), drawing a view from a distant steeple on a sunless London day, a circular effect (see Pl. IA). William Poel, in his model (1897), and J. H. Farrar, in the Topham Forrest reconstruction (1921), came to the same result.

What now is the size of the ground plan? This is not so easy to decide. The sole evidence we possess is from the Fortune contract, but there is a difficulty about this evidence, namely that it relates to a square theatre. The facts are as follows: the Fortune contract specifies five figures relating to plan-size

    (a) the frame of the house was to be 80 ft. square outside,
    (b) and 55 ft. inside,
    (c) the first 'storey' was to be 12 ft. 6 in. deep,
    (d) the stage was to be 43 ft. wide,
    (e) the stage was to extend to the middle of the yard.

From this we perhaps tend to think unjustifiably that all Elizabethan stages were 43 ft. wide and all Elizabethan theatres 80 ft. in diameter. But I would go so far as to say that, in my view, we must give up one or other of these two figures if we seek to plan a 'round' theatre—we must make the stage narrower or we must make the house wider.

I have tried to illustrate this matter in the diagram, Fig. 1. It shows, in thick lines, the plan of the Fortune and (so far as it goes) shows the plan exactly according to the information of the contract. (We might almost say it is remarkable in that it is a diagram of an Elizabethan theatre that possesses no element that is conjectural!) But I have then superimposed a polygonal plan

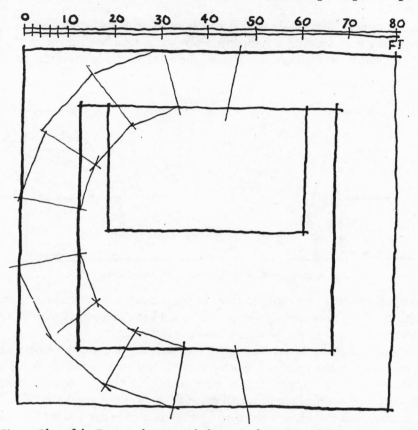

Fig. 1. Plan of the Fortune theatre, with diagram of a sixteen-sided theatre imposed.

upon it; we at once see how much space we lose by cutting off the corners, how much we have reduced the capacity of the building and crowded too close on the stage. Let us now construct another diagram to show the effect of this crowding-in on the stage.

In Fig. 2 we incorporate the dimensions of the contract which relate to heights. There are four specific figures:

(a) the foundations were to be made at least 1 ft. above the ground,
(b) the first 'storey' was to be 12 ft. high,
(c) the second 11 ft.,
(d) and the third 9 ft.

Let us set these up in relation to the square Fortune plan and we have what is shown on the right-hand side of Fig. 2. We can take a further step and, since we know the width of the yard, we can set up the opposite galleries on the left of the diagram. But we have to enter into conjecture when we add the stage, for its height is not specified.

Suppose we follow Walter Hodges's lead and put in a fairly high stage, say 5 ft. 6 in., and then represent upon the stage, and well to the side, an actor to scale (see Fig. 2). It will already be apparent to a student of theatrical sight-lines that it is going to be fairly difficult to see that actor from the adjacent upper gallery. We may define how difficult by estimating a height for the railing of the gallery and drawing a sight-line from the actor's head through the top of this railing. To any spectator on the right of that line the actor is totally invisible.

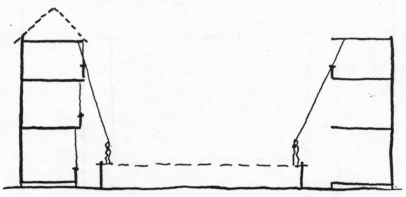

Fig. 2. Suggested section through the Fortune theatre.

But we have still omitted one complicating factor, namely the mysterious 'jutty forwards' of 10 in. in 'either' of the two upper galleries. If, on the left gallery in Fig. 2, we represent this (as far as we can understand it) the problem becomes still greater.

Some people claim that the Elizabethans ignored such disadvantages. At present I am not concerned to take sides in the matter; I merely state that, if you built a 43 ft.-wide stage in a sixteen-sided theatre (where this problem is most acute), then any extension of the diameter of the frame *beyond* 80 ft. would help those gallery sight-lines; or, if you built an 80 ft.-diameter sixteen-sided theatre, then a *narrower* stage than 43 ft. would fit better and would also help those gallery sight-lines.

To speak in figures, I would ask for at least a 92 ft.-diameter polygon round a 43 ft. stage, or at most a 31 ft. stage inside an 80 ft. polygon (of sixteen sides).

2. THE DETAILS OF THE FRAME AND AUDITORIUM

In the details of the frame, the Hope contract (relating incidentally to a 'round' theatre) offers us more information than the Fortune contract, since it gives us the dimensions of many of the timbers. The following classes of timbers are specified:

Inner principal posts, by which we understand the posts supporting the galleries on the inner, or yard, face;

prick-posts, for which see below;

breastsummers, which are horizontal beams spanning an opening on a façade—as for example the stretch of gallery-front between two posts;

binding joists, by which we understand horizontal transverse timbers, running from the inner face to the outer face of the frame and binding the two faces together.

What is least clear in the above is the position of the prick-posts. The *New English Dictionary* defines prick-posts as "...the posts in a wooden building placed between the principal posts at the corners. Also the posts framed into the breastsummer, between the principal posts, for strengthening the carcass of a house." Thus one's first inclination is to put the prick-posts on the inner face, supporting the middle of the breastsummers between pairs of principal posts, but there are three observations to be made here. First, it is obviously undesirable to have more posts than necessary on the inner face since any post is likely to trouble spectators. Secondly, the length of any breastsummer in a sixteen-sided frame of 55 ft. diameter is only some 10 ft. long and seems to need no centre support. Thirdly, the Hope Theatre was related to the Swan Theatre in shape; we have De Witt's sketch of the interior of the Swan, and in that sketch there is a very curious feature about the columns in the galleries, namely that there are shown *more* columns in the voids above the balcony-fronts than against the balcony-fronts themselves. Perhaps in so rough a drawing one may be little inclined to credit minor discrepancies. But there is also a major discrepancy here. At the 'ingressus' steps *where the gallery front is cut away*, there is *still* shown a post descending to the level of the top of the front but stopping there. It must, thus, either stop in mid-air or be situated some way within the frame and stop on one of the degrees inside. This would appear to be more than a 'discrepancy' and to amount to a deliberate statement of fact, for the same thing happens in cruder drawing on the right-hand side of the sketch. One explanation would be that De Witt saw two rows of posts, one on the façade, and one within under the binding joists.

I am well aware of the tenuity of this reasoning, save in one incontestable point—that is that a post *is* shown at the steps which does *not* stand on the balustrade, and therefore (as I believe) cannot be an 'inner principal post' but could be a prick-post set half-way back in the gallery, and thus the prick-posts would be posts intermediate between the inner and outer faces of the frame (see Figs. 3 and 4 and Pl. IVA).

It is not specified whether the heights of the galleries are to be reckoned in the clear, or as between floor and floor; in the latter case we should have to deduct a figure for the thickness of floor and joists. A modern architect might suppose the former to be the more likely, but there is one important fact to be noticed.

In specifying the dimensions of the plan, the Fortune contract gave 80 ft. as the outside measurement of the building, and 55 ft. as the inside measurement across the yard. Subtract one from the other and we get 25 ft. to be occupied by the two galleries—that is 12 ft. 6 in. exactly, as the depth of the galleries. Thus, on plan-measurements it is certain that wall-thicknesses were *not* deducted, and measurements were thus not given in the clear. It seems likely, then, that the same system would be used of vertical measurements, and if so then the heights of the galleries are to be taken as from floor to floor.

Each gallery contained seating. This is shown in De Witt's Swan (on which theatre the Hope was based), and specified in the Fortune contract.

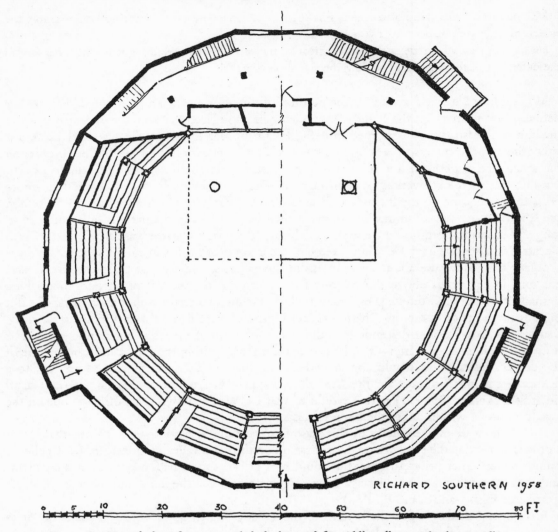

RICHARD SOUTHERN 1958

Fig. 3. Conjectural plan of a sixteen-sided playhouse: left, middle gallery; right, lower gallery.

The lowest gallery—some 10 ft. 10 in. deep (that is 12 ft. 6 in. less the thickness of two 10 in. posts or walls) and some 11 ft. 2 in. high (that is 12 ft. less a 9 in. deep binding joist and a 1 in. thick floor-board)—would just accommodate five rows of seats (at 2 ft. 2 in. intervals), stepped on degrees for better viewing of 1 ft. 2 in. high, thus leaving 6 ft. 6 in. headroom on the top degree (see Fig. 4).

The second gallery—11 ft. 8 in. deep (that is the depth of the first gallery plus a 10 in. jutty)— is not so easy to seat, although it actually offers more floor space than the first gallery, because the seat degrees here have to be stepped more steeply if any view of the stage is to be possible, and the clear height is now only 10 ft. 2 in.; therefore only three risers of 1 ft. 4 in. would already bring us to 6 ft. 2 in. from the joists above. The resultant four rows of seats would leave 3 ft. of space unaccounted for at the back of the gallery (see Figs. 3 and 4). (In these calculations, a 5 ft. 6 in. high stage is postulated, with a 10 ft. 6 in. gap between it and the first gallery front.)

The top gallery is either 11 ft. 8 in., or 12 ft. 6 in., deep (according as we read the jutty of 'either' upper gallery to mean 'both together' or 'one in succession to the other'). Here the seating problem is still greater; we have only, presumably, 8 ft. 2 in. headroom, and the seat degrees must be very steep—one 2 ft. 6 in. step alone brings us to 5 ft. 6 in. below the joists, which might be just tolerable to an Elizabethan. The resultant two rows of seats take up only 4 ft. 4 in., leaving the remarkable space of either 7 ft. 4 in. or 8 ft. 2 in. of this gallery unusable for seating! (see Fig. 4).

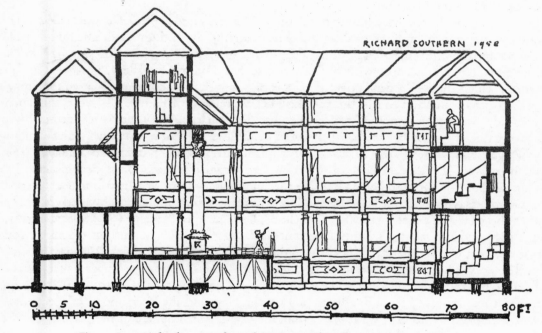

RICHARD SOUTHERN 1958

Fig. 4. Longitudinal section through Fig. 3, incidentally suggesting details of the hut as a two-storey source of flying effects.

At first the above offers a considerable problem to the investigator, but fortunately it can be straightened out fairly adequately upon the considerations which follow.

To begin, let us study a fresh point. Quite apart from the seating, both contracts specify something else to be included in the galleries, namely "divisions" or "particions". In detail, the Fortune contract asks for "ffower convenient divisions for gentlemens roomes, and other sufficient and convenient divisions for Twoe pennie roomes", and the Hope contract for "...two Boxes in the lowermost storie fitt and decent for gentlemen to sitt in; And shall make the particions betwne the Rommes as they are at the saide Plaie house called the Swan".

Here we have to make some guesses. The four Gentlemen's Rooms at the Fortune may be similar to the two Boxes fit for gentlemen at the Hope; if so they would be in the lowest gallery.

The partitions between the Rooms at the Hope may be similar to the convenient divisions for Twopenny Rooms at the Fortune; if so, they would imply that some parts at any rate of the galleries here also were subdivided, or even partly enclosed—in other words, were something like rooms as we know them today (even to the point that the ceilings were plastered).

Lambard's "penny at the gate" in *The Perambulation of Kent* presumably let a visitor into the yard. His "another at the entrie of the Scaffolde" might seem to support a supposition that the *Twopenny* Rooms were (like the Boxes or Gentlemen's Rooms) in the first gallery. But another interpretation is possible; that Lambard's second penny gave entrance not to the first gallery alone, but to the scaffold (or frame) in general and thus, it seems, to *any* of the galleries. Therefore the middle gallery at any rate may have consisted of Twopenny Rooms also, and thus have been partitioned like the first.

Now, was the third gallery similar to the others? Here a puzzle arises. De Witt labels the two rooms by the stage in his lowest gallery *orchestra*, or seats of the distinguished. The middle gallery (and presumably the remaining portion of the lowest gallery not shown in his sketch) is *sedilia*—lesser seats. All this accords with our progress so far. The upper gallery, however, he labels *porticus*, which means "a walk covered by a roof supported on columns"—an ambulatory or strolling-place. But add to this the very cryptic last remark of Lambard's—your third penny you paid "for a quiet standing". Now, because of the particular system of collecting by successive gatherers in an Elizabethan playhouse, it follows inevitably that the "quiet standing" (whatever it may mean) was *beyond* the Twopenny Rooms, since it cost an *additional* penny. But it can only have been 'beyond' them in one of two directions in the circumstances; that is above them or through them—outside the playhouse frame. Was there, in fact, anything outside the playhouse frame? Oddly enough, two prints (though one possibly derives from the other) bear evidence that there was. The Globe, both in Speed's view (*Shakespeare Survey*, I, Pl. VIIIB) and in Delaram's James I portrait (*ibid.* I, Pl. X) shows a curious extension round its lower part outside the first gallery. Can this contain the 'quiet standing'? It may be so; but another possibility, it would seem, is strongly hinted already; that the upper gallery was not 'Rooms' but the 'quiet standing'. The *porticus* suggests standing as well as strolling. It was quiet in that it was removed from the distractions of the play, and the interruption of spectators. It was overlooked by no one, yet it was within the exciting atmosphere of the play. Therefore it was (exactly like the gallery slips of the eighteenth-century playhouse) eminently suited for the special purposes of popular gallantry.

However this may be, our argument about the seating is unaltered: the first gallery could contain five rows, the second four, the third two. This is the practical limit, however the remaining space might be used. And, it should be noted, this is not because any theory of sight-lines lays down that it should be so, nor is it an arrangement that could be improved by having a still wider theatre. It is simply *because the galleries are not high enough to allow headroom for more degrees.* And whatever we do not know about the theatre, we do know the gallery heights.

With this definite conclusion let us now turn to look more in detail at the partitions. Study of diagrams shows that, speaking generally, any partitions among the audience would be a nuisance if they reached ceiling-high. Such partitions would most likely radiate from the 'inner principal posts', cutting the gallery into a series of wedges (see Fig. 3), and, for reasons of vision, would almost certainly not be more than about elbow-high (see Fig. 4 and Pl. IVA).

There are, however, two places where we might expect a variation. These are in the Gentlemen's Rooms on either side of the stage. The Hope contract refers to these as 'Boxes'. This may suggest more seclusion and thus higher partitions. But if the Gentlemen's Rooms were indeed provided with ceiling-high partitions, it would be inconvenient to have them, like the others, radiating from the principal posts, because thus the occupants of the boxes would be set to face the centre of the theatre, not the stage; and all but the very front occupants would lose sight of any balcony scene. It would seem better to turn these partitions to point more towards the back of the stage, thus giving a sense of obliquity as opposed to the radial 'wedges' of the Twopenny Rooms (see Fig. 3 and Pls. II and IV A). Here it may or may not be relevant to note Jonson's allusion in *The Magnetick Lady* (1632) to "the oblique caves and wedges of your house". By chance perhaps, this is exactly what we have produced.

A further point. In the middle gallery, though dwarf partitions radiate from the posts, yet we should notice that a full ceiling-high partition *could* come all round at the back of the fourth row of seating, because beyond this is (so far as we have discovered at present) waste space. This would make the wedges still more resemble 'rooms'. (And incidentally make our 'waste space' quite dark.)

We have shown that we do not suppose the top gallery would come under the appellation 'rooms'. In that case it would not be partitioned.

Having reconstructed our galleries so far, the next point profitable to consider is access. Access to the yard itself was possibly by a short passage traversing the frame at a point facing the stage (Pl. II). You paid a second penny to enter the 'scaffold' or galleries, and De Witt very obligingly informs us exactly where you entered. He shows two flights of *ingressus* steps directly next to the orchestra boxes. But, if these boxes were flanked by a ceiling-high partition, a good half of the people in the Twopenny Room directly adjacent to them would be unable to see the stage fully (Fig. 3). Thus the steps here seem placed in an admirable position, otherwise unsuitable for the use of spectators.

These steps, we suppose, led up to the top seatway of the first gallery; after which a spectator might pass along this seatway right round to the front of the theatre, provided the inter-room partitions stopped at the fourth row of seats (an arrangement which is exactly adopted in Georgian theatre side boxes), and take his place in whichever room he fancied. Thus access is provided to the lower gallery generally.

To reach the middle gallery a staircase would be needed. It is interesting to notice that both contracts specify staircases as being 'without'. The Hope contract says "two stearecasses without and adioyninge to the saide Playe House in such convenient places, as shalbe most fitt and convenient for the same...". What are these "convenient" places, whose convenience is twice mentioned in one phrase? Hollar's view shows them some eighth of the way round the house from the front, on either side. If we so place them on our plan, we find they occupy the bay next to the stairs, Fig. 3. (At first one is puzzled that they should not come fully opposite the stairs, and thus flank the house symmetrically. But Hollar distinctly says not.) Upon proceeding up them to the middle gallery, we see why; for we emerge into what at present we have admittedly left as a dark, waste space (this we shall clarify with a later piece of evidence), but we *do* emerge at an excellent strategic position, namely behind the centre of the demi-lune of seating—with three bays to our right and three to our left. Undoubtedly this is the most fit and convenient place to discharge people into the gallery on entering, or to collect them as they prepare to leave. And, once again, it is a sensible piece of planning.

The upper gallery is reached by a further flight in the same staircase tower.

Finally, we have to consider the access to the Gentlemen's Rooms. These (probably with the special charge of Twelve Pence) were approached not through the common yard but from the tiring-house. This is easy enough to arrange if we partition-off, at their back, a short corridor from the tiring-house. (Such a corridor would, incidentally, connect the tiring-house with a point near the head of the *ingressus* steps and, if it were provided with a door there, would allow actors to enter the auditorium and approach the stage from the side by 'vaulting' the stage rails.)

Next, let us consider the possibility of lighting all these 'rooms', stairs, and 'conveyances'. In our arrangement, daylight adequately reaches all parts of the galleries save two—the corridor to the Gentlemen's Rooms and the space round the back of the middle gallery. (To these we should perhaps add the staircase towers outside the frame, into which, however, it would be easy to build windows.)

Now look at Hollar's exterior of the Globe. The stair-towers are obscured by trees, but apart from them windows are visible in two places. First in a ring, running round the centre of the theatre at the level of the middle gallery (cf. Pl. IA). To the best of our belief these could illuminate nothing but the underside of the middle-gallery seating *unless* our ceiling-high partition was a fact, and our waste space a well-lit corridor of access, with doorways opening out of it up steps into each room, exactly like the box-corridors in a modern opera house (Pl. II).

Thus our project fits all into natural place, save for the last detail of the dark, short, Gentlemen's-Room corridors either side. These would be cut by a chord taken through the house parallel with, and somewhat in front of, the tiring-house façade. The second, and only other, position in Hollar's exterior where we find windows is exactly at this particular point, where two are shown close together, just visible above the tree-tops. They thus come exactly at the sole remaining place in the auditorium where we could else provide no light; in other words, at the sole remaining place where, if our reconstruction be correct, windows would be required (see Pl. IA).

3. THE INTERIOR AND THE STAGE BACKGROUND

First, concerning the interior decoration in general, we should remark that since there was no proscenium arch or front curtain, there was consequently no visual separation of the background of the stage from the surrounding auditorium. In fact the stage was within, and part of, a unity which consisted of the galleries and passages of the theatre—some of them for the principal use of actors, some of them for the principal use of spectators, but all jointly used. Even the stage was used by both, and hence the stage entrances must have been used by audiences on occasion, while the balcony over the stage was a sort of recognized no-man's-land, shared quite indiscriminately by Lords or Players as the exigencies of the show demanded (Pl. IVB). Thus the whole was a unity.

In considering the decorative character of this complex unity, I am inclined to be influenced by three things. First, I believe that such details of columns as De Witt shows indicate the Renaissance style (the Renaissance style was already used in England for interior architecture as early as 1533—for example, the stalls in King's College, Cambridge), and that since the first public playhouses were novel buildings, put up commercially and dependent on attracting public favour, they therefore had to be 'up-to-date' and—at any rate so far as their superficial decoration went—in the 'latest style'. This style was that of the Renaissance. Again, many stages and triumphal arches had been erected in Holland before 1596 that were already thoroughly Renaissance in style.

Secondly, I am influenced by a number of direct references which allude to the theatres as being 'painted'. Thus, Edmund Spenser opens *Thalia* with a question beginning—

> Where be the sweet delights of learning's treasure,
> That wont with comic sock to beautify
> The painted theatres...?

and in a letter from Gabriel Harvey to Edmund Spenser, we read of—

> sum newe devised interlude, or sum malt-conceivid comedy fitt
> for the Theatre or sum other paintid stage.

Both 'stage' and 'theatre', then, could receive the epithet 'painted'. In addition we have Van Buchel's statement, accompanying De Witt's sketch in his commonplace book, that the London theatres were *visendae pulchritudinis*. And there are many such comments, both from friends of the theatre and from enemies.

Thirdly, I am (perhaps most of all) impressed by the categorical statement of Van Buchel's that the theatre interiors were rendered *ob illitum marmoreum colorem, nasutissimos quoque fallere possent.*

The case seems proved for a colourful interior with early-Renaissance columns, and with false marbling (Pls. IIIA, IVA and IVB).

As to the style of the marbling, there are wooden columns painted to imitate marble on several of the pageant cars in Van Alsloot's painting of The Triumph of Isabella. The marbles chiefly represented would appear to be *vert antique, sienna*, and a white marble.

Coming now to our major problem—the one on which we have least unequivocal information—the tiring-house façade; we must, if we reconstruct the theatre, make some decisions. We cannot omit an area and write 'doubtful' in its place. And the line I have taken may very well prove ill-advised, but it is only fair to state what it is: I feel that since we have so little positive evidence about the façade, it would be well to establish all we could about the kinds of popular stages in use just before, and in, this period—both at home and over the Channel—such a stage, indeed, as Burbage's company might have used in the inn-yards and elsewhere before he built the Theatre in 1576. I have named the kind of stage I have in mind 'The Booth Stage'.

The essence of the Booth Stage, as I see it, is that it possesses (*a*) a platform of boards on temporary supports, which can be raised fairly high for performances in the open air before a standing audience (with possibly, though not inevitably, a curtain or hanging to surround that platform below and hide the supports); (*b*) a 'booth', or curtained space, at the back of the platform, probably composed of four uprights at the corners, with four cross-bars connecting them to hold the surrounding back and side curtains and (*c*) the front curtain, generally not drawable but arranged so as to provide three entrances: that is, the actor could enter at either side by slipping round the edge of the curtain, or in the centre by parting a central slit between the two halves of the curtain. (*d*) The top of the booth is left open, or, at any rate, some possibility is offered of playing over the top of the front curtain—often by means of a ladder behind it. (*e*) A flight of steps may occasionally be seen, by which actors can descend from the platform to the ground where the audience stand.

The above, again as I see it, is a relatively highly organized stage, in that it is evolved in all details to offer the simplest, but fullest and most practical variety of settings and effects that the performances of the time could demand. There may be slight variants, but in the main I would be prepared to suppose this was the pattern of the normal travelling stage of the Middle Ages, and the source of the stage in the Elizabethan playhouse.

To explain its development into the Elizabethan playhouse one has to make only the simplest modifications; the slightly awkward entrances round the edges of the curtain may become regular doors; the curtain itself remains between them, but is capable, on particular (and relatively rare) dramatic occasions, of being parted in the centre to disclose a small discovery-space; and the primitive method of playing upper scenes from the top of a ladder set behind the curtain gives place to a rigidly-built balcony running from side to side. Here (but for some small development in the elaboration of brought-on or 'thrust-out' furniture and properties) we would appear to have the full technical system of the most developed Elizabethan or Jacobean public playhouses.

The illustrative evidence for the above is to be found as follows: For the first phase—the primitive Booth—see the sketch of a stage in Cambrai Library, said to date from 1542; also the many variants of the painting attributed variously to Pieter Balten and to Pieter Breughel the younger (for example, that in the Fitzwilliam Museum, Pl. IB); further, the stage in Scarron's *Comical Romance*, and that in one of the designs in Callot's *Balli di Sfessania*. For the second phase —intermediate developments toward the elaboration of the public playhouse stage—see Van der Meulen's painting in the Liechtenstein Gallery, Vienna; a similar painting in Drottningholm Theatre Museum (Pl. VA, to be described below); and the etching by Van der Venne reproduced in *Theatre Notebook*, IX (1954), 5 ff., and *The Times*, 8 September 1953. For the third phase—in the playhouse itself—we have no farther to seek than our old, controversial friend, the frontispiece to Kirkman's *The Witts*. All these stages are intimately related as regards technical form and practicalities, and (as it seems to me) tradition and development.

With such an approach we may perhaps begin to feel inclined to interpret the salient problem of the De Witt sketch—namely the blank, centre wall between the doors—on the supposition that De Witt visited the theatre when the play being performed was one (of the many) which do not happen to call for use of a discovery-space, and thus the central curtain or arras was never parted in his presence, with the result that he supposed it a mere decorative hanging against a solid wall. Otherwise his general scheme is entirely within this tradition.

As for developing, now, the architectural detail that he indicates so slightly, there is a print of a street stage in Brussels, of 1594, which shows a façade in style so very conformable to De Witt's that I have taken from it the few developments needed to bring his sketch into line with the description of the theatres which accompanies it (see Pl. IIIB for the print, and for the description of the theatres see *Shakespeare Survey*, 1, 23 f.).

PLATE I

A. EXTERIOR VIEW OF A MODEL RECONSTRUCTION, MADE BY RICHARD SOUTHERN FOR THE BRITISH COUNCIL IN 1954, OF A 16-SIDED ELIZABETHAN PLAYHOUSE

B. DETAIL FROM 'A VILLAGE FÊTE' (1632), ATTRIBUTED TO PIETER BREUGHEL THE YOUNGER (FITZWILLIAM MUSEUM)

PLATE II

GENERAL VIEW OF THE MODEL RECONSTRUCTION

Details of gallery seating are illustrated in the cut-away to the right. In the foreground are
represented the foundations

PLATE III

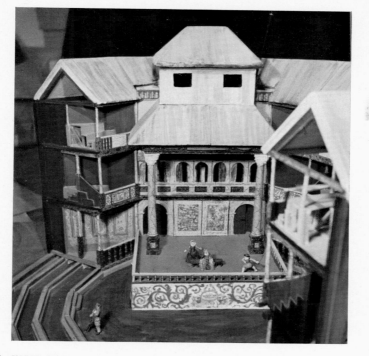

A. VIEW OF THE STAGE TAKEN AS NEARLY AS POSSIBLE FROM THE
VIEWPOINT OF THE DE WITT SKETCH

B. A STREET SCENE ERECTED IN BRUSSELS IN 1594

PLATE IV

A. THE INTERIOR OF THE MODEL, SHOWING THE STAGE AS IF SEEN BY
A SPECTATOR IN THE LOWEST GALLERY

B. SKETCH BY RICHARD SOUTHERN SHOWING THE AUDIENCE
AT A PERFORMANCE

I owe to Agne Beijer the privilege of reproducing, I believe for the first time, the painting in Pls. VA and VB, in which the stage is so interesting as to warrant a brief description.

The painting is in oil and is undated and unsigned. It bears some likeness to a similar subject in the Liechtenstein Gallery, which is by F. van der Meulen and represents Brussels about 1660.

The stage, seen to the right of the middle distance, is enlarged in Pl. VB. We see a high platform, possibly between 6 ft. and 7 ft., and upon it a shallow booth with a roof falling to the back. The façade of the booth is what is so exceptionally interesting; it consists of four white-and-gold uprights, forming three intervals of which the centre is wider than the others. The top

R.S.

Fig. 5. Sketch showing possible interpretation of the references to 'two doors' and to a 'middle' or 'farther' door. (See W. J. Lawrence, *The Physical Conditions of the Elizabethan Public Playhouse* (1927), pp. 16 ff.)

is framed across with a sort of fascia-board, covered with green material embroidered in gold. Between the uprights hang three green curtains, apparently not capable of being drawn (at any rate as far as concerns the side ones) because entering figures have, as we are shown, to drape them aside. The notable feature of the curtains is that they do not reach the full height of the uprights, but leave a gap at the top of some 4 ft. to 5 ft., exactly corresponding to the openings of the 'upper stage' of a conventionally restored Elizabethan public playhouse. Through the gap, the dark interior of the booth is plainly seen.

Suspended above in the centre opening is a whitish, oblong shape. So far as I can ascertain, this now bears no traces of lettering, but some hazy suggestion of a frame or border seems visible—was it a 'locality-board'?

The platform itself, besides its seven actors, bears two other interesting items; on the right-hand side are two members of the audience sitting on the stage; and from the adjacent stage 'door', a table and a chair have been 'thrust out'—indeed, the action of the player behind the chair might well mean that we have here an actual picture of a piece of furniture caught in the act of being 'thrust out'.

This street stage contains in essence every feature we believe to have been necessary in a play-house stage, and contains them very simply and without straining. It would appear not equipped for flying-effects, and perhaps not for trapwork, but apart from these 'sensations', we could present upon it any play out of the classic range of Elizabethan drama.

Couple now this picture with the Van der Venne print (again showing a low curtain), and add them to the Brussels print of 1594, and we are able to develop the Swan sketch to the kind of reconstruction shown in Pl. III A and in my print in Pl. IV B, where I have endeavoured to give, also, something of the impression of the massed audience, as well as of the possible lighting effect which might result if the sunlit actors played opposite an auditorium in shadow, and against a façade upon which the 'shade', or 'cover', partly cast its own shadow. Further, the print adds a point to the model-reconstruction by recognizing that, if the stool-holders occupied the part of the stage shown, the floor of the Gentlemen's Rooms would have to be raised above that of the rest of the lower gallery, to permit any view across to the stage. And finally, opportunity is taken to incorporate a *projecting* (instead of recessed) discovery-space, of the sort shown in the Van der Venne print in which the canopy and curtains might well serve for the discovery of, say, a throne.

Thus far, then, it seems justifiable to go in reconstructing a practical Elizabethan theatre upon the evidence at present available to us.

THE DISCOVERY-SPACE IN SHAKESPEARE'S GLOBE

BY

RICHARD HOSLEY

This paper[1] proposes the theory that the tiring-house of the First Globe was essentially similar to that of the Swan as pictured in the De Witt drawing of 1596. Thus the Globe tiring-house would have been equipped with two (or three) double-hung stage-doors. (Probably there were three rather than two doors, but since the problem of discoveries is essentially the same in the one case as the other we may leave the question temporarily undetermined.) Each door (since as wide as high) would have been some 7 ft. or 8 ft. wide and (since hinged on the outside) would have opened upon the stage. When fully opened, either door (or a presumptive third door) would have discovered a considerable space within the tiring-house; and this space might have been discovered by drawing aside curtains instead of opening a door if we accept the expedient of fitting up hangings in front of the open doorway. Such a 'discovery-space' (behind an open doorway in the tiring-house façade) must be distinguished in what follows from that other kind of discovery-space known as the 'inner-stage'.

I

The Elizabethan 'inner-stage', as commonly reconstructed, may be defined as a curtain-covered recess in the tiring-house wall, measuring some 7 ft. or 8 ft. in depth and 20 ft. or more in width, and persistently used for actions localized in 'interior' scenes (since these occasionally require such properties as beds, tables, chairs, and the like).

The first thing that strikes us about this 'inner-stage' is that the term itself apparently never occurs in Elizabethan documents. Moreover, there does not seem to have been a generally employed alternative term. Perhaps the closest we can come to it is the periphrastic "*middle of the place behind the Stage*" in which a "*brazen Head*" is to be set in Greene's *Alphonsus King of Aragon* (*c.* 1587). Without question this is important evidence for the Elizabethan discovery-space. However, the term is not quite the same as *inner-stage* (in fact it is quite different), nor does it necessarily imply the sort of playing-area usually understood by that term. For example, it may well designate the space behind a middle door in the tiring-house wall. Again, the term *study*, occasionally used in Elizabethan stage-directions calling for discoveries, designates a discovery-space only when a study is required by the fiction of the play in question. In other fictional situations the discovery-space is referred to as a *shop*, a *tent*, a *cabin*, a *tomb*, a *closet*, a *porch*, a *countinghouse*, and so on.

Next we may recall that the concept of an 'inner-stage', though occasionally regarded as a fact, is no more than a theory by which a number of investigators since the early nineteenth century have sought to explain the 'internal' evidence of discoveries in Elizabethan dramatic texts. That evidence is capable of alternative explanation. And so is the 'external' evidence of contemporary pictures showing tiring-house curtains. For example, the 'curtains' in the *Roxana* vignette may well be hangings fitted up along a tiring-house wall. In fact there is no un- ambiguous evidence whatsoever for an Elizabethan 'inner-stage'.

Finally we may note a theory that the proscenium arch 'evolved' through gradual enlarge- ment of a proto-alcove we have come to know as the 'inner-stage'. But this theory may not be invoked to support that of an 'inner-stage' without lapse into circular argument. In any case it is probable that the proscenium arch, as its name implies, originated through enclosure of the stage itself—the *proscænium*. This is the theory proposed by Richard Southern in *The Open Stage* (1953).

With these considerations in mind we may approach the question whether there was an 'inner-stage' in Shakespeare's Globe (always understanding by this term the elaborate recessed playing-area referred to above). Since there is no relevant external evidence, we must depend on the internal evidence of the plays. Here let us confine our attention to a group of plays designed for performance presumably at the Globe and in no other theatre. These are the thirty extant plays first performed by the Chamberlain-King's Men between the spring of 1599, when the Globe was built, and the autumn of 1608, when the King's Men may have begun using the Blackfriars as well as the Globe.

A scene-by-scene examination suggests that twenty-one of these thirty plays were produced without a single discovery or 'concealment' (deliberate closing of a discovery-space so as to hide a player or property from view of the audience): *As You Like It, Every Man out of his Humour, Henry V, Julius Caesar*, and *A Warning for Fair Women* (1599); *Alarum for London, Hamlet* and *Twelfth Night* (1600); *All's Well That Ends Well* (1602); *The London Prodigal* and *Sejanus* (1603); *The Fair Maid of Bristow, Measure for Measure*, and *Othello* (1604); *King Lear* (1605); *Macbeth* and *A Yorkshire Tragedy* (1606); *Antony and Cleopatra* and *The Miseries of Enforced Marriage* (1607); *Coriolanus* and *Timon of Athens* (1608). (The dates are approximate, and the other nine plays in the group are listed on pp. 43-4 below.)

If the reader will tentatively accept this proposition, we may follow one of its implications to a conclusion. Twenty of these twenty-one plays have actions localized in interior scenes. (The exception is *Alarum for London*.) Yet over two-thirds of these interior actions were demonstrably produced without discovery or concealment. It follows that there was not an 'inner-stage' at the Globe, for if there had been it would presumably have been used in these twenty plays.

That the twenty plays here referred to were produced without discovery or concealment is suggested by absence from the substantive texts of any stage-direction or dialogue calling for or implying the opening or closing of curtains or other discovering agency. In the past, proponents of the 'inner-stage' theory have met this difficulty by recourse to two assumptions. The first is that Elizabethan dramatic texts are largely deficient in directions for staging. It is true that a few texts are without stage-directions and that others occasionally lack an important direction, either because the text in question was printed from a manuscript to which the direction had not been added or from which it had been excised, or because the direction was omitted in the course of printing. But by and large Elizabethan dramatic texts are well-furnished with stage-directions. Not, generally, with such as are sometimes supplied in present-day texts "in order to help the reader visualise the action": "*After she leaves the room, X throws himself down in a chair; he lights a cigarette and sits puffing abstractedly as—the curtain falls.*" But, generally, with such as will account for the salient needs of Elizabethan production: "*A bed thrust out*", "*Enter X above*", "*X arises in the midst of the stage*", "*Enter X at one door, Y at another*", "*X draws a curtain discovering Y*", and so on. Since it cannot be demonstrated, the assumption that evidence is largely missing from our texts cannot be refuted; but for the same reason it may be rejected with impunity.

The other assumption is more important. It is that the unqualified term *Enter* in Elizabethan stage-directions can mean 'is discovered', a sense not recorded by the *Oxford English Dictionary* and not current in the modern theatre. (Occasionally the term *Enter* does seem to have borne the sense 'is discovered', when qualified in the direction by allusion to a discovery-space, as in Marlowe's *Doctor Faustus*, "*Enter Faustus in his Study*"; or in dialogue by the requirement of discovery, as in Fletcher's *Sea Voyage*, "*Sure this Curtaine will reveale. Enter Albert*".) In the nature of things this assumption (like the one concerning evidence) is not capable of demonstration; hence in the nature of things it also may be rejected. Throughout Elizabethan drama the unqualified term *Enter* seems to have retained the full force of its Latin original (*introire, intrare*) in implying the idea of motion: "To go or come into...; to pass within the boundaries of..." (*O.E.D.*). The unqualified term *Exit* seems also to have retained its original meaning (*exire*) suggestive of motion.

(I do not press the interpretation that the unqualified terms *Enter* and *Exit* generally meant no more than 'comes on stage' and 'goes off stage', for this is a conclusion of the present argument, and in any case we are here concerned only with an assumption occasionally invoked to explain the absence of a certain class of evidence. But in passing I would point out that once these terms are accepted at face value we may suppose that practically all 'entrances' and 'exits' in Elizabethan drama were walk-ons and walk-offs.)

The argument against an 'inner-stage' at the Globe is based not only on absence of evidence for discovery or concealment in these twenty-one plays. There is also occasional evidence in stage-directions that the players walked on stage at the beginning of actions localized in interior scenes; and if so the actions in question did not begin with discoveries. 'Walk-on directions' (as they may be called) have occasionally been noticed by editors and other commentators, but they have not, apparently, been noticed systematically and their significance has been largely ignored by investigators of the 'inner-stage' persuasion. They are of several kinds, the following list including all examples noted at the beginning of interior actions in the twenty plays under discussion. Scene-locations in inverted commas are by Kittredge or Gifford, otherwise by the present writer.

One kind of walk-on direction involves reference to doors:

(1) *Henry V*, v, ii (F): "*Enter at one doore, King Henry, Exeter, Bedford, Warwicke, and other Lords. At another, Queene Isabel, the King, the Duke of Bourgougne, and other French*" ("The French King's Palace").

(2) *Antony and Cleopatra*, III, ii: "*Enter Agrippa at one doore, Enobarbus at another*" ("Caesar's house").

(3) *Timon of Athens*, I, i: "*Enter Poet, Painter, Jeweller, Merchant, and Mercer, at severall doores*" ("Timon's house").

(4) *Ibid.* III, vi: "*Enter diverse Friends at severall doores*" ("A banqueting hall in Timon's house").

Another kind calls for bringing on stage a "sleeping", "injured", "dead", or otherwise non-ambulatory player:

(5) *A Warning for Fair Women*, sc. 19 (sig. G4 in Q): "*Enter John Beane brought in a Chaire, and master Barnes, and master James*" (a room).

A third kind calls for bringing properties on stage:

(6) *Coriolanus*, II, ii: "*Enter two Officers, to lay Cushions, as it were, in the Capitoll*" ("The Capitol").

(7) *Timon of Athens*, I, ii: "*A great Banquet serv'd in*" ("A room of state in Timon's house").

A fourth kind calls for a player to enter and immediately seat himself (instead of being discovered seated):

(8) *A Warning for Fair Women*, sc. 21 (H3v): "*Enter some to prepare the judgement seat to the Lord Maior, Lo. Justice, and the foure Lords, and one Clearke, and a Shiriff, who being set, commaund Browne to be brought forth*" (a court of justice).

(9) *Othello*, I, iii (Q): "*Enter Duke and Senators, set at a Table with lights and Attendants*" ("A council chamber").

(10) *Coriolanus*, I, iii: "*Enter Volumnia and Virgilia, mother and wife to Martius: They set them downe on two lowe stooles and sowe*" ("A room in the house of Marcius").

And a fifth kind of walk-on direction involves qualification of the verb *Enter* by a participle or adverb expressing the idea of motion:

(11) *A Warning for Fair Women*, sc. 25 (K1): "*Enter Anne Sanders and her keeper following her*" (inside a prison).

(12) *Every Man out of his Humour*, IV, i (Q): "*Enter Fungoso, Fallace following him*" ("A Room in Deliro's House").

(13) *Ibid.* IV, ii: "*Enter Deliro, with Macilente, speaking as they passe over the Stage*" ("Another Room in the same").

(14) *Ibid.* V, vi: "*Enter Deliro, Fungoso, Drawer following them*" ("A Room at the Mitre").

Evidence of dialogue for walk-ons and walk-offs seems also to have been imperfectly appreciated. There is, to be sure, a useful essay by Warren D. Smith on 'entrance-announcements', or the sort of remark one player makes to another in order to identify a third who is appearing on stage—"Here comes so-and-so." ('The Elizabethan Stage and Shakespeare's Entrance Announcements', *Shakespeare Quarterly*, IV, 1953.) Generally entrance-announcements shed no light on whether a given action began with a walk-on, for of necessity they almost always occur in the midst of an action, when players are already on stage.

In plays with 'Presenters' remaining on stage, however, entrance-announcements can be very instructive. One of our twenty Globe plays is of this type, *Every Man out of his Humour* (Q). Apart from choral commentaries by the Grex, this play has eighteen individual actions, of which fifteen are localized in interior scenes. References by the Grex to entering players suggest that eleven of these fifteen interior actions began with a walk-on instead of a discovery:

(1) II, ii in Q (iv–vi in F): "*So sir, but when appears Macilente againe? Enter Macilente, Deliro, . . . here he comes, and with him Signior Deliro a merchant*" ("A Room in Deliro's House").

(2) III, i (i–vi): "*Stay, what new Mute is this that walkes so suspiciously? Enter Cavalier Shift*" ("The Middle Aisle of St Paul's").

(3) III, iii (ix): "*Here comes Macilente and Signior Briske freshly suted, . . . Enter Macilente, Briske*" ("An Apartment at the Court").

(4) IV, i (i–ii): "See who presents himselfe here?... *Enter Fungoso, Fallace following him*" ("A Room in Deliro's House").

(5) IV, ii: "*Enter Deliro, with Macilente, speaking as they passe over the Stage*" ("Another Room in the same"). No entrance-announcement is possible since the action is not preceded by a choral commentary; however, the action begins with a walk-on direction.

(6) IV, iii (iii–vi): "Stay, here comes the Knight Adventurer....I, and his Scrivener with him. *Enter Puntarvolo, Notarie, with Serving-men*" ("Puntarvolo's Lodgings").

(7) IV, iv (vii): "Behold here hee comes, very Worshipfully attended, and with good variety. *Enter Fungoso with Taylor, Shoe-maker, and Haberdasher*" ("A Room in Deliro's House").

(8) IV, v (viii): "O here they come from seal'd and deliver'd. *Enter Puntarvolo, Fastidius Briske, serving men with the Dog*" ("Puntarvolo's Lodgings").

(9) V, i: "Here come the Gallants,... *Enter Puntarvolo, Fastidius Briske, Fungoso, and the Dog*" ("The Palace Stairs").

(10) V, ii: "Here they come,... *Enter Puntarvolo, Saviolina, Fastidius Briske, Fungoso*" ("An Apartment in the Palace").

(11) V, iii: "*Enter Shift*" ("The Palace Stairs"). No entrance-announcement is possible since the action is not preceded by a choral commentary.

(12) V, iv (iv–vii): "I, here he comes:... *Enter Carlo*" ("A Room at the Mitre").

(13) V, v (viii): "*Enter Macilente and Deliro*" ("A Room in Deliro's House"). No entrance-announcement.

(14) V, vi (ix): "here comes the Pawne and his Redeemer. *Enter Deliro, Fungoso, Drawer following them*" ("A Room at the Mitre").

(15) V, vii (x–xi): "*Enter Briske and Fallace*" ("The Counter"). No entrance-announcement is possible since the action is not preceded by a choral commentary.

One of the three exterior actions also begins with an entrance-announcement.

More generally informative than entrance-announcements are what may be called 'walk-off cues', by which is meant such tags of closing dialogue as "Come with me", "I'll follow you", "Let's in to dinner", and so on. The reader will of course have noticed these dramaturgical aids to the player in gracefully getting himself and his fellows off stage without benefit of blackout or curtain-drop. Walk-off cues crop up in Greek tragedy, Roman comedy, and medieval drama, and they occur throughout Elizabethan drama with a frequency that is surprising when one first begins systematically to notice them. They do not usually occur in soliloquies, for when a person alone decides to leave a place he need not communicate his intention to anyone, and a single player does not have a traffic problem in walking off stage. But when two or more players are on an 'open' stage the careful dramatist usually gives them one or more walk-off cues. The device seems to have two theatrical functions. First it prepares the audience for the players' imminent departure from view, and in this respect the walk-off cue is also (in a sense) 'realistic', for when two people leave a place they must usually come to some sort of verbal agreement about their leave-taking. The other function is to regulate the exit of two or more players at a single door: if one of the players is to precede the other off stage (for occasionally players go off two or three abreast), the order of their going must be clearly implied by the script in order to avoid hesitation or collision. Especially interesting examples are those in which one player, a person of rank, orders a second to precede him and a third to follow him off stage.

The device of the walk-off cue may conveniently be illustrated from *Macbeth*, *A Warning for Fair Women*, and *The Miseries of Enforced Marriage*.

In *Macbeth* there are twenty-nine individual actions, of which fourteen are localized in interior scenes. Dialogue suggests that twelve of these interior actions ended with a walk-off rather than a concealment:

(1) I, iv: "Let's after him, Whose care is gone before, to bid us welcome:...*Exeunt*" ("The Palace").

(2) I, v: "*Exeunt*" ("Macbeth's Castle"). No walk-off cue (two players exit).

(3) I, vii: "Away,...*Exeunt*" ("Macbeth's Castle").

(4) II, ii: "Retyre we to our Chamber:...*Exeunt*" ("Macbeth's Castle").

(5) II, iii: "Therefore to Horse, And let us not be daintie of leave-taking, But shift away:...*Exeunt*" ("Macbeth's Castle").

(6) III, i: "Ile call upon you straight: abide within,...*Exeunt*" ("The Palace").

(7) III, ii: "So prythee goe with me. *Exeunt*" ("The Palace").

(8) III, iv: "Come, wee'l to sleepe:...*Exeunt*" ("Hall in the Palace").

(9) III, vi: "*Exeunt*" ("The Palace"). No walk-off cue (2 players exit).

(10) IV, i: "Come bring me where they are. *Exeunt*" ("A cavern").

(11) IV, ii: "Run away I pray you. *Exit crying Murther*" ("Macduff's Castle").

(12) V, i: "Looke after her,...So goodnight,...Good night good Doctor. *Exeunt*" ("Macbeth's Castle").

(13) V, iii: "Bring it after me:...*Exeunt*" ("A room in the Castle").

(14) V, v: "Arme, Arme, and out,...*Exeunt*" ("Within the Castle").

Twelve of the fifteen exterior actions also end with a walk-off cue.

In *A Warning for Fair Women* there are twenty-six individual actions, five involving Presenters and thus unlocalized, twenty-one constituting the fiction proper. Of these twenty-one actions, eleven are localized in interior scenes. Dialogue suggests that each of these interior actions ended with a walk-off rather than a concealment:

(1) Sc. 4 (B3v in Q): "come Roger let us go,...*Exeunt*" (a room).

(2) Sc. 5 (C1v): "Ile folow you" (a room). No exit-direction.

(3) Sc. 12 (F2v): "Ile up into the Presence....*Exeunt*" (a buttery).

(4) Sc. 13 (F3): "go thou and watch For master Brownes arrival from the Court,...In the meane space I will go after her" (probably a room). No exit-direction.

(5) Sc. 15 (G1): "come my lords, lets in,...*Exeunt omnes*" (a court of justice).

(6) Sc. 16 (G2): "farewel Nan,...God be with you, good Captaine....Farewel, gentle Hodge" (probably a room). No exit-direction.

(7) Sc. 18 (G3v): "Come master Maior,...farewell good neighbor Brown....*Exeunt*" (a room).

(8) Sc. 19 (G4): "Come, Ile go along with you. *Exeunt*" (a room).

(9) Sc. 20 (H2): "Farewel George Browne,...*exeunt om.*" ("*at the Court*", Q).

(10) Sc. 21 (H3v): "Jailer, away with them....*Exeunt*" (a court of justice).

(11) Sc. 25 (K1): "The time is come sweete hearts, and we must part, That way go you, this way my heavie heart. *Exeunt*" (within a prison).

Eight of the ten exterior actions and one of the five unlocalized actions also end with a walk-off cue.

In *The Miseries of Enforced Marriage* there are thirteen individual actions, of which six are localized in interior scenes. Dialogue implies that each of these interior actions ended with a walk-off rather than a concealment:

(1) Sc. 2 (sig. B2 in Q): "come get you in:...*Exeunt*" (a room).

(2) Sc. 5 (D3v): "Why then lets come and take up a new roome,...*Exeunt*" (a room).

(3) Sc. 6 (E2): "Well then, I will go tel him newes of his of-springs. *Exit*" (a room).

(4) Sc. 7 (E4): "weele first to the surgeons....*Exeunt*" (probably a room).

(5) Sc. 12 (H3v): "Ile stay his journey, least I meet a hanging. *Exeunt*" (a room).

(6) Sc. 13 (K1v): "And in your eies so lovingly being wed, We hope your hands will bring us to our bed. FINIS" (a room). No exit-direction.

Five of the seven exterior actions also end with a walk-off cue.

The incidence of walk-off cues in the interior actions of these three plays is exceptionally high. Nevertheless walk-off cues occur in over two-thirds of all interior actions in the twenty plays under discussion. (The incidence is approximately the same in exterior actions, and also in actions of each kind in the ten plays not under discussion.) Limitation of space forbids printing further examples, but the phenomenon may easily be verified in a text of the reader's choice.

To sum up the argument from our twenty Globe plays: walk-on directions, entrance-announcements, and walk-off cues, in view of the absence of any evidence for discovery or concealment, suggest that, in over two-thirds of the interior actions of these plays, the players were not discovered or concealed within a discovery-space but rather walked on and off stage. In general the actions of these plays (excepting those of *Sejanus* which begin with character-lists in the neo-classical style) begin and end with stage-directions employing the term *Enter* or *Exit*. Hence we have evidence that the unqualified terms *Enter* and *Exit* generally meant no more than "comes on stage" and "goes off stage".

II

Let us return to our chief source of information about the Elizabethan stage, the Swan drawing. This does not show curtains. But absence of curtains does not mean that discoveries were not effected at the Swan, even as we see it in the De Witt sketch. We must recognize that a discovery can be effected without curtains in a tiring-house whose doors open out upon the stage. The Swan doors evidently did open out, and being also some 7 ft. or 8 ft. wide they would have disclosed a space adequate to the needs of most Elizabethan discoveries. A few examples may suffice to illustrate the convention of discovery by opening a door:

(1) Anon., *Arden of Feversham*, v, i: "*Then they lay the body in the Countinghouse.... Then they open the countinghouse doore, and looke uppon Arden. Ales.* See Susan where thy quandam Maister lies" (c. 1592, theatre unknown). One player reclining; also a concealment.

(2) Dekker, *The Shoemakers' Holiday*, III, iv: "*Enter Jane in a Semsters shop working, and Hamond muffled at another doore, he stands aloofe. Ham.* Yonders the shop, and there my faire love sits" (1599, Rose). One player seated.

(3) Chapman, Jonson, and Marston, *Eastward Ho*, I, i: "*Enter Maister Touch-stone, and Quick-silver*

at severall dores, ... At the middle dore, Enter Golding discovering a Gold-smiths shoppe, and walking short turns before it" (1605, Blackfriars). One player standing.

(4) Anon., *The Second Maiden's Tragedy*, line 1926 in the Malone Society Reprint: "*On a sodayne in a kinde of Noyse like a Wynde, the dores clattering, the Toombstone flies open, and a great light appears in the midst of the Toombe; His Lady as went owt, standing just before hym all in white, Stuck with Jewells and a great crucifex on her brest*" (1611, Blackfriars or First Globe). One player standing.

(5) Fletcher, *The Island Princess*, II, v: Armusia, in search of the imprisoned King, forces open a door: "*The King discover'd*" (1619–21, Blackfriars or Second Globe). One player.

(6) Fletcher and W. Rowley, *The Maid in the Mill*, v, ii: The King forces the lock of a "closet" in which Otrante has incarcerated Florimel: "*Florimell discovered*" (1623, Blackfriars or Second Globe). One player.

(7) Massinger, *The Renegado*, III, vi: Asambeg, going to release the imprisoned Paulina, "*opens a doore, Paulina discovered comes forth*" (1624, Cockpit). One player standing.

(8) Massinger, *The Guardian*, III, vi: "*Enter Severino (throwing open the doors violently) having a knife*" (1633, Blackfriars). One player standing.

The possibility of discovery by opening a door necessarily modifies our interpretation of numerous Elizabethan discoveries. Nevertheless, we know from contemporary stage-directions that many discoveries were effected by opening curtains of some sort, and we know also, from a letter by John Chamberlain describing a hoax perpetrated by Richard Vennar in 1602, that the Swan was capable of being fitted out with 'curtains' and 'hangings'. (See T. S. Graves, 'A Note on the Swan Theatre', *Modern Philology*, IX, 1911–12.) It will be remembered that Vennar had promised an expensive entertainment called *England's Joy*, to be performed by "certain gentlemen and gentlewomen of account". The response was enthusiastic but there was no play; and Vennar absconded, only to be apprehended almost immediately and bound over "in five pound to appear at the sessions". "In the meane time [writes Chamberlain] the common people, when they saw themselves deluded, revenged themselves upon the hangings, curtaines, chaires, stooles, walles, and whatsoever came in theire way, very outragiously, and made great spoile; there was great store of goode companie, and many noblemen."

Presumably some of the 'hangings' here referred to were stage-hangings concealing trestles or posts beneath the open stage. But how might 'curtains' or 'hangings' have been fitted to the tiring-house that we see in the Swan drawing? One method would have been to set up a curtained booth against the tiring-house façade, as suggested by George F. Reynolds in *The Staging of Elizabethan Plays at the Red Bull Theater* (1940) and by C. Walter Hodges in *The Globe Restored* (1953). Another method would have been to fit hangings along the front of the tiring-house, thus hiding one or both of the stage-doors and possibly the whole length of the tiring-house façade. That some such arrangement was occasionally resorted to is shown by the *Wits* frontispiece (1662), which depicts a player entering from behind an arras apparently concealing a door.

Furthermore, essentially the same arrangement may well be pictured in the *Roxana* vignette (1632). (And also in the *Messalina* vignette, 1640, but since this may have been influenced by the earlier picture we may not, in this respect, regard the two illustrations as independent sources of information.) The curtains or hangings in the *Roxana* vignette are usually interpreted as concealing the opening of an 'inner-stage'. Possibly they do, but if so it is curious that the picture fails to show the stage-doors we should then have to imagine on either side of the presumptive 'inner-stage'. Doors may, of course, have been omitted from the sides of the picture as a result of cropping (though even in this case the hangings might still conceal only a middle door in the tiring-house wall). On the other hand, it is possible that no doors are shown in the *Roxana* vignette because the curtains are hangings which conceal them.

The general interpretation is supported by Florio's definition (1598) of the word *scena* in the classical sense of tiring-house: "a skaffold, a pavillion, or fore part of a theater where players make them readie, being trimmed with hangings, out of which they enter upon the stage."

Accordingly I would suggest that hangings were occasionally fitted up along the façade of the Swan tiring-house in front of its open stage-doors, the leaves of each door having been swung open through 180° and lying flat against the tiring-house façade. (Alternatively, the hangings might have been fitted up in front of one door only, or behind one or both of the doors.) Thus the players, in the rigid situation of a permanent tiring-house, would have recreated the flexible situation of the curtained booth which they presumably used as a temporary tiring-house in performances away from a regular theatre.

In addition to making possible a variable stylistic *décor*, the arrangement of hangings in front of open stage-doors would have had three practical advantages. First, it would have eliminated much opening and closing of doors by enabling the players to enter and exit by slipping through openings in the hangings. Second, the arrangement would have made readily available an 'arras' behind which an eavesdropping player might 'hide', either completely disappearing or remaining partly within view of the audience as desired. And third, the arrangement would have permitted discovery of a space of indeterminate depth some 7 ft. or 8 ft. wide by means of drawing aside or looping up the hangings in front of one of the open stage-doors, the hangings being manipulated by attendant players or by stage-keepers. (On stage-keepers see Leslie Hotson, 'False Faces on Shakespeare's Stage', *The Times Literary Supplement*, 16 May 1952.) If masking were considered necessary, a curtain backing might also have been fitted up a few feet behind the doorway.

III

Let us now consider evidence for the Globe discovery-space. Discoveries are required in nine of our thirty Globe plays:

(1) *The Merry Wives of Windsor* (1600), I, iv (F): "goe into this Closset [Q: *He steps into the Counting-house*]:...dere is some Simples in my Closset,...O Diable, Diable: vat is in my Closset?" One player (Simple) "goes into" the discovery-space; a concealment. He is then discovered (possibly by door).

(2) *Satiromastix* (1601), I, ii: "*Horrace sitting in a study behinde a Curtaine, a candle by him burning, bookes lying confusedly*". One player seated, a table; by curtain.

(3) *Thomas Lord Cromwell* (1602), II, i–ii: "*Cromwell in his study with bagges of money before him casting of account.*" One player seated, a table.

(4) *Ibid.* III, ii: "*Go take thy place Hodge,....Hodge sits in the study, and Cromwell calles in the States....* Goe draw the curtaines, let us see the Earle, O he is writing.*" A player (Hodge, who will impersonate the Earl of Bedford) "goes" and sits "in" the discovery-space; a concealment. He is then discovered seated at a table; by curtains.

(5) *Ibid.* IV, v: "*Enter Gardiner in his studie, and his man.*" One player (possibly two).

(6) *Troilus and Cressida* (1602), III, iii (F): "*Enter Achilles and Patroclus in their Tent. Ulis.* Achilles stands i'th entrance of his Tent." Two players standing.

(7) *The Merry Devil of Edmonton* (1603), Induction: "*Draw the curtaines....*Behold him heere laide on his restless couch,...And by him stands that Necromanticke chaire, In which he makes his direfull invocations,...And in meane time repose thee in that chayre....*Sit downe....*Enough, come out." One player (Peter Fabel) discovered reclining on a day-bed, a chair; by curtains. Another player (Coreb) sits in the discovery-space and then "comes out".

(8) *Volpone* (1605), I, i–v (F): "next, my gold: Open the shrine, that I may see my saint. Haile the worlds soule, and mine." Property only (Volpone's gold), presumably upon a table.

(9) *The Revenger's Tragedy* (1606), I, iv: "*Enter the discontented Lord Antonio, whose wife the Duchesses yongest Sonne ravisht; he Discovering the body of her dead to certaine Lords:...*A prayer Booke the pillow to her cheeke." One player reclining; also a concealment.

(10, 11) *The Devil's Charter* (1607), Induction: "*Enter, At one doore betwixt two other Cardinals, Roderigo in his purple habit close in conference with them, one of which hee guideth to a Tent, where a Table is furnished with divers bagges of money, which that Cardinall beareth away: and to another Tent the other Cardinall, where hee delivereth him a great quantity of rich Plate.*" (10) Properties only (bags of money), upon a table. (11) Property only (rich plate), presumably upon a table. This direction is part of the evidence for three doors in the Globe tiring-house.

(12) *Ibid.* I, iv: "*Alexander in his study with bookes, coffers, his triple Crowne upon a cushion before him.*" One player seated, a table.

(13) *Ibid.* IV, i: "*Alexander in his studie beholding a Magicall glasse with other observations....* Let me looke forth. *Alexander commeth upon the Stage out of his study with a booke in his hand....Exit Alexander into the studie.*" One player seated, a table. He "comes out of" the discovery-space "upon" the stage.

(14) *Ibid.* IV, iv: "bring forth her ransome hither. *Barbarossa* [on stage] *bringeth from Caesars Tent hir two boyes....Exeunt with the boyes....*Behold thy children living in my Tent. *He discovereth his Tent where her two sonnes were at Cardes.*" Two players seated, a table.

(15) *Ibid.* IV, v: "*Enter Alexander out of his studie....Exit Alexander into his study....Bernardo knocketh at the study. Alex.* What newes man?...*Alexander upon the stage in his cassock and nightcap with a box under each arme.*" One player, who subsequently comes "upon" the stage.

(16) *Ibid.* V, vi: "*Alexander unbraced betwixt two Cardinalls in his study looking upon a booke, whilst a groome draweth the Curtaine....They place him in a chayre upon the stage, a groome setteth a Table before him.*" Three players, one seated in a chair; by curtain. The seated player is then carried on stage and a table is set before him.

(17) *Ibid.*: "*Alexander draweth the Curtaine of his studie where hee discovereth the divill sitting in his pontificals.*" One player seated; by curtain. This and the preceding discovery occur during the same action and apparently in the same discovery-space.

(18) *Pericles* (1608), V, i: "May wee not see him?...Behold him." One player (Pericles) seated or reclining (since "asleep"); he is then presumably carried on stage.

These discoveries have three noteworthy characteristics. First, they are few and infrequent, twenty-one of the thirty Globe plays requiring none and seven of the remaining nine only one each. (*The Devil's Charter* is exceptional in Elizabethan drama in requiring so many as eight.) Second, the Globe discoveries are essentially 'shows', or disclosures, of a player or object invested with some special interest or significance. (Alternatively they might be described as *tableaux vivants* and still-lifes.) Furniture is involved only in so far as the discovered player requires something to sit or lie upon so that he may be shown effectively (a stool, chair, bench, or day-bed); or in so far as something is required in order to show him at a characteristic activity (a table for his book, standish, candle, triple crown, magical glass, bags of money, or game of cards); or in so far as the discovered object must rest upon something in order to be properly visible (a table for Volpone's gold or Roderigo's money-bags). Unless a 'show' is to be presented, necessary furniture is always carried on stage; and unless a non-ambulatory player is to be specially 'shown' (and even, occasionally, when he is, for example Discovery number 16), he also is carried on stage. Thus properties or non-ambulatory players are carried on in seven of the nine plays requiring discoveries. In *Merry Wives* (F) a buckbasket is twice carried on stage (III, iii, IV, ii). In *Satiromastix* a banquet is 'set out' (IV, i), a chair (the King's 'State') is 'set' under a canopy (V, ii), and Cælestine 'enters' in a chair (*ibid.*). In *Thomas Lord Cromwell* servants 'bring out' a banquet (III, iii). In *Volpone* (F) the supposedly impotent protagonist is 'brought in' (IV, iv–vi) and Corbaccio is carried on stage (V, i–ii). In *The Revenger's Tragedy* a furnished table is 'brought forth' (V, iii). In *The Devil's Charter* Lucretia 'brings in' a chair "*which she planteth upon the Stage*" (I, v), two Pages 'enter' with a table (IV, iii), a cupboard of plate is 'brought in' (V, iv), a spread table 'enters' (*ibid.*), and Alexander (having just been discovered) is 'placed' on stage in a chair, whereupon a table is 'set' before him (V, vi). In *Pericles* Thaisa is carried on stage in a chest (III, ii).

A corollary may be developed. A 'setting' at the Globe (when there was one) was usually created by one or more properties placed on stage within full view of the audience by 'servants' or stage-keepers. (Compare the Swan drawing, where a bench at the front of the stage apparently creates as much of a setting as necessary for the action depicted.) It is true that a Globe setting was also occasionally created by discovered furniture, which must therefore have been placed within the discovery-space before this was opened to the sight of the audience. In such cases, however, the discovery-space was used not in order to conceal preparation of the setting but in order to permit the sudden display of a player who (if so much as a single property were discovered with him) would automatically be seen in a setting of one sort or other. Discoveries in the Globe plays are primarily shows of persons or things themselves inherently interesting. They are never (as in the proscenium-arch theatre) conveniences for the sake of arranging furniture out of sight of the audience.

Third, the Globe discoveries do not involve any appreciable movement within the discovery-space, the discovered player in one instance being 'dead' and remaining within the discovery-space (9) and in all others being discovered as it were *en tableau* and subsequently leaving the discovery-space for the stage, as is indicated either by a direction to that effect (13, 15, 16) or by evidence in dialogue or stage-direction that he later walked or was carried off stage. (Since they could not involve movement, the three discoveries of objects are not considered here.) It may be further pointed out that our texts afford no sign of closing the discovery-space after a discovery, presumably because it was automatically and unobtrusively closed when the attention of the audience was no longer directed to the 'show' (8) or when the discovered player had left it for the stage. (The latter explanation is confirmed by 17, which occurs during the same action as 16 and apparently in the same discovery-space, the initially-discovered player leaving the discovery-space and then returning to it in order himself to discover another player.) There are only three formal 'concealments' (1, 4, 9).

We may now inquire into the physical conditions of the Globe discovery-space. It is perhaps inexact to speak of a single discovery-space at the Globe, for an action in *The Devil's Charter* requiring discoveries (10, 11) in two separate places suggests that there were (or could be) at least two. For convenience, however, and because 'multiple' discoveries are rare in Elizabethan drama, we may continue to speak of a single discovery-space. (On multiple discoveries compare Dekker and Middleton's *Roaring Girl*, a Fortune play of *c.* 1610: "*The three shops open in a ranke.*") Our evidence tells us three things about the Globe discovery-space. First, it was equipped with a curtain or curtains (2, 4, 7, 16, 17). Second, it was off stage, or outside and somehow distinct from the main playing-area, for in one action the discovered player is directed to come on stage out of it (13), and in two others he walks or is carried from discovery-space to stage (15, 16). (Compare also 1, 4, 7, and 15, in which players 'go into' or 'come out of' the discovery-space.) And third, it need not have been deeper than 4 ft. or wider than 7 ft., for no discovery is of more than three players (twelve out of a possible fifteen are of only one) or of more or larger properties than a table and two seats (14) or a day-bed and chair (7).

These conditions would have been fulfilled if the Globe discovery-space was behind an open doorway in the tiring-house wall (usually, we may suppose, the middle doorway of three) essentially similar to the doorways in the Swan drawing and fitted with hangings as in the *Wits* frontispiece or the *Roxana* vignette, for such a discovery-space would have been (1) curtained, (2) off stage, and (3) indeterminately deep and some 7 ft. or 8 ft. wide. The theory is suggested by the fact that Elizabethan discoveries were occasionally effected by opening a door, it accounts for discoveries in two (or three) separate places since the other two doorways might easily have been used simultaneously in the same capacity, and it harmonizes with the fact that Globe discoveries were few and infrequent 'shows' or *tableaux* not involving appreciable movement within the discovery-space.

Finally the theory accords with the fact that certain Globe plays apparently produced without discovery nevertheless allude to 'curtains', 'hangings', or an 'arras'. In *A Warning for Fair Women*, Tragedy the Presenter says to the audience: "But now we come unto the dismall act, And in these sable Curtaines shut we up, The Comicke entrance to our direful play" (C4v). In *Every Man out of his Humour* (Q) Fungoso has the following walk-off cue: "Is this the way? good truth here be fine hangings. *Exeunt Puntarvolo, Briske, Fungoso*" (v, i). And in *Hamlet* Polonius hides behind "the Arras" (Q1). Then, having been stabbed through the arras ("dead for a Ducate"), he apparently falls forward upon the stage, for Hamlet later drags him off: the Folio text reads "*Exit Hamlet tugging in Polonius*" (III, iv). This evidence suggests that the curtains or hangings at the Globe were not intended primarily to effect discoveries. They *might* effect discoveries; but discovery was not their chief *raison d'être*.

NOTE

1. Read (in preliminary form) at the Eighth International Shakespeare Conference at Stratford-upon-Avon, 2 September 1957. The underlying research was completed while the writer held a fellowship of the John Simon Guggenheim Memorial Foundation.

'PASSING OVER THE STAGE'[1]

BY

ALLARDYCE NICOLL

During the past few years many attempts have been made to reconstruct the staging of Elizabethan plays, and in these attempts the usual assumption is that the players' actions were confined to the main platform jutting out into the yard, to such space behind doors or curtains as provided opportunity for discoveries, and to the upper stage. Only occasionally has the suggestion been put forward that for some scenes or situations part of the yard was also put into histrionic service.[2] Hitherto this suggestion has, in general, been ignored, since no valid evidence has been brought forward to support it—and indeed it well may be that no amount of research could ever succeed in proving beyond doubt that any important dramatic actions took place down in the arena assigned to the groundlings.

Perhaps, however, we should do wrong if we were to make a specific search for documentary support (or the opposite) of any theory concerned with important dramatic actions of this kind. Such matters must be explored step by step; and the first step would seem to be to limit ourselves strictly to the simple inquiry whether Elizabethan actors ever had the opportunity of making their appearances otherwise than by the normally-used doors. If we do this, the possibility of reaching, if not absolute certainty, at least a reasonable measure of assurance, may lie within our grasp.

I

Strangely, no attempt has been made in any of the numerous modern studies of the Elizabethan playhouse to consider the use of the word 'stage' in play directions. The significance of the term for Elizabethans is not in the slightest doubt. Once or twice we may find such a reference as appears in *Hoffman*, where the hero closes the 'stage'—that is to say, draws shut the curtain on a space discovered at the rear of the platform; but a reference of this kind may be regarded as an exception to a general rule that for the actors 'stage' had its obvious significance of the normal acting area. Now, this being so, we should not have expected to find any employment of the term in play directions save for a limited number of particular situations which demanded exact reference to the platform. Thus, for example, the direction in the 1603 Quarto of *Hamlet*, "The Gost vnder the stage", or that in *Antony and Cleopatra*, "Musicke of the Hoboyes is vnder the Stage", clearly requires mention of the stage to make evident what is intended. So in the plot of 2 *Seven Deadly Sins* the instruction that a tent should be "plast one the Stage" had to employ the word 'stage' to indicate that this tent was not merely simulated by the drawing-back of a curtain before one of the façade doors but was a temporary structure set out on the acting area itself.

We may go further still, and agree that the use of the word was necessary, too, in *Henry VIII* where

The Bishops place themselues on each side the Court in manner of a Consistory.... The rest of the Attendants stand in conuenient order about the Stage.

This direction in *Henry VIII* is but one among a considerable number wherein similarly the preposition 'about', varied by such other prepositions as 'on' or 'upon', is related to the noun 'stage'. Characters are bidden to walk "once about the Stage" (*The Misfortunes of Arthur*), to "meet on the stage", to "march vpon the stage" (*2 Edward IV*), to march "about" the stage (*Woodstock* and *2 If You Know Not Me*), to "meete at the midst of the stage" (*The Turk*). It seems apparent that all these directions indicate fundamentally the same action; the players enter by a door or doors and then step widely over the acting area: when Romeo and the maskers are bidden to "march about the Stage", they are intended to do just that, to walk about the boards.

II

In addition to the prepositions 'about', 'on' and 'upon', however, there is another which, when we start to examine its use carefully, seems to belong to an entirely different category. In directions involving the word 'stage', much more frequently employed than the prepositions already mentioned is the word 'over'. Perhaps our first thought in connection with this term is that it might well be equivalent to 'aloft' and thus refer to the open space above the doors in the tiring-house façade; if so, 'over the stage' would mean 'in the gallery'. Undoubtedly 'over' is very occasionally used in this sense, but a different significance obviously attaches to it when it appears in a phrase, 'pass over the stage', which occurs so frequently, in such a wide variety of plays, as to make us believe that it was a definitely technical theatrical term, having for dramatists and actors a precise meaning. The facts we have to consider, therefore, are (1) that in play-directions 'over' is familiarly associated with the verb 'pass' and (2) that, although the word 'stage' occurs in other phrases, its use in 'pass over the stage' appears to outnumber the others. The question is: what did 'pass over the stage' actually imply?

In seeking an answer to this query, one thing immediately attracts our attention. Almost always the direction 'pass over the stage' applies to one of two movements—to a stately procession, or to the walking across of one or more persons, passers-by, who do not speak but are observed and commented upon by others. In *The Shoemakers' Holiday* the Lord Mayor and a company "passe ouer the stage"; in the *Nero* of 1624 Poppea and her attendants "passe ou[er] the Stage in State"; in *The Revenger's Tragedy*

the Duke, Dutchesse, Lusurioso her sonne, Spurio the bastard, with a traine, passe ouer the Stage with Torch-light.

These three examples may be sufficient to serve as illustrations of the processional emphasis. The second device, that of passers-by, appears early in the plot of *The Dead Man's Fortune*, where we find a direction:

Enter panteloun whiles he speaks Validore passeth o'r the stage disguisde.

In *A Wife for a Month* it is an old lady who thus goes across; in *The Double Marriage* some fourteen characters are similarly seen "passing ouer"; in *Monsieur Thomas* the passage is made by a group of physicians, in *The Loyal Subject* by a gentleman and his lady, in *The Little French Lawyer* by a girl and her nurse; in *Coriolanus* a kindred action shows Valeria, Virgilia and Volumnia "passing ouer the Stage"; the entry of Mosca "passant" in *Volpone* clearly belongs to the same category. In each of these instances—and the examples might readily have been multiplied—the silent figures who thus 'pass over the stage' are observed and commented upon by others.

III

After having noted these facts we may turn to the more difficult problem of interpretation. Where did the passers-by appear before the audience, what did they do and whither did they go? If, as seems certain from its frequent use, the term was a technical one, presumably with a specific and well-recognized meaning, we need not hope to find any explanations in the texts themselves: neither dramatists nor actors would have felt called upon to elaborate.

Two possibilities may first be briefly examined and dismissed. (1) The characters might have been supposed to come in at one door and to go out by another. No very deep theatre sense is required to show that for a processional movement this would have been hopelessly ineffective; after all, the doors in Elizabethan theatres cannot have been much more than 12 ft. apart and any such 'passage over the stage' would certainly have proved flat, stale and unprofitable. This possibility, therefore, may be summarily rejected. (2) The second possibility is that the characters, entering by one door, moved outwards on the acting area, round the posts, making a great sweep over the platform and turning to make their exit by the other door. For processions this might not have been unimpressive; in fact, it would have been precisely the same as the movement demanded when an army is bidden to march on or about the stage.

Before accepting such an interpretation of the phrase, however, several considerations must make us pause. Where the term 'pass over the stage' is employed for passers-by the situation almost always involves other characters observing them, and generally the processional passages likewise introduce observation and comment by other characters. Thus in *The Revenger's Tragedy*, before the ducal party "passe ouer the Stage" there is an "Enter Vendici". Vendice, therefore, like all the observing characters, is kept theatrically distinct from the silent figures in the procession, and since he has a long soliloquy-commentary upon the Duke and his companions it is evident that he must take up a position well to the front of the platform. Suppose he does so; suppose the procession perambulates the acting area: how could he effectively be kept distinct from the others, how could he avoid becoming involved in the sweeping train? No skilled actors, no 'producer', would permit such a disposition of the players. And if it were to be suggested that instead of moving to the front of the platform Vendice took his stand at, let us say, one of the posts, the situation would not only be worse, it would become absurd; in that case his long poetic commentary could only have been spoken from the midst of a circle, over the heads of the processional figures. This certainly will not do.

Further confirmation comes from a study of the similar situation in *Coriolanus*. The direction reads:

Enter two Senators, with Ladies, passing ouer the Stage, with other Lords.

At first glance this looks like an instruction for a general processional entry introducing all the characters mentioned, but the dialogue proves that this was not intended. The only speech in the scene is that by the First Senator beginning "Behold our Patronnesse, the life of Rome", which is greeted by "All" with a cry of "Welcome Ladies, welcome". The "Ladies" are silent. Quite clearly the direction, so far from being single, is threefold: (1) first, two Senators enter, (2) then appear the Lords (the "All" referred to in the speech-heading), while (3) the "Ladies" make their passage over the stage. This, except for the presence of the Lords, is exactly the same as the situation in *The Revenger's Tragedy*, and to it the same comments apply.

Before proceeding further in the inquiry, we may note another movement which, although the full phrase 'pass over the stage' is not used, evidently involves a kindred action. In *Macbeth* we read:

Enter a Sewer, and diuers Seruants with Dishes and Seruice ouer the Stage,

and this is paralleled in *Thomas Lord Cromwell* by "the meate goes ouer the Stage". There is nothing gorgeously processional here, just the servitors carrying in the plates to a banquet, and it is hard indeed to believe that these servitors entered by one of the doors, uselessly bore their dishes round the full area of the platform and then went out again. Such action would have been meaningless, and a study of the Elizabethan theatre indicates that the players were admirable in their profession and consequently not given to presenting meaningless movements in the progress of their dramas. Once more, the supposition that a mere perambulation of the platform was intended must be set aside.[3]

IV

Clearly, the interpretation which would best fit the movements suggested in the phrase 'pass over the stage' is an entry of actors in the yard and their walking onto and over the platform. Thus we return to the basic question with which we started, and ask: is there any evidence to show that, even occasionally, players did in fact make their appearance otherwise than by the doors?

At the very beginning of such an inquiry, attention may be drawn to the fact that often, although not invariably, the characters who 'pass over the stage' are not given an initial "Enter" in the directions. In *The Revenger's Tragedy* it is "Enter Vendici", while the Duke and his companions simply "pass ouer the Stage"; similarly in *Coriolanus* we may attach the "Enter" to the Senators but not to the ladies. Perhaps, however, no distinction was intended—although the fact itself is worthy of passing note, even if the occasional omission of the word "Enter" may have been due simply to implication of entry included within the verb 'pass over'.

Greater help in our investigation comes to us from the consideration of still another word which occasionally crops up in play directions—the 'ends' of the stage, sometimes varied by the 'corners' of the stage. A particularly interesting and informative series of entries in *John a Kent* may be taken first. At the beginning of the episode in question John a Cumber "opens the doore" representing the castle gates. The rear façade, therefore, stands for the castle itself. During the following action four Antiques or Antics are raised by John a Cumber's power and made to go into this castle. First, "ffrom one end of the Stage enter an antique", then "ffrom the other end of the Stage, enter another antique", "ffrom vnder the Stage the third Antique", and, finally, "The fourth out of a tree, if possible it may be". Let us proceed to interpret these directions as what they must have been in fact—the instructions given by an author to an Elizabethan acting company. He is not sure whether the players can provide a trick tree; hence his qualification in connection with the fourth entry. He knows, however, that a trap is available for the third, and he knows, too, that the first and second can come in from the 'ends' of the stage. With this example from *John a Kent* may be taken another from *The Silver Age*. In this play Hercules, going to Hades, *sinkes himselfe: Flashes of fire; the Diuels appeare at euery corner of the stage with seuerall fire-workes. The Iudges of hell, and the three sisters run ouer the stage, Hercules after them: fire-workes all ouer the house.*

This situation clearly introduces what was not infrequent in the Elizabethan playhouse, a complete and sudden change of locality determined by the presence of an actor or actors: Hercules is first shown on earth and descends, by a trap, as going to hell; almost immediately after, on his reappearance, he is supposed to be under the earth, and the acting area, which a moment before had represented the upper world, now represents the nether regions. It has been suggested by some that this direction in *The Silver Age* proves the existence of four or even five traps, but such a supposition is quite untenable. The only other supporting evidence comes from the companion drama, *The Golden Age*, with its "Enter at 4 seuerall corners the 4 winds: Neptune riseth"—but in both these plays there is a clear distinction between "riseth" and "sinkes" on the one hand and "appeare" and "enter" on the other. In any event, it is reasonable to suppose that, even had such traps existed, they would not have been placed at the corners. These traps may be dismissed completely from our minds. Whence, then, did the Devils come? Obviously from under the platform, with a clambering up at each corner. The Devils' entrances, however, are not so important as that of the Judges and Hercules who "run ouer the stage". Such persons could, it is true, have made an entry at one of the doors, but since Hercules just before had gone down in a trap, it seems much more probable that they and he appeared, as the Devils did, from beneath the platform. Once more theatrical commonsense seems to call for such a movement. If we accept this interpretation, we could also suppose entries at yard level from under the platform for the two Antiques in *John a Kent*. It seems obvious that the author, Anthony Mundy, sought for his Antiques entries out of the common and we can hardly suppose that the first two were intended tamely to come out of doors close to the castle gates: something special was designed for them. It looks, accordingly, as though we have part of the evidence for which we were seeking—indicating that on occasion players stepped out from under the stage at the yard level and then made their way up on to the main acting area.[4]

V

This is helpful; but it still leaves us with a question. We turn to another play, *A Warning for Fair Women*. This is, in essence, a realistic drama, dealing with a contemporary murder. At the same time, it introduces a few symbolic dumb shows, and one of these reads:

The Musicke playing, enters Lust bringing forth *Browne* and *Roger*, at one ende mistres *Sanders* and mistres *Drurie* at the other, they offering cheerefully to meete and embrace, suddenly riseth vp a great tree betweene them.

As in *John a Kent*, we are confronted with a scene in which the author clearly seeks for an uncommon effect, and it may reasonably be guessed that the employment of "at one ende" and "at the other" instead of the usual "at one door" and "at another door" is intended to signify an effect different from that of normal entries. In the absence of any other information, however, we cannot be quite sure. Certainty, on the other hand, seems to come to us in *The Fair Maid of the Exchange*. The third act of that drama opens in the "Exchange"—clearly Gresham's Royal Exchange, the central court of which was lined with shops or booths. A Boy is discovered in such a shop, which presumably was discovered at the centre of the façade wall. A girl, Phillis, also appears in the shop; there is some talk between the pair, and then Phillis "sits and works in the shop". Immediately after this,

Enter M. Richard Gardiner booted, and M. William Bennet, two gentleman, at one ende of the stage.

 Ben. Kinde *Dicke*, thou wilt not be vnmindfull of my dutie
To that same worthy Arts-master, *Lyonell Barnes.*
 Gard. Thy love, sweet *Will*, hath chainde it to my memory.
 Ben. Then with this kinde imbrace I take my leaue,
Wishing thou wert as safe arriu'd at *Cambridge*,
As thou art at this present neere the Exchange.
 Gard. And well remembred, kind *Will Bennet.*
Others affaires made me obliuious
Of mine owne; I pray thee goe to the Exchange.
I haue certaine bands, and other linnen to buy,
Prethee accompanie me.
 Ben. With all my heart.
 Gard. Sure, this is a beauteous gallant walke;
Were my continuall residence in London,
I should make much vse of such a pleasure:
Methinkes the glorious virgins of this square
Giues life to dead strucke youth; Oh heavens!
 Ben. Why how now *Dicke*?
 Gard. By my sweete hopes of an hereafter blisse,
I neuer saw a fairer face then this:
O for acquaintance with so rich a beautie.

On this, the two gentlemen move over to the shop. The situation seems perfectly plain and unambiguous. The shop is supposed to be set on one side of the Exchange; Gardiner and Bennet, "booted", have come from a distance, not into, but "neere" the Exchange; after their first few lines they walk across, enter the square and see Phillis in her shop. The normal reference to entry by means of a door is, properly, abandoned in favour of an entry "at one end of the stage", and, when we consider the effect aimed at, this can mean only an entry at the yard level. Nothing could be more definite and precise.

The actors in both these plays, however, are not impersonating devils, antics or denizens of Hell; they represent ordinary humans. At once we realize that for them an appearance from under the stage would have been entirely inappropriate. Not only so: whereas devils and antics may clamber up the sides or corners of the platform, quite obviously neither the ladies in *A Warning for Fair Women* nor the gentlemen in *The Fair Maid of the Exchange* could be expected to indulge in any such indecorous acrobatics.

We are thus confronted by a double problem. On the one hand, examination of the phrase 'pass over the stage' does seem to demand the interpretation already indicated, of entry by the yard and movement on to the platform, and further examination of the word 'ends' or 'corners' forces us to believe that these yard entries were in fact made; yet, on the other hand, the only place of entry at the yard level which seems fully substantiated by documentary evidence is the space underneath the acting area. It is at this point that we are forced to move from the consideration of definite fact to a consideration of hypothetical assumptions. If we believe that the evidence concerning the movement involved in 'passing over the stage' is valid, and if we reject the possibility of entry by the characters concerned from under the acting area, then logically we *must* postulate another means by which actors could come out into the yard. Such an assumption, fortunately, offers no serious strain to our credulity. In the Swan Theatre drawing there is a large 'Ingressus' at each side of the acting area in the yard wall. However we interpret its function, whether it was a means for the audience to get into the theatre from outside or whether it was designed to allow spectators to reach the first gallery, it could easily have been connected with the players' tiring-house: indeed, it would have been rather peculiar had it not been so connected. The 'Ingressus', therefore, provides us with precisely what we were looking for. True, it is removed from the tiring-house itself, but in none of the actions designated as 'passages over the stage' in the play directions is there any call for an actor to make an entry, an exit and an immediately following re-entry at another place. The passers-by and the processions move on and off: that is all.

The second assumption, that there was provision in the Elizabethan theatre for some way of stepping up on to the acting area from the yard, although there is no positive evidence to support it, finds justification in the long-standing tradition in booth-stages of ladder-like steps from the ground to the raised acting level, associated with the tradition of steps from stage to floor in Renaissance court theatres, English as well as French and Italian. If there were two sets of such ladder-like steps, probably movable, at each side of the Elizabethan public theatre, set fairly close to or even against the façade wall, then we should have precisely the 'one end' and the 'other end' cited in the play directions. At the same time, their presence, coupled with means of entry by the 'Ingressus', would provide just what would be necessary for the effective carrying-out of a dignified 'passage over the stage'.[5]

One objection might, perhaps, be raised here; but it is an objection which, although at first appearing valid, can be dismissed after a moment's consideration as academic rather than practical. What, it may be said, about the problem of clearing a lane for the actors through the groundlings in the yard? The answer is obvious. Spectators, except for those few who go to be seen, want to see, and a glance at the Swan drawing shows that the strip of yard from the 'Ingressus' to the tiring-house wall offers a location from which the greater part of the action would have been quite invisible. Without doubt the groundlings, being sensible folk, must have tended to crowd into that part of the yard which faces the platform; and if ever such a crowd gathered as to leave space for some spectators only in the rear portion, the players must have regarded the occasion as a truly extraordinary gala-afternoon.

VI

Taking everything under consideration, therefore, it would appear that we have to accept as the most reasonable, effective and practical interpretation of the phrase 'pass over the stage' a movement from yard to platform to yard again. Thus only could Vendice in *The Revenger's Tragedy* be offered an adequate position for delivering his soliloquy while the corrupt ducal company passes by in long-extended procession; Wendoll's soliloquy in *A Woman Killed with Kindness* as others go "ouer the stage" would have the same force; the characters in *The Fair Maid of the Exchange* would set the action by coming from a distance to the booth; the "Lieger Embassadours" in *The White Devil* would be differentiated from those who observe them. With this concept in mind, we should, perhaps, be prepared to reconsider a number of related directions, such as that which appears in *The Atheist's Tragedy*. There

Enter Borachio *warily and hastily ouer the Stage, with a stone in eyther hand.*

After a few words he "Descends", and our first thought is of a trap. A closer examination of the scene, however, suggests something different. Taking our cue from the words "ouer the Stage", we might well believe that Borachio comes in from one side of the yard, "warily and hastily" steals across the platform and then gets down on the other side, where he lies concealed. Thus, after D'Amville has thrust down Montferrers, Borachio can appropriately say:

> I lay so fitly vnderneath the bancke
> From whence he fell,

and the location can be described as "the grauell pit". While it is true that the directions are not quite clear, the scene would have been much more effective, acted thus, than it would have been if resort had been made to the use of a trap. In fact, we should have here a variant of the procedure which Sir E. K. Chambers believed was commonly employed to suggest action at the banks of rivers: "as a rule", he says, "the edge of the stage" seems to have been used for this purpose.[6]

Sometimes, even when the preposition 'over' is used with a verb other than 'pass', we may suspect the same movement. In 2 *Edward IV* "Jockie is led to whipping ouer the stage", and the situation is so closely akin to the others that it can reasonably be placed in the same category. Still further, it might be suggested that in some plays, particularly those written by young dramatists who had not as yet fully mastered their technical playhouse vocabulary, certain scenes, although not specified as involving movement "over the stage", were so intended. A particularly interesting example of this occurs in *Every Man in his Humour*. The 1601 Quarto, representing the text of the comedy as written and played in 1598, tells us that Giuliano enters, "goes out agayne" and re-enters, while other characters standing on the platform comment on his appearance. The comedy, however, was later rewritten by Jonson, with an English setting and characters, and as such was printed in the Folio of 1616. There, the person corresponding to Giuliano, now named Downright, "walkes ouer the stage" and then, after making his exit, returns. The nature of the scene, with the silent figure observed and commented upon by others, at once indicates that "walkes ouer" is equivalent to the familiar "passes over"; and consequently we must presume that the action indicated by this phrase remains concealed in the 1601 Quarto's entry and "goes out agayne".

If the conclusions reached in this scrutiny of 'passages over the stage' are valid, then Elizabethan performances must indeed be conceived of as possessing a kind of additional dimension, providing means of presenting dignified and spectacular processions and of effecting distinctions between separate groups of characters. How far we may go beyond this remains uncertain, but in the debate concerning the precise method by which some particular scenes were presented on Shakespeare's stage, we should certainly not confine our attention to the main acting area, to 'discoveries' and to the appearance of characters 'above'; we should also take into consideration action at the rear portions of the yard and across the platform.

To 'pass over the stage' seems indeed to have been an important part of Elizabethan stage practice.[7]

NOTES

1. This article formed part of a presidential address delivered to the Society for Theatre Research on 30 April 1958.

2. C. Walter Hodges, in 'Unworthy Scaffolds' (*Shakespeare Survey*, 3 (1950), 95), has stated his opinion that "there is more than a little reason to believe that Elizabethan stage practice did occasionally include, if only for its stunt value, a certain amount of action in the yard".

3. *The Antipodes* provides three examples of the use of 'pass over the stage', of which two have special interest in this connection: (1) "Hoboyes. A service as for dinner, passe over the Stage, borne by many Servitors richly apparreld, doing honor to Letoy as they passe"; (2) "These persons passe over the Stage in Couples, according as he [i.e. the Doctor] describes them."

4. Richard Hosley, to whom I am indebted for many useful comments, has drawn my attention to one direction which seems to suggest that a 'passing over' character enters by a door. This is in *The Hog hath lost his Pearl*: "Enter Lightfoote, a country gentleman, passing ouer the stage, and knocks at the other dore"—but this single reference from a non-professional play ("Divers times Publikely acted, by certaine London Prentices") cannot outweigh the many other references cited above.

5. Sir E. K. Chambers, *Elizabethan Stage*, III (1923), 29 and 40, finds evidence in the plays of Whetstone and Lyly for "a convention by which action on the extreme edge of a stage, or possibly on the floor of the hall or on steps leading to the stage, was treated as a little remote from the place represented by the setting in the background"; these he calls 'approach' episodes. He further states (p. 90) that he could not find evidence for a similar convention in the public theatres; but, if the interpretation of 'passing over the stage' is correct, then we have a direct continuation of the Whetstone-Lyly device. J. W. Saunders ('Vaulting the Rails', *Shakespeare Survey*, 7 (1954), 69–81) has argued for movement from yard to platform and has suggested that the 'Ingressus' might have been used as a place of entrance, without, however, providing any clear evidence from play-directions. In the present volume of *Shakespeare Survey*, p. 30, Richard Southern suggests the possibility that actors may on occasion have come in by this yard entrance and indicates how this entrance was probably connected with the 'back-stage' area.

6. Sir E. K. Chambers, *op. cit.* III, 107: see also pp. 51, 58 and 90.

7. Dr N. J. Sanders has drawn my attention to a scene in Greene's *Alphonsus* which well illustrates the necessity of taking into account the possibility, indeed likelihood, of these entries from the yard. At the end of the first act the stage is cleared with an "*Exeunt*", yet a direction immediately following specifically calls for the players who have just left the stage to re-enter in martial order and, once they are "in", for Venus to enter at the beginning of act II. Sir Walter Greg, in his Malone Society edition, assumes a compositorial error of "*Enter*" for "*Exit*"; but the intention seems to be to provide some action between the two acts (a device used elsewhere in the play, at the end of II. ii and after the exit of Venus in act v). Hence we might well assume that the direction: "*Enter* Belinus, Albinius...*with the souldier[s], assoone as they are in, strike vp alarum a while, and then enter* Venus" means what it says—that these actors did come in again, making a passage across the stage from the "Ingressus", leaving Venus free to come in by one of the doors or from above. As Dr Sanders points out, such an arrangement would make the first lines of her speech much more effective and would make her declaration, "From banisht state as you haue plainely seene, He...marcheth in the Ensigne of the King", literally true for the audience.

THE ACTOR AT THE FOOT OF SHAKESPEARE'S PLATFORM

BY

J. L. STYAN

In the original staging of Shakespeare's plays for the public theatre, one factor that can be reckoned with is a wide and deep platform—the contract for the Fortune requires that its stage shall "containe in length Fortie and Three foote of lawfull assize and in breadth to extende to the middle of the yarde". This remarkable platform allowed the actor freedom to act either remotely upstage or intimately on the perimeter with his feet among the spectators. If we argue from an upstage entrance and this special feature of depth, from the logic of acting and the modulations of a scene, it is not only possible to consider the actor's position on the stage relative to the audience, but we can gain a little more insight into the Elizabethan kind of theatrical vitality.

How did this actors' freedom help to shape a scene in Shakespeare? As might be expected, we find an urgent hint thrown out by Granville-Barker. Discussing soliloquy in the introduction to his *Prefaces*, and writing with his customary feeling for the actor in relation to the audience, he said, "Soliloquy becomes the means by which [Shakespeare] brings us not only to a knowledge of the more secret thoughts of his characters, but *into the closest emotional touch with them too*.... Time and again he may be feeling his way through a scene for *a grip on his audience*, and it is the soliloquy ending it that will give him—*and his actor*—the stranglehold..." (my italics).

But was the soliloquy the only occasion for the actor to narrow the physical gap between himself and his audience? Shakespeare was of course not unaware of the acting opportunities of his three-dimensional platform. We need to see the action of his plays, not only as scenes played out by actors, but more as actors playing to an audience. What has rather stiffly been called the actor's 'direct address' to the audience, usually with reference to the soliloquy, is better seen as but one small, if striking, part of a whole stage technique which takes into account the actor playing to or away from his spectators. Soliloquy takes our attention because it is the extreme use of an actor's convention which actually pervaded the whole play. B. L. Joseph has reminded us that "Elizabethan acting did not make our modern distinction between monologue and dialogue" (*Elizabethan Acting*, p. 132). A play written by a dramatist thinking in terms of an open stage is likely to use dialogue which, while it is not always soliloquy or aside, is yet often directly addressed to the audience. More important, such a play is likely to have the shape and quality of its speech and movement controlled by a feeling for the spectator that we today, trained to the playing of a proscenium stage, must make a special effort to understand.

The actor who knows the force of the pull towards the 'footlights' will feel the practical principle behind this. The impulse of the actor to present himself at close quarters to his audience must have been strong on an open stage with the spectators on three really tight sides of him. And the playgoer who witnesses movement on an unlocalized stage will know how such a stage sharply emphasizes the presence of the actor and helps him to manipulate the feelings of the

56

spectator. What has been called "the eloquence of emptiness" permits a direct relationship between actor and spectator. When did Shakespeare feel the pull of the actor towards his audience? When did he encourage it with his dialogue?

These were some of the occasions when the playwright evidently did send the actor downstage:

(1) Sometimes upon entrance, the actor introducing himself and what he stands for, establishing the emotional relationship with the spectator, often to prepare him for an irony to come. Banquo's open revelation of his suspicions serves for an example of this.

(2) When the actor points out another character in order to establish a relationship between them, or to define the feeling with which the playwright wishes the audience to surround his second character. Thus Romeo indicates and embellishes the dancing Juliet; Philo prepares us with a judgment on his general, Antony; Ulysses clinches our view of Cressida.

(3) When a character is to comment upon the scene, without himself leaving it, as when the Doctor diagnoses Lady Macbeth's trouble, or when Thersites diagnoses the misery of Troilus.[1] The downstage position of the commentator is used to mark behaviour which demands criticism, the nearness of the observer to the spectator itself compelling such criticism.

(4) When it is important to the meaning of the scene for one or more characters to be clearly distinguished from the rest, sometimes because the stage is heavily populated, but often because the playwright wishes to explore the dramatic situation of an individual versus the rest, making distinctions between characters and providing visual ironies within the framework of the scene itself: Cordelia refuses to answer Lear as her sisters do; Malcolm and Donalbain hold a private conference in, and in spite of, a crowded and exciting scene.

(5) When the revelation of a secret is to make the audience temporary collaborators in a deceit, without necessarily claiming their sympathy, as when Edmund makes his confession before Edgar and Gloucester enter. The place of hero or villain in the affections of the audience may determine his place on the platform.

(6) To suggest contrasting values of sincerity between characters, as between Hamlet and Claudius in their carefully juxtaposed "soliloquies".

We shall look at these instances. Trying to catalogue examples which demonstrate such great variety shows how freely characters seem to move, as it were, out of and back into the scene. It is as if the scene takes the actor upstage from time to time, reducing him to a character in a play-within-a-play, while release from the situation allows him to become in part a spectator, bringing him downstage as if to identify himself with his audience. This movement may often correspond with S. L. Bethell's "depersonalisation of character" (*Shakespeare and the Popular Dramatic Tradition*, ch. 5). It follows that the foot of the platform is sometimes used as neutral ground that is even less localized than the acting area nearer the façade of the tiring-house. Direct and indirect address seem to be used at a time when the poetic drama, by definition non-naturalistic, refreshes and compels its audience by methods that lie outside the immediate action of the scene. Such moments may be subtly woven into the scene itself.

A straightforward entrance which demonstrates a fully dramatic use of the platform's depth is that introduced by Banquo's only soliloquy (III, i),

Thou hast it now, king, Cawdor, Glamis, all.

Banquo partly extends our own tentative thoughts on Macbeth's conduct, and articulates them. His physical position and movement on the stage from the time when he enters by the upstage door, sees, perhaps (as others have suggested), the throne of the new king set in the study, and then moves downstage to impart his confession to the audience from a pivotal point, reinforces the emotional relationship in which he stands to us. His intimacy with us is directly related to the dramatic meaning.

The sennet is sounded, and Banquo, confident that he has our sympathy, rhetorically calls for our silence as much as his own with a downstage whisper:

> But hush, no more.

And he must turn his back on the greater part of the spectators to greet the King and Queen, following with his movement the direction our eyes have taken as we see the full state procession with its lords and attendants. This sudden, exciting transition from an almost empty stage to a crowded one, from a downstage to an upstage action, is a common trick of Shakespeare's, but here it stresses the distinction between private truth and public deceit, which is explored as a major theme in the structure of the play.

If Macbeth is to be seated on his throne, it is in the nature of practical stage grouping for Banquo to remain with his back to us, our representative as the innocent, partly detached observer, so that we receive fully the emotional implications of the sly questioning that follows, as if its evil intention were directed against us too. Meanwhile, to answer Macbeth's questions, Banquo must move upstage, withdrawing himself into the stage picture, but not before we have been so prepared that we weigh up the meaning of the sequence with a renewed intensity of interest. In this way Shakespeare the producer controls his audience by the agency of his actor's movement.

Romeo's first sight of Juliet (I, v) is an example of an indirect address, whereby one character directs our response to another:

> *Romeo.* What lady is that, which doth enrich the hand
> Of yonder knight?
> *Servant.*   I know not, sir.
> *Romeo.* O, she doth teach the torches to burn bright!
> It seems she hangs upon the cheek of night
> Like a rich jewel in an Ethiope's ear;
> Beauty too rich for use, for earth too dear!
> So shows a snowy dove trooping with crows,
> As yonder lady o'er her fellows shows.

When Capulet and his cousin have 'retired' to talk over old times, Romeo must here be downstage to be clear of the dancers. He is thus looking upstage at Juliet dancing, that is, looking where the Elizabethan audience is looking, while at the same time speaking into its ear. Given these primarily illustrative lines, he not only warmly suggests, as if by soliloquy, that he has fallen in love, but he also supplies a verbal commentary to establish the boy-actor as a beautiful girl; his words paint and adorn her. The movement upstage catches the eye, the voice downstage catches the ear, both creating an initial impression of Juliet which is to persist throughout the play, though enlarged and refined as the play develops.

At the opening of *Antony and Cleopatra*, Philo's is a pretended conversation with his guest Demetrius: Shakespeare opens the dialogue with a *Nay, but...*, veiling in a partly naturalistic fashion another address to the audience.

> Nay, but this dotage of our general's
> O'erflows the measure...

presents us directly with the superficial view of Antony, a view we are to modify. But what must strike us is that, since Antony and Cleopatra enter after Philo and Demetrius, and since Philo continues his commentary after Antony, Cleopatra and their retinue have disposed themselves about the platform against his

> Look, where they come:
> Take but good note....

Shakespeare is certainly using all available depth to stage an effective visual as well as verbal irony. For Antony and Cleopatra must play out their first love scene,

> If it be love indeed, tell me how much...,

framed upstage between the pillars, and seen through the critical eyes of these Roman officers.

Ulysses' comment on Cressida as she moves upstage to the door (*Troilus and Cressida*, IV, v) is typical of a stage pattern whereby one character passes judgment on another for us. This instance is interesting since Ulysses is evidently looking upstage at her as she walks off:

> Nay, her foot speaks; her wanton spirits look out
> At every joint and motive of her body.
> O, these encounterers, so glib of tongue,
> That give accosting welcome ere it comes....

Ulysses, like Romeo, is reinforcing the skill of the boy-actor as he moves. More important, he is formally embodying, from a relatively downstage position and from the audience's physical viewpoint, an acknowledged set of values upon which Shakespeare in this play is embroidering.

To imagine the Doctor and the Gentlewoman upstage *with* Lady Macbeth during her sleep-walking scene (v, i) is to forget the spectators. A grouping which effectively uses the depth of the stage is fully suggested by the dialogue. Shakespeare is careful to prepare Lady Macbeth's entrance with words that both gather suspense and indicate the meaning of what we are to see. The Doctor's comment,

A great perturbation in nature, to receive at once the benefit of sleep, and do the effects of watching!

is a sly example, surely, of an indirect address to the audience. To convey the excitement of this, the Doctor and the Gentlewoman must be placed downstage. Lady Macbeth may enter upstage where it may be convenient, since dramatically it is not she who matters as much as the meaning to be deduced from her behaviour and statements. The excitement gains ironically, of course, because we see her through uninformed eyes; but much of this would be lost with any other grouping.

After pressure has been put on us by the Doctor's ejaculations, "Do you mark that?", "Even so?", he clinches the meaning of the scene and finally stimulates a larger interest with,

> Foul whisperings are abroad: unnatural deeds
> Do breed unnatural troubles: infected minds
> To their deaf pillows will discharge their secrets:
> More needs she the divine, than the physician.

While Shakespeare almost incidentally creates the character of the Doctor in the rhythmic repetitiveness of his lines, his character is given the double function of being both *dramatis persona* and chorus, which is precisely the advantage of the deep stage.

v, ii of *Troilus and Cressida* is a scene of visual originality. In it the eavesdroppers, Troilus and Ulysses, are themselves the object of eavesdropping by Thersites. Every comment Thersites makes on Cressida is a comment on Troilus's idealism: while Cressida in her flirting with Diomedes is staged as a specimen for her former lover's dissection, Troilus himself suffers like treatment, in this manner:

> *Diomedes.* How now, my charge!
> *Cressida.* Now, my sweet guardian! Hark, a word with you.
> *Troilus.* Yea, so familiar!
> *Ulysses.* She will sing any man at first sight.
> *Thersites.* And any man may sing her, if he can take her cliff; she's noted.

Thersites's "any man" is every man in general and Troilus in particular. In a scene of three groups, Diomedes and Cressida, Troilus and Ulysses, and Thersites, none of the groups is at the centre of the action—the effect of the drama lies in the ironies set up by the physical relationships between the groups. It is therefore important that we in the audience feel these ironies by the nearness of Troilus relative to Cressida, and by the greater nearness of Thersites relative to Troilus. Only on an Elizabethan platform could such a scene have been conceived.

Delicate ironies helped by grouping in depth abound in Shakespeare. Malcolm and Donalbain, as Ronald Watkins has suggested (*On Producing Shakespeare*, p. 293), hold their quick debate (II, iii) on their future course of action against a crowded and lively stage: they speak, indeed, at the climactic moment of Lady Macbeth's fainting, and Shakespeare has considerably sandwiched their words between Macduff's line,

> Look to the lady,

and the same line repeated by Banquo, encouraging us to follow the central action from the point where our attention had to leave it. It is evident from this that the author wants Malcolm and Donalbain to speak downstage, and the reason is not far to seek. Macbeth's public and effusive statement,

> Who can be wise, amazed, temperate, and furious...,

with its prolixity amid the brief, stunned phrases of the others, is to be immediately balanced by an intimate honesty from the other party so closely affected by the murder of Duncan:

> Let's away;
> Our tears are not yet brew'd.

The upstage-downstage arrangement of the action sharply marks the contradiction in the scene.

The court scene in Act I of *King Lear* also presents a crowded stage. The elder daughters are identified as soon as they are addressed by Lear and when they speak. Cordelia must wait till last—yet is it not important that we begin to know her feelings before she utters her "Nothing, my lord"? As has been recognized, Shakespeare gives her words before the narrative requires them, because he sees that the *audience* requires them. Unfortunately, as one of three sisters facing Lear, Cordelia's words may well be lost: but the author provides for this.

The words Cordelia is given to speak are usually marked in the edited directions as 'aside'. Closer definition is wanted. Her words involve a movement away from the sisters whom she repudiates. This movement follows naturally from what she hears Goneril say, but it brings her unnaturally outside the acted scene: her words therefore suddenly take our attention. The unexpected full view of Cordelia's face, isolated among the crowd of courtiers, helps to distinguish these words as a form of speech. They are close to a direct address to the audience, and they are characteristic of soliloquy in that they immediately illuminate Cordelia's mind. The brevity and simplicity of

> Love, and be silent,

separates her from the loquacious Goneril. And the movement assists our impression of her sincerity.

What lies behind the effectiveness of Shakespeare's device is what makes Banquo, Romeo, Philo, Ulysses, the Doctor and Thersites play to the audience: here it is Cordelia's instinct to pass downstage, leaving Goneril and Regan upstage in their deceit, her turning away itself being a comment. Thereafter we judge the elder sisters for what they are, and are predisposed to sympathize with Cordelia. We are at the same time prepared fully to appreciate the value of her "Nothing", while still able to enjoy its shock.

It is worth noticing that in the same act Edmund's "Nothing, my lord" to his father Gloucester is, in the stage grouping, given a visual echo to Cordelia's. Edmund's

> Thou, nature, art my goddess

is spoken downstage in soliloquy: this is the villain's confession. At the entrance of Gloucester at the door upstage, Edmund must turn to greet him, just as Cordelia had to turn back into the play when Lear addressed her with, "Now, our joy". The verbal echo of "Nothing, my lord", is made ironic, not only because of Edmund's initial confession, but, quite simply, because Edmund conceals his forged letter in full sight of the audience, thereby forcing us to join in the deceit. But Cordelia spoke the truth; Edmund lies. Thus his words underline Cordelia's sincerity, and are emphasized by a parallel stage position.

Edmund persists in challenging our regard by movements of confidence towards us in this scene. Upon the entry of Edgar, we are again involved in his pretence, even to the extent of being given, as it were, the villain's wink:

Pat he comes like the catastrophe of the old comedy: my cue is villanous melancholy, with a sigh like Tom o' Bedlam. O these eclipses do portend these divisions! fa, sol, la, mi.

The implied 'wink to the audience' is sustained throughout the sequence that follows, up to his,

I am no honest man, if there be any good meaning toward you.

And this pretence is strengthened by the physical relationship with the audience that the open stage allows.

Finally, in the scene of Claudius' prayer (*Hamlet*, III, iii), there would seem to be two soliloquies, since neither character speaks to the other or is heard by the other. But each offers a different convention of speech, the difference being marked by the actor's proximity to the spectator. Although both are private, Claudius' speech is not confidential as Hamlet's is. Each character is debating with himself, but the spectator does not join in Claudius' debate. When we hear Claudius plead

Forgive me my foul murder,

we do not plead with him: we view him objectively. This effect would be promoted by his total disregard of the audience.

Hamlet's case is different, for we are in sympathy with him.

O, this is hire and salary, not revenge,

is the speech of a man deliberating with himself, but it is also the choric comment of a downstage address, directing us to place a valuation upon his proposed killing of Claudius. When he asks,

and am I then revenged,
To take him in the purging of his soul,
When he is fit and season'd for his passage?

this is at once the rhetorical question of a chorus and a direct question to the audience. And so Hamlet moves back into the scene, into character and into the situation once more.

The contrasting attitude the spectator will have to each character is emphasized by the grouping on the deep stage, Claudius remote, Hamlet close. This whole effect has a parallel in the visual image we retain of the court scene of I, ii, in which Claudius sits in public state, offering himself with his glib speech for our criticism, as it were in a play-within-a-play among his court. There too he is suddenly brought sharply into relief, first by the emptying of the stage and then by the private comments of Hamlet's first soliloquy, their contrasting tones of voice being marked by the downstage and upstage positioning of the actors.

In acknowledging the nature of his platform in these ways, Shakespeare had in mind what force could be added to the flow of his drama, with what emphasis he could mark the significant statement, what special response he could persuade from the spectator, what variety of tone and feeling he could create within the framework of a scene. In addition, speech at the centre of the Elizabethan theatre must have been generally quieter and lower in tone than speech upstage: a glance over the soliloquies confirms this. The 'ranted' speech is the speech from the throne and the declamation in battle. But, as the actor knows, lower tone permits a greater control over intonation and a greater variation in pace: in general the soliloquy at the foot of the platform invites a more musical and quicker speech. This is related to the confidential nature of such speech, and offers a distinctive heightening of its quality and intensity.

Such clear-cut subtle effects must be constantly subdued, if not suppressed, on the flatter proscenium stage. Yet today's producer should be aware of the shades of interest his actor ought to kindle, and he should know when downstage effects are being suggested. He must contrive such effects by means other than those of proximity to the audience. The most flexible and subtle agency on the stage remains the actor's voice, and since the behaviour of the voice is directly related to the behaviour of the body, it would seem that special use must be made of speech. We accept that when the voice whispers, the body enacts the whisper; when the voice roars, the body enacts the roar. It follows that when the body is to any extent restricted, the voice must create a compensatingly stronger impression if the same effect is to be communicated as when the body is free. The producer must therefore look to the speaking of the verse if the full variety of Shakespeare's deep stage is at all to be reproduced within the picture frame.

NOTE

1. I would not suggest that occasions may not be found when one character is passing comment on another from a position upstage, but this arrangement seems to be dictated by a special situation. Here are three scenes whose grouping is determined by the need to eavesdrop: (1) In *Much Ado About Nothing* it is likely that Benedick will be hidden upstage in the 'arbour' to overhear Don Pedro, Leonato and Claudio, and that it is from this position he speaks his asides, though these are intended only to let the audience know that he can 'hear' what is being said by the conspirators. (2) In *Twelfth Night* we may presume that Sir Toby, Sir Andrew and Fabian hide upstage from Malvolio if we believe that the 'box tree' was introduced as a property, though this is not certain. (3) We can be more certain of the prison scene in *The Two Noble Kinsmen*, since we are told directly that the captive Palamon and Arcite overhear "*Emilia and her Servant, below*". It is therefore from above that they comment on her beauty.

ELIZABETHAN STAGE-PRACTICE AND THE TRANSMUTATION OF SOURCE MATERIAL BY THE DRAMATISTS

BY

RUDOLF STAMM

Harley Granville-Barker, in his study of *Hamlet*, says of Shakespeare: "The play as it leaves his hands is not a finished product, only its performance makes it that."[1] This conception of a text as a kind of theatrical score requiring the actor and the producer to bring it to life has practical consequences for the student of Shakespearian as well as many other kinds of drama. The study of dramatic structure, speech patterns, imagery, characters, ideas, and meanings in a play cannot be independent, but demands a clear idea of the play-in-performance in the reader's mind. A similar awareness should direct those investigating such practical matters as stage-structure and methods of acting and production. The play-in-performance as a governing idea renders impossible both the purely literary interpretation of a theatrical text and the purely technical interest in matters of theatrical research.[2] Considering the present state of our knowledge of the texts and of the methods of production in the Elizabethan and Jacobean theatres, it now seems particularly promising and necessary to study the relationship between the playwright's words and stage events, to correlate what the actors spoke and did, what the spectators heard and saw. It leads to the comprehension of what we may call a play's theatrical physiognomy—the *ensemble* of all those features of a text that define, explicitly or implicitly, its realization on the stage for which it was originally written. This article can only glance briefly at the most important features.

Our first question concerns the relation between speech and action. Does the play contain the two extreme forms of representation, pantomime on the one hand and purely declamatory reports, soliloquies and dialogues on the other? What is the proportion of these forms to the scenes in which both speech and action are present? No less characteristic for a play than this proportion are the qualities of each of the three types of scenes. Where speech and action appear together, the methods of combining the two elements demand our full attention. Naturally, we must study the texts as originally printed and disregard many of the improvements of the later editors. If we do this, we are struck by the modest part played by the stage directions. By far the most frequent are "Enter" and "Exeunt", and most of the directions about other stage events are equally terse. "They stab Caesar" and "Dies" are good instances of this. They simply tell what happens, and leave us completely in the dark as to how it happens. The most valuable pointers concerning how things happen are contained in the speeches themselves. They direct the movements, gestures and facial expression of the actors, but only where the playwright, instead of relying upon established acting conventions, creates new combinations of speech and action to express new meanings. Sometimes a dramatist attempts a double representation, in word and action. The suicide of Cassius and Banquo's first speech to the Weird Sisters are examples, containing invaluable information about the methods of Elizabethan acting. The study of such passages is the best preparation for the more numerous speeches in which gestures and stage events are only implied, instead of being explicitly mentioned. The hints may be in the meaning, rhythm, punctuation or the typography of the original text. The student of such features will be most attracted by the scenes where speech-action is the main medium, but he should not neglect the declamatory ones. They had their functions in all the forms of Elizabethan drama, and were never completely abandoned by Shakespeare. They must be accepted and understood as an integral part of the theatrical texts of the period.[3] The question as to how the declamatory passages were rendered in the theatre is difficult to answer. Probably the conventional means of rhetorical delivery were freely used and, therefore, the explanations given by Bertram Joseph in his *Elizabethan Acting* can be particularly helpful here.

Another basic problem is the relationship between the dramatist's words and the stage setting. It resembles the relationship between word and action in one important respect. Those neutral scenes which have only the vaguest definition of place and time correspond to the declamatory passages where actions and gestures are left undefined. The setting of a scene is defined only when it has a specific function. In studying the collaboration between the stage-picture and its mental image we shall have to range from the simple expedient of naming the place at the opening of a scene to various forms of word-scenery, some of them highly atmospheric and intimately connected with the moods of the characters and the meaning of their fate. The use of such demonstratives as 'this', 'that' and 'yonder', and of the gestures demanded by them, deserves close attention, because they are the most obvious connecting links between speech and action, imagination and the stage.

Nearly all these problems have been discussed by Granville-Barker and others,[4] but they have not been consistently co-ordinated. When this work has been done, interesting affinities and differences will emerge, which will help us to relate plays with a similar physiognomy—on the lines of George F. Reynolds, Gerald E. Bentley and Richard Hosley—to the acting companies and stages for which they were written. Moreover, a new approach to the plays themselves will be open, capable of supplementing the results of the more familiar approaches through language, imagery, structure, characters, and ideas. It should prove equally valuable to the scholarly interpreter in his study or in front of his experimental stage and the producer and actor in the modern professional theatre.[5] In these artists it can sharpen the sense for the difference between methods which are in harmony with the texts and others that clearly go against them.[6]

We turn now to a subsidiary question: What place has the study of sources in the inquiries we have outlined? Kenneth Muir's *Shakespeare's Sources* (vol. 1) draws together hundreds of facts, effectively stimulating our curiosity about source study. Are the changes undergone by source material in the hands of the playwright significant for those scholars only who want to understand an author's ideas, allusions, characters,[7] and meanings? On the contrary, because the playwright has the play-in-performance before his mind's eye while he is transmuting source material, the comparison of a text with its sources can help the student of a play's theatrical physiognomy, too.

As an example of this we may compare the opening scenes of *Antony and Cleopatra* with the corresponding account in North's Plutarch. The relation between the play and its source is so close and clear here that it forms an unusually good basis for a comparison.

To begin with, let us call to mind how Plutarch marshals his facts. Before coming to the first meeting of the lovers, he offers a thorough discussion of Antony's character, followed by a striking description of his luxurious and wild life at Athens. Then he recounts the exchange of civilities between him and the queen of Egypt, and draws a glowing picture of Cleopatra's splendour, never more remarkable than during her arrival on her barge and the subsequent festivities. Plutarch endeavours to explain the overwhelming fascination she had for Antony, mentioning her not quite perfect beauty, her numerous abilities and unrivalled charm. A number of anecdotes illustrate the lavish life of the couple at Alexandria: eight wild boars roasted for a single dinner; Antony's son a reckless spendthrift; Cleopatra always with Antony, sometimes walking the streets with him at night in a "chamber-maid's array", full of resources in planning entertainments and pranks. One of these, her fooling him by having a salt-fish put upon his hook when he was fishing, is reported in some detail. After this leisurely description Plutarch's story begins to move. Bad news about the disasters of his wife and brother in Italy and the successes of Labienus in Asia rouse Antony. He prepares to fight the Parthians, but is recalled to Italy by Fulvia. Before he can meet her, he hears of her death. His reconciliation with Octavius Caesar, the new political arrangements of the triumvirs, and the new marriage with Octavia are summarized rapidly. Then the conflict and patched-up peace with Sextus Pompeius are given again in greater detail.

We shall now observe how this circumstantial account is turned into a stage-worthy text by Shakespeare. In search of the right beginning he pounces, with his experienced eye, on the point where Plutarch's story begins to move. Antony is in the coils of Cleopatra, but being Antony nevertheless, he is, from the beginning, torn between the two forces whose conflict is the play's leading theme: between Egypt and Rome, imagination and will-power, the senses and the intellect, to mention only some of its manifestations and significances. The opening is made by Philo, who, acting as a kind of prologue, expresses the Roman view of the situation and confronts Antony's present with his former self.

> Nay, but this dotage of our Generals
> Ore-flowes the measure:[8]   (I, i, 1–2.)

'Nay' implies an angry gesture of revulsion. The third little word 'this' presents an interesting problem. As we have pointed out above, demonstratives of this kind, as well as the deictic gestures required by them, are of considerable importance for our purpose. They usually point to parts of the stage, to figures or properties on the stage, or to objects, places or events to be imagined beyond its limits.[9] The 'this' before us, however, is of a more abstract quality. It points to Antony's condition; it summarizes the entire situation in which the play opens. Its implications are the only place-indication for the spectator, and also the only time-indication. The time quality is felt when the 'this' sentence is followed by

> those his goodly eyes
> That o're the Files and Musters of the Warre,
> Haue glow'd like plated Mars.

'This' implies the present, 'those' the past. They can hardly have been entirely non-gestic. 'This' seems to call for a vague, generalizing gesture, probably in the direction where Antony and the queen will presently appear. 'Those' would draw Philo's look in another, possibly, the opposite direction, a look beyond the present into the past, accompanied by a gesture of disappointment and loss. The passage on Antony's eyes is remarkable in another respect. It continues:

> Now bend, now turne
> The Office and Deuotion of their view
> Vpon a Tawny Front.

Antony's former and his present self, the proud warrior and the compliant lover, are presented in terms of facial expression. Before the spectator catches a glimpse of the protagonist, he visualizes imaginatively two conflicting expressions on his face, which contain, as it were, everything that is going to happen in the play. Before Demetrius can give any answer, Antony and Cleopatra make their formal entry. Theatrical convention prevents them from hearing and being disturbed by the speaker's devastating remark about "The triple Pillar of the world transform'd into a Strumpets Foole". This disgusted commentary is accompanied by no less than four invitations to concentrate attention on the approaching couple. They are addressed to the audience as well as to Demetrius:

> Looke where they come.
> Take but good note, and you shall see in him....
> Behold and see. (I, I, 10–13)

These demonstrative verbs were certainly accompanied by appropriate gestures.

The first exchange of words between Antony and Cleopatra is in complete contrast to what precedes and what follows it. Four end-stopped lines, three of them of a very regular metrical structure, still breathe the rhythm of the formal entry, and demand statuesque declamation rather than speech-action. For a moment Shakespeare interrupts the lively flow of the speech-action in order to reveal, through another medium, one of Antony's basic attitudes, before it is broken by the news from Rome. Only here do we find the couple in that initial situation so carefully and lengthily described by Plutarch. The fact that the playwright cut down the historian's introduction so drastically does not mean that he had no use for its characteristic details. They were either boldly summarized in Philo's biased opening speech or resolved into the speech-action of many a following scene or, as we shall see, digested into reports, and inserted between the speech-action at suitable places.

The static seconds, the seconds of declamation, are succeeded by something new and different as soon as the messenger announces:

> Newes (my good Lord) from Rome.

From Antony there comes only a contemptuous "Grates me, the summe", charged with two powerful gestic impulses. Cleopatra is stung into vehement speech-action. In it she reveals her fiery temperament, jealousy, possessiveness, wit, powers of impersonation, and she continues to do so in the following scenes, where we see her struggling in vain against the "Roman thought" that has struck Antony and, later on, sending and receiving messages to and from Rome. In defining herself she gives reality, life, and power to our conception of Egypt, just as, in later scenes, Caesar and Octavia give reality, life, and power to our idea of Rome. But our conception of Egypt is fed and enriched by much else beside Cleopatra's speech-action. There are the scenes of her women and courtiers with their loose talk and manners. And, thirdly, there are the reported events and inset descriptions that offer considerable help to the spectator's imagination. Very little of what appears in speech-action in these early Cleopatra scenes is based on Plutarch. Not one of the lively anecdotes concerning the Alexandrian revels is staged; they are all reserved for occasional reporting.

Plutarch's remark that Antony and Cleopatra used to mix with the common people at night is the basis of the following proposal:

> No Messenger but thine, and all alone, to night,
> Wee'l wander through the streets, and note
> The qualities of people. Come my Queene,
> Last night you did desire it. Speake not to vs. (I, i, 52–5)

The first sentence requires the tones and gestures of not entirely convincing encouragement. The second begins with an invitation to the queen to move and leave the disagreeable presence of the messenger without having heard his news, and it ends with a second attempt to overcome the reluctance visible in her behaviour. The final negative imperative is addressed to the messenger, and implies that the latter has once more tried to obtain Antony's permission to speak. The whole passage is thoroughly integrated in the uneasy controversy of the scene. Through it the audience set foot in Alexandria for the first time. The hints that give a certain concreteness to the place of the scene are accompanied by corresponding time indications: 'to-night' and 'last night' introduce new and concrete time relations, very different from the general and abstract ones implied by the 'this, and 'those' in Philo's opening speech. In the course of the scene Shakespeare moves from the general to the particular.

Another use of Plutarch's anecdotes is made in Caesar's speech at the beginning of the first Roman scene of the play (I, iv). It adds vivid details to our knowledge of the goings-on in Alexandria:

> From Alexandria
> This is the newes: He fishes, drinkes, and wastes
> The Lampes of night in reuell: Is not more manlike
> Then *Cleopatra*: nor the Queene of *Ptolomy*
> More Womanly then us. Hardly gaue audience
> Or vouchsafe to thinke he had Partners. (I, iv, 3–8)

A particular virtue of this enumeration consists in the inclusion, among the new details, of one fact the audience have witnessed in I, i: Antony's reluctance to listen to the messenger. Furthermore we hear:

> Let's graunt it is not
> Amisse to tumble on the bed of *Ptolomy*,
> To giue a Kingdome for a Mirth, to sit
> And keepe the turne of Tipling with a Slaue,
> To reele the streets at noone, and stand the Buffet
> With knaues that smels of sweate. (I, iv, 16–21)

This rhetorical flashback both defines Caesar's critical attitude to Antony's behaviour and amplifies our impressions of the earlier Egyptian scenes. When Caesar receives the bad news of Pompeius' successes, he turns away from Lepidus and the messenger, and invokes the absentee Antony directly, painting a striking word-picture of the famous warrior's former self:

> *Anthony,*
> Leaue thy lasciuious Vassailes. When thou once
> Was beaten from *Medena*, where thou slew'st
> *Hirsius*, and *Pausa* Consuls, at thy heele
> Did Famine follow, whom thou fought'st against,
> (Though daintily brought vp) with patience more
> Then Sauages could suffer. Thou did'st drinke
> The stale of Horses, and the gilded Puddle
> Which Beasts would cough at. Thy pallat then did daine
> The roughest Berry, on the rudest Hedge.
> Yea, like the Stagge, when Snow the Pasture sheets,
> The barkes of Trees thou brows'd....   (I, iv, 55–66)

This is the impassioned plea of the skilled orator, devoid of gestic and other acting impulses. Here Shakespeare relies upon the traditional methods of rhetorical delivery. He sometimes moves quite close to North's diction, without neglecting his opportunities for heightening it. Even a rhetorical passage like the one before us is subtly attuned to the peculiarly dynamic mode of the whole play. This is achieved by imagery conceived in the spirit of dramatic and theatrical representation. The same methods are illustrated by the description of Cleopatra on her barge in II, ii, where some of the most striking details in Shakespeare's source take the form of a reminiscence. Another of Plutarch's Egyptian anecdotes appears in the same form, but is completely absorbed by the speech-action of a typical Cleopatra scene (II, v). The amusing fishing incident receives a very peculiar and moving emotional colour because it is recounted when Cleopatra, disconsolate and impatient without Antony, is at a loss how to while away her hours.

There is a striking example of one anecdote being actually staged, in the scene on Pompey's galley (II, vii), where Menas tempts his master. Here Shakespeare makes the most of the acting values in Plutarch's lively story. His Menas does not simply tell Pompey of his plan of cutting the cable and afterwards the throats of the three world-sharers. He finds it extremely difficult to approach his master, who is enjoying the conviviality and the drinking, and can hardly be made to listen. The passage abounds in impulses towards movement and gesture, as the following fragment of it shows:

> *Pomp.* Go hang sir, hang: tell me of that? Away:
> Do as I bid you. Where's this Cup I call'd for?
> *Men.* If for the sake of Merit thou wilt heare mee,
> Rise from thy stoole.
> *Pomp.* I thinke th'art mad: the matter?
> *Men.* I haue euer held my cap off to thy Fortunes.
> *Pomp.* Thou hast seru'd me with much faith: what's
> else to say? Be iolly Lords.   (II, vii, 59–65)

These speeches are important as pointers to fascinating and somewhat complicated stage events, which count for much more in the performance of the play than the words themselves. We cannot undertake their scenic interpretation here; if we could, we should derive considerable help from the piece of stage property mentioned in "Rise from thy stoole".

Thus we find that the comparison between a play and its source renders us particularly sensitive to all those features in it that characterize it as a text intended for a certain kind of stage performance. We have observed how a theatrical opening takes the place of a lengthy historical exposition, how the dramatist uses much of Plutarch's introductory material later in the play in order to create, by a variety of methods, a striking experience of his hero's existence in Egypt and Rome; we have noticed the appearance of direct and indirect acting impulses in the speeches of many scenes, but also the juxtaposition of speech-action and declamation. *Antony and Cleopatra* is famous for its many scenes, but Shakespeare hardly ever finds it necessary to give his places any local qualities and atmosphere. This is different in *Julius Caesar*, where the information offered by Plutarch, and amplified from other sources, concerning the horrors and strange portents of the night before Caesar's assassination is important for a whole series of scenes, in which the strategy of word-scenery can be studied. In *Romeo and Juliet*, to mention a play of an entirely different order, Shakespeare's treatment of the local and atmospheric descriptions in Brooke's poem is a new and individual problem again. A glance at these two plays tempts us to stress once more, by way of conclusion, the necessity of repeating the study of theatrical physiognomy, and of what we can learn about it from the comparison with the sources, in the case of every individual play.

NOTES

1. *Prefaces to Shakespeare*, 3rd series (1937), p. 5.
2. A striking example of a successful reinterpretation of a text in terms of its original performance is contained in *The Medieval Theatre in the Round* (1957) by Richard Southern. Here *The Castle of Perseverance*, which led a very modest existence in the books of literary scholars before Southern took it up, is brought back to its pristine vitality and splendour in a painstaking process of reconstruction, equally remarkable for its elaboration of technical details and its imaginative grasp of the performance as a whole.
3. Valuable information concerning the history of this type is offered in *Die Tragödie vor Shakespeare. Ihre Entwicklung im Spiegel der dramatischen Rede* (*Schriftenreihe der Deutschen Shakespeare-Gesellschaft*, N.F., Band v, Heidelberg 1955) by Wolfgang Clemen.
4. It is not necessary to enumerate the contributions made by Richard Flatter, John W. Draper, Alfred Harbage, Bertram Joseph, Ronald Watkins and other scholars in recent years, but we wish to draw attention to the important Basle dissertation by Arthur Gerstner-Hirzel on *The Economy of Action and Word in Shakespeare's Plays* (Bern 1957), the first detailed examination of Shakespeare's use of, and methods of indicating, gestures, and to an article by Robert Fricker on 'Das szenische Bild bei Shakespeare', *Annales Universitatis Saraviensis*, v (1956), 227–40, elucidating the playwright's art of charging stage-events and properties with meaning. Besides, we mention two recent studies of his use of word-scenery, one by Anton Müller-Bellinghausen: 'Die Wortkulisse bei Shakespeare', *Shakespeare-Jahrbuch*, xci (1955), 182–95 (this is a summary of a comprehensive Freiburg doctoral dissertation, unfortunately not available in print), the other by the present writer: *Shakespeare's Word-Scenery* (Zürich und St Gallen, 1954).
5. The author of this essay hopes to substantiate these claims in a study devoted to the theatrical physiognomy of a series of Shakespearian plays.
6. The best recent attempt to develop this sense is Alfred Harbage's *Theatre for Shakespeare* (University of Toronto Press 1955).
7. Charlotte Ehrl stresses their importance for the student of the characters in *Sprachstil und Charakter bei Shakespeare* (*Schriftenreihe der Deutschen Shakespeare-Gesellschaft*, N.F., Band vi, Heidelberg 1957), 175–7.
8. Quotations are from the facsimile edition of the First Folio prepared by Helge Kökeritz (1955), but line references are given according to the Globe edition.
9. Arthur Gerstner-Hirzel, *op. cit.* pp. 88–96, has an interesting chapter on the various functions of deictic gestures.

THE MADDERMARKET THEATRE AND THE PLAYING OF SHAKESPEARE[1]

BY

NUGENT MONCK

The question which is constantly being put to me is: "Why choose an out-of-the-way place like Norwich for a theatrical experiment?" My answer must be biographical.

Norwich, a city of 130,000 inhabitants, has always been cut off from the rest of England by rather bad communications. It is not on the Great North Road, and such roads as existed when our Maddermarket began led to Norwich and to nowhere else save the sea.

This relative isolation created in the city a spirit of independence; the inhabitants made everything they needed, and by the fifteenth century were able to export woollen goods dyed with the root of the Madder, for which was created a special Madder Market. The prosperity of the city is reflected in the forty remaining perpendicular-style churches of this period, all within the city walls. The place is very much alive and many municipal experiments have been tried out here, such as lighting the streets by electricity and inaugurating the first free library to be put on the twopenny rate. There was a fairly large, educated audience ready to hand; the idea of giving Shakespeare's plays upon the kind of stage for which they were written seemed both acceptable and respectable, and we received a warm support in our venture.

The Norwich Players, a group of enthusiastic young amateurs, were formed as far back as 1911, but we had no money and most of our takings went in renting various buildings. I realized that we must have a place of our own where we could work, and act. By looking around Norwich I found the remains of a medieval great hall with a fine chestnut roof. This room, which was attached to an old inn, the owner had long wanted an excuse to restore. We provided that excuse, and thus we were able to open in January 1914 with a mystery play. Great things were planned for the autumn—but by August 1914 we had all scattered, never to act together again.

When I returned from the 1914–1918 war (my return was not until 1920) I was presented by deed of gift with a sixteenth-century house, on condition that I made Norwich my permanent home. I accepted, and immediately started reconstructing the Norwich Players. There came into the market a building that had been built in the late eighteenth century as a Catholic chapel. In the following century it became a baking-powder factory, and finally, in the twentieth century, a highbrow playhouse! As someone pointed out, I always had an elevating tendency! This building we acquired by donations, guarantees, and a little money I had inherited. What attracted me to it was that the roof was held up on three sides by wooden pillars braced together with a gallery half-way up: it already looked like an Elizabethan playhouse. All it needed was a stage, and a small balcony above it.

I asked William Poel down for a week-end before I signed any documents, as he was the one man then living who had any practical ideas about the Elizabethan stage. He thoroughly approved, and offered good advice—none of which I took, as his ideas were too expensive.

71

All these negotiations took place in July 1921, and after we had paid £600 for the chapel we had very little left to do anything with. I bought two hundred Georgian chairs at 1s. 6d. each. Then there was trouble over the electricity; the city accountant would not allow any work to be done until £100 had been paid in cash. We had not got this money, so I sold the chapel's vestry to the Corporation for £100, provided I could have it on a lease at £5 a year. The current was in within twenty-four hours. We were happy in our architect, a man of taste with an instinctive sense of proportion; happy also in our contractor, who, when his workmen had gone, took off his coat and continued to work alongside the architect—both working voluntarily. We were happy in our workmen too, who, when their union forbade overtime, said, "There's no-one else who understands the job", and came back and went on with it. The Players themselves, after their own work was finished, came in and gave a hand.

We fixed a date—23 September 1921, at 8 p.m. The Norwich Players would then present *As You Like It* in their own playhouse, the Maddermarket Theatre. We had given ourselves a month. "You'll never do it" said the city engineer—who had come down to see if he could help in any way. "We must or break", I answered. I was already broke, without a penny in the world, and fed by my Players. But the spark had been lit, and a burning enthusiasm spread to everyone. They worked with the faith that can do anything, and the determination that their theatre should be opened. They worked in many ways; some took tickets to badger their friends to buy, some worked in the box office (money was already beginning to come in), others on the wardrobe.

On 23 September I arrived at 9.30 a.m. The antique chairs were just arriving from store; a woman was waiting with a plan and the numbers ready to tie on. By noon the contractor handed over "for the present" and the workmen were out by 12.30. At 2 p.m. six charwomen started on the floor, and by 6 p.m. the chairs were in order. By 7 p.m. the performers were all in their two small dressing rooms—fearfully cramped up. At 7.30 p.m. the doors were opened to a small queue and the programme sellers were showing the advanced bookers to their seats. At 7.50 p.m. the call "beginners please" went round the theatre, and at 7.58 p.m. I struck the gong so as to be sure that we began at 8 p.m. punctually, and the doors were closed against late-comers. During the one interval at 9 p.m. W. B. Yeats formally opened the theatre. So the first practical model of a sixteenth-century stage since Shakespeare's day came into being with this performance of *As You Like It*.

It was not a particularly good performance for we were all exhausted and had yet to learn the subtleties of our theatre, but the audience was enthusiastic. The Players felt rewarded. Most of the press next morning, however, misunderstood our purpose. They said we were retrograde or throwing away what time had given to the theatre. They missed the scenery, the footlights, and, above all, the proscenium; they also missed the names on the programme. The Players are always anonymous.

The Maddermarket Theatre was modelled on the Fortune Theatre, and is about 40 ft. square. The stage does not extend sufficiently into the audience, but we could not afford to lose a row of seats. There are three entrances each side, to the forestage, the middle and under the balcony; also an entrance each side, above, on to the balcony.

Certain plays seem to need steps direct from the stage to the balcony, so that you can see the performers going up or down. Many writers have suggested this, but have never settled the exact position. Originally the steps may have been temporary, pushed into position according to the need of the play. Such a staircase—in three parts—is in use at the Maddermarket. It can be placed under the balcony if not required throughout a play, or otherwise stored in the scene dock. I have used this staircase for *The Tempest, King Lear, Hamlet* and *Timon of Athens*. In these plays part of the action takes place on the staircase, welding the two levels together. There are curtains across the balcony and the under-balcony, and a large pair to shut out the middle stage from the forestage. These are used for punctuation, the actors closing (or opening) first one, and then, after a few words, the other.

Upon this platform stage the Norwich Players have given all Shakespeare's plays with the exception of *Henry VIII*, which we presented in the garden of the Bishop's Palace because we wanted much larger audiences to raise money for the theatre. The play makes a good 'pastoral', and the interior scenes can be played within a pavilion standing on steps, curtained between its front pillars.

There are two things necessary to remember in the staging of a play. First, the geographical location must be fixed in the audience's mind. If the place remains unchanged, the characters should come in and go out on the same side. If a messenger is sent out by (let us say) the left, and later re-enters by the right to deliver his message, it can then be presumed that he is now in another place. Secondly, the verse must be spoken swiftly and with clarity, as William Poel insisted. This does not mean gabbling, for the rhythm must be preserved. When in doubt where the accent comes, one can refer to the scattered capital letters of the First Folio; they do not always help, but they do give one ideas for interpretation.

Hamlet's advice to the Players ought to be implanted in every young actor's heart, but stars and older performers do not dream of acting upon this advice. In speaking, in coming on to the stage, and in waiting for applause, much time is wasted. If the characters enter on the forestage as the curtains close much time is saved.

I will now consider the application of these points in relationship to some of the plays.

In *Love's Labour's Lost*, if the balcony is considered as a high-road above the King's garden, which is the main stage, the forestage can be used for the comedians. The high-road effect allows all the important entrances and exits to be taken above, and a more impressive effect is gained if the messenger of the French King's death stands alone above the gaiety on the middle stage.

In *Romeo and Juliet*, the balcony has several uses. It is, of course, kept for the first balcony scene, and for the second when Romeo secures his escape by the rope ladder, which Juliet unties, and throws after him. This is the one play where I think it is justifiable for the Prologue to make the location clear by coming on with a placard announcing 'Verona', turning it slowly, and showing 'Mantua'. This just gives time for the apothecary's shop to be set behind the front curtain, after which the Prologue can return and reverse his placard. For the last scene of all, you return to the balcony. Juliet is upon the tomb below; there is a grating before the balcony so that the impression is given that you are looking down into a crypt—this, of course, is done by the lighting. Juliet's head should be towards the audience, so that when Romeo addresses her he is facing the audience. Juliet can easily turn when the Friar awakens her. The Duke and the crowd speak from the balcony; only the parents are below, save for their two torch-bearers, who close the curtains after everyone has filed out.

A Midsummer Night's Dream should be treated as a masque—the forestage for the rude mechanicals, the centre stage for the court and also the forest, the gallery for the sleeping Titania and Bottom; for the wedding scene, the Duke and Hippolyta are on the balcony.

In *As You Like It* the balcony can be used for the watching of the wrestling, and perhaps not again until the final scene.

For *The Merchant of Venice*, I put Shylock's house in a corner of the balcony. The remainder of the balcony is used as a bridge over a canal. In this play it is important that the caskets be treated with great respect: I have them brought in by three choristers under the direction of a priest. This accentuates the vow imposed upon everyone to be silent as to which casket contains the portrait of Portia. It also allows Bassanio to face the audience while he is choosing; the boys circle round him till he makes the right choice. If the caskets are put on a table, the three casket scenes become too static. Shylock must be treated seriously and played with well-dressed dignity.

It is important in *Troilus and Cressida* that the geographical situation be clear to the audience from the beginning: that the balcony is Cressida's room; that under the balcony is Priam's court; that the middle stage is the Greek camp with the balcony and under-balcony shut out (by folding book wings) leaving three Renaissance tents; and that the forestage is mostly Greek, but sometimes Trojan. With this arrangement the production is fairly simple and the play can be played swiftly. It breaks down at the last scene, the battlefield, played mostly on the forestage. (This scene should be set as the test piece for young producers. The old method of cutting it altogether makes nonsense of the play.)

The Tempest—this lovely comedy is so essentially artificial that it is best treated as a masque (like its forerunner, *A Midsummer Night's Dream*). We begin with a shipwreck; the boat can be placed in the balcony on rockers and can be rocked by the ship's crew—care should be taken that they move in the same direction! To the keel of the ship is attached a large sheet of muslin with a suggestion of waves painted upon it. Under this Ariel and his sprites create the storm by throwing up the muslin and dancing as it slowly descends upon them again. The middle curtains are opened by two nymphs, who then join the dance. The steps down and Prospero's cave are hidden by the muslin sea and by the lighting and black-out of the wreck. Two nymphs close the curtains; Prospero and Miranda walk on the forestage in the darkness and Prospero begins that very boring scene (boring except when played by Sir John Gielgud). It must be played very quickly with suppressed excitement. In all probability this scene was written in order to allow time for the wreck to be cleared away (exactly three minutes). If Prospero enters after this upon a full stage and looks round the house for applause (which he will undoubtedly get if he waits long enough), the sympathy of the audience will be lost almost before the play begins. Prospero is not a pleasant character: he has been a bad ruler who loved his books more than his dukedom and thus gave his enemies every justification for giving him the push. He seems to be utterly selfish towards his daughter, who has no means of escaping from him, and is downright cruel to both Ariel and Caliban.

Ferdinand should make his first entrance on the balcony and come down the steps so that Miranda, standing below with her back to the audience, gets the full view of Prince Charming. The other part of the island can be suggested by closing the stone door to Prospero's cave, making it look like solid rock, and adding a single tree. Ariel's banquet can be taken on the balcony so that the trick will pass unnoticed by the audience in the flash and the thunder. The goddesses can sing from there, and the shepherds dance their folk dance on the stage below. Part of the greatness of the play lies in the gradual softening of Prospero, as he watches the effect of love upon the young couple. His enemies can come down the steps and be drawn into his magic circle, and the final exit can be made through Prospero's cave from which the back wall has been removed, showing the sea beyond; and as the stage gradually becomes empty, Caliban can be left on the highest point, looking in the direction that the ship is supposed to be moving, while Ariel—who probably cared less for his master—closes the curtains. If the play is played quite simply, with the songs which were written for it, the effect upon the audience should be like music in a great church—and that is probably what the author expected.

When I say that a play is easy to put on stage, I do not mean that it is easy to interpret, but that it is not difficult actually to present it on the boards. The interpretation of *Hamlet* has filled many volumes, but the producer and his actor must decide on a definite characterization, and stick to it throughout the tragedy, or come to grief. They might do worse than to take the First Quarto (1603), that curious text which tells us so much about the stage business and so little about the poetry. Was Shakespeare, when he wrote it, thinking of his own son Hamnet, who died at the age of eleven? Hamnet's twin sister was about seventeen when Shakespeare was probably composing the play. There is evidence in the text that Hamlet was meant to be played as a young undergraduate, and in our version at the Maddermarket Hamlet is always acted by someone young. From the very beginning of the play we stress the point that Ophelia is going to have a child by him. We take our hints for this from an old Scandinavian legend behind the source material, from Laertes' attitude to the love of Hamlet and Ophelia, from Hamlet's "Nymph, in thy orisons, be all *my* sins remember'd", and from Ophelia's own words in her mad scene, "O, how the wheel becomes it", meaning that the farthingale hides her disgrace.

These remarks are not those of a scholar, not of an original thinker, but of a man who has spent his life trying to put Shakespeare simply on the stage. I started fifty-six years ago, and I am among the few who have given the whole cycle to the public.

The one gift that is necessary for a producer to have is common sense; a sense which seems strangely lacking when people come to deal with the stage. We may have scenes of great beauty, costumes historically correct, but the producer's common sense may not stretch to seeing how the audience will take it, nor why the gallery first-nighters boo! These things do not happen at Stratford-upon-Avon, because the audience know what they are going to see, and treat what they are shown with reverence. The situation is different if you are giving Shakespeare to a working-class audience between the ages of sixteen and twenty. There is no knowing what will raise a loud burst of ironic laughter, for these audiences are intelligent and quick to take up points; they are also readily moved by sincerity. Such audiences are very good training for the producer, and we may hope that they, in their turn, learn something.

NOTE

1. It is with sorrow that we have to record the death of Nugent Monck, on 21 October 1958. This article is based on a paper which he delivered at the Shakespeare Conference, Stratford-upon-Avon, on 5 September 1957.

ACTORS AND SCHOLARS: A VIEW OF SHAKESPEARE IN THE MODERN THEATRE

BY

RICHARD DAVID

Here am I presuming to adjudicate between actors and scholars, when I am not an actor and certainly no scholar. My only excuse is the old saying that "the onlooker sees most of the game"; and certainly in the last eight years and more I have been kept busy peeping at it from the touchline. For I have had the job, the very delightful job, of reporting for *Shakespeare Survey* on current productions. The delight lies in this, that my reporting has not had to be hurried, and I have had full time to browse. The regular critic, poor man, must telephone his notice to his paper as soon as the performance is ended—sometimes, we suspect, well before; and that is that. The *Survey* reporter, however, can wait to garner in not only the initial, the overall, impression of a production, but later amplifications and modifications of these first reactions. In other words he can go back and back, to see the play at different stages in its run and to concentrate in turn on particular elements in it.

I am always fascinated by the changes that come over a production during a long run. The first night, with which the regular critic must be content, is seldom the best, though it often has an attack and what I can only call a purity or integrity that may later a little evaporate. Only a series of performances will mould the company of actors to the play as an old glove to the hand, though the course of time is likely also to produce a coarsening of effects that were at first precise and cleanly made.

Repeated visits also enable the reporter to check his findings point by point. One evening he can close his ears and survey the visual presentation as it unrolls, on another listen to the pattern of the verse; now seeing the play as a whole, its continuity and development, now watching for particular points. Repetition will etch on his memory groupings, gestures, intonations that have from the start excited him, but with an excitement whose causes he cannot at first stay to apprehend. Unlike the regular critic, to whom his first nights are routine professional engagements, the *Survey* reporter can sometimes take his family with him as additional eyes and ears. My own visual memory for colours is peculiarly bad, so in the first interval I turn to my companions with "That Council scene was brilliant; help me to fix it. Now that dress the Queen wore—was it green or beige?" "It was green," says my wife; "Oh no," says my daughter, "it was a sort of yellow shot with pink"; "I should have called it silvery-mauve," says my son. Luckily on our way out after the play we pass the designer's original sketch, which is on exhibition; the dress is light blue.

All this by way of apologia—but also as introduction. I hope you will forgive the autobiography for the sake of its three morals, which underline all I shall have to say. First, the art of the theatre is a complex and multifarious one. The effect of a stage performance is a composite effect, made up of innumerable elements; spectacle and personality and sound and intellectual pattern and many other things. In the second place this art is shifting and impermanent, for no two performances of a play will be anything like the same. And, thirdly, the audience's reception of it will be highly subjective, much more so, I think, than with any other art, because of the excited, almost hypnotic state of those by whom it is received. I do not believe my family is abnormally unobservant; it is just that no two spectators will ever see precisely the same thing. Let us then remember the multiplicity, the instability, the insubstantiality of the theatrical art as qualities that are of its very essence, and inescapable.

The subtitle of this paper refers to Shakespeare "in the modern theatre", but I had better make it clear at once that in my opinion the last four words are superfluous. For it is the first article of my belief that outside the theatre Shakespeare can have only the thinnest and most unsubstantial of existences; and since, inescapably, we are moderns, it is only in the modern theatre that we can hope to find him whole.

Some years ago the members of the International Shakespeare Conference at Stratford attended a performance of *Macbeth*, which was by no means the least effective of that season's productions. I sat just behind two very distinguished Shakespearian scholars, and could not help hearing them warmly agreeing that they would always much prefer hearing the play read to seeing it acted. This seemed to me profoundly shocking, like suddenly discovering that your husband is a notorious poisoner wanted by the police. For out of the theatre Shakespeare, like a concert performance of opera or an orchestral work transcribed for piano, lacks a dimension. Shakespeare, the whole Shakespeare, makes his effects only in terms of acting, of human actors actually present. Even the process of filming or televising blurs the immediacy and dulls the impact of his work, which needs the embodiment of flesh and blood.

Of course—and here I speak on the scholars' side—there are still actors whose Shakespeare is every bit as tenuous and lacking in body as that of the worst pedant. To match my two professors I can produce a recent Shylock who wrote in an extra appearance for the character and prolonged his final exit by two whole minutes of what Hamlet would have called "damnable faces". He did not trust Shakespeare as a dramatist. His helping-out of the text, like the 'improvements' of those actors and directors who 'tidy up' Shakespeare's scenes and rearrange their order, was just as much a denial of Shakespeare's dramatic powers as is the scholar's neglect. And so the scholar dismisses the actor's art as presumptuous mountebankery, while the actor disables the scholar's judgment, branding it with the worst word in his vocabulary—'literary'.

In truth the actor's and the scholar's gifts must help each other out where Shakespeare is concerned, and both are essential if the plays are to be so presented as to reveal the true 'form and pressure' of Shakespeare's intention. Except in and through the actor the scholar cannot properly 'realize' Shakespeare, any more than even the best musician can judge the full impact of a symphony from reading the score or an engineer assess the performance of a machine from its blue-print. The medium in which Shakespeare expressed himself was not words, simply, but spoken words; what he had to say was said not merely in literary terms but specifically in terms of the theatre—and by this I do not mean the historical Elizabethan or Jacobean stage, but that peculiar combination of qualities, some of which I have already touched upon, that complex mode that has always marked off the theatrical art, making it in some ways more akin to games of skill than to the more orthodox fine arts. But the scholar is equally indispensable to the actor, for however unchanging this essential quality of 'theatre' the theatrical modes that Shakespeare employs, and especially that of language, are over three hundred years old. Without the scholar to interpret, it is often hard to tell what he is driving at, though once you have the secret it is generally surprisingly easy to put it over on the stage, even to an audience that has not been so prompted.

In any collaboration between actor and scholar it is vital that each should remain true to himself. The scholar as he leans towards the actor must be careful to retain his scholarly standards, the actor as he listens to the scholar must continuously test what he hears against his own theatrical sense. Otherwise you will have the scholar bowled over by a theatrical *tour de force* such as Peter Brook's *Titus Adronicus* and accepting as good Shakespeare something that is merely good acting and not Shakespeare at all; or, worse still, the actor who in his anxiety to avail himself of scholarly knowledge takes over a scholar's interpretation that his own instinct should have told him is theatrically non-viable. Then the actor who follows the scholar in order to make his performance good Shakespeare as well as good theatre is led to produce something that is neither good Shakespeare nor any longer good theatre, for example a *Hamlet* with the Prince as villain or an *Othello* in which the hero is Iago.

It is not, however, such major misunderstandings that I mean to discuss here, still less the deliberate distortions of those actors and directors who regard Shakespeare as an old-fashioned barnstormer whose plays must be turned upside down and tricked out with new ideas before they can be decently presented to a modern audience. Most serious interpreters of Shakespeare do now recognize him to be a consummate dramatic artist, whose least effect is carefully calculated. The Director of the Memorial Theatre, in the 1956 production of *Othello*, restored Shakespeare's Clown, so regularly cut, and was delighted to find that his scene seemed to provide a pause, a point of rest, just where it was wanted. Nor do I have to enlarge on the more obvious occasions where the actor needs the scholar's advice: the jokes that require elucidation, the hard or obsolete words to be translated. There is a more subtle and all-pervading distortion, or so it seems to me after seven years' reporting, that ruins nine out of ten modern productions. It has changed its character a little since Granville-Barker denounced it, but its name is still the same—realism.

I said earlier that acting was clearly akin to games of skill. At least we should all, I think, admit that some of the pleasure of watching a good actor is the same as that of watching a good athlete. One of the signs of a major dramatist is that he presents his actors with a game to play in which the rules are so harmonious and well-judged that the actor's skill in following them and taking advantage of them is beautifully apparent. I suggest that the rules of the Shakespeare game are unusually complicated and strict; and that unless they are very precisely observed the play becomes a shambles. What then are these rules?

We know that the conventions of the Elizabethan theatre were, by our standards, extraordinarily artificial. There was little or no scenery, and the audience had to be prepared to accept at successive moments the same bare permanent structure as a council-chamber, a field of battle, a bedroom, a garden, the battlements of a fortress, a dungeon. A similar code governed action. It was assumed that any character, on putting on a simple disguise, became instantly unrecognizable to his nearest and dearest. If he took one pace to the front and spoke straight out he was inaudible to his fellow-actors; and he was not thought to be behaving oddly if, left alone on the stage, he unburdened himself of his most secret thoughts in a speech of some dozen or sixteen lines. We may suspect that the very style of speaking and playing was, whatever Hamlet says, more rhetorical and formal than anything we ourselves have seen, with set gestures, as in Indian dancing, to express each particular emotion. Then again the female parts were played by men and boys. I am sure we must not think of this as a clumsy makeshift or of its effect as in any sense puerile. Rather must it have contributed its own element of stylish stylization, something akin to the art of the castrato singers described by Goethe in these terms:

I reflected on the reasons why these singers pleased me so greatly, and I think I have found it. In these representations, the concept of imitation and of art was invariably more strongly felt, and through their able performance a sort of conscious illusion was produced. Thus a double pleasure is given, in that these persons are not women, but only represent women. The young men have studied the properties of the female sex in its being and behaviour; they know them thoroughly and reproduce them like an artist; they represent, not themselves, but a nature absolutely foreign to them.

Last, but not least, the plays were for the most part written in verse, not a natural but a highly artificial mode of speech.

Now the last thing I am suggesting is that Shakespeare should be played only on a replica of the Globe stage (if we knew what it was—we do not), that the actors should be set to semaphore their emotions, and that women should be banished again from the boards. These things are deader, by two hundred years, than the dodo, and we cannot resurrect them. But they did each and all of them contribute to Shakespeare's intended effect, and we must somehow translate them into our own terms.

Unfortunately the predominant modes of staging and playing today are at the opposite extreme to those of the Elizabethans. The Victorian-Edwardian vogue for drawing-room comedy, Stanislavsky's Chekhov productions in Russia, Reinhardt's elaborations, and now The Method in America, all call for extreme naturalism, an illusion created by a mass of fine detail. Of course there have been vigorous rebels against this tradition, but the very extremism of their reaction makes them equally unsuitable as presenters of Shakespeare. Shakespeare, who even in so political a play as *Coriolanus* considers always the individual human predicament, who employs all his resources to work upon the sympathies of the audience, who made so much of the idiosyncrasies of his own company of actors, cannot be played in a style that generalizes every particular, that, in the Brechtian sense, deliberately 'alienates' the audience, and that reduces the actors to puppets. Better Shakespeare swathed and smothered in naturalism than Shakespeare balletized or mimed out of humanity.

Over the staging I think that modern producers have for the most part achieved a very satisfactory compromise. The point of the Globe stage, as they have learned, is that it allowed, first, a very close and direct relation between actor and audience and, second, the rapid succession, the juxtaposition, of scenes extraordinarily disparate. Within each act of a play by Ibsen or Chekhov there are of course infinite variations of mood and tempo, but in an Elizabethan play these variations are very much more rapid and more violent. You can see this writ large in such plays as *As You Like It* or *Henry V* which are built, almost on the music-hall prescription, of a series of 'turns', the cross-talk comedians following the sentimental singer, heroics alternating with knockabout, and lyricism with feats of strength; but the pattern is just as varied, though perhaps more subtly so, in every other play of Shakespeare. It is seldom nowadays, as fifty years ago, that this tumultuous flow is dammed up by endless scene-changing or dissipated in over-elaborate production. But though staging may be suitable enough, the conventions of action sometimes give trouble. For instance, there are still actors and directors who are afraid of the soliloquy. When Paul Rogers played Touchstone at the Old Vic he carried a large Fool's Head on a stick and confided his quips to this instead of to the audience. As Falstaff, the same actor kept his page always with him, and addressed to him the great homilies on Honour and on Sack. Neither Touchstone nor Falstaff ever engaged with the audience and the direct sympathy which is the life-blood of the comic act was never aroused. Again, in the Old Vic *Cymbeline* in 1957 the wicked queen was provided with a Confidant in the shape of a Court Fool, crippled and degenerate, who followed her everywhere and gleefully shared her secret plottings. The presence of a hearer on the stage reflected the queen's utterances back upon herself so that they never got through to the audience, who made no direct contact with the queen as a person. The effect of this (the opposite of that intended) was that she became less real, more a stock villainess, than if she had employed the 'unreal' convention of the soliloquy.

This, I think, illuminates the nature of theatrical illusion and the standard fallacy of those who seek to create it by way of realism. Here is another example to bring out what I mean. You may remember the Stratford season of 1951 and the series of histories of which *Henry IV Part One* was the high-light. All went magnificently until the death of Hotspur. Michael Redgrave acted the corpse, if I may so put it, to the life. The war was not far away, and many people had vivid memories of just what a dead body was like, its soggy lumpishness as you lifted it. Yet Redgrave's perfect realism did not help the illusion; instead the mind revolted, refusing to accept what it knew to be impossible. For the mind, it is clear, is not actually taken in by stage illusion, though both the realists and their opponents argue as if it was. It merely accepts the stage event, if consistently presented, as a working hypothesis, in the same way as a mathematical theorem is seen to be valid, significant, and in that sense 'real', but not in the same category as an event in 'real' life. When (to quote a famous chestnut) the lady in the gallery screamed out a warning to Othello, she did not imagine that what was happening on the stage was true, that the play had invaded her world, the world of real life; it was rather that she had been drawn into the world of the play.

Since I first wrote this I have, I must confess, been shaken by another story, told me by Sir Barry Jackson. It concerns a play in which an actor was supposed to burn his hand on a red-hot stove. At this point a lady in the audience was heard to remark indignantly: "What a thing to leave about on the stage!" There is here, I admit, a clear confusion between real life and stage life. But on my side I can claim that part of the point of Sir Barry's story was that the lady had never been in a theatre before, and I shall still maintain that an experienced audience will, as Goethe implies, surrender *consciously* to the stage illusion, accepting 'for the sake of argument' (so to speak) the reality of what it sees. Excessive realism, by offering the audience too much to swallow, breaks the rules of the game and bursts the illusion it seeks to support. It is for this reason that stage fights are so peculiarly tricky to handle. To be too convincing is as dangerous as to be unconvincing. If after three laborious and swingeing parries the victim drops his sword and collapses, we shall giggle; but if the duel is realistically prolonged, with pauses in which the combatants take hissing breath, we shall giggle again, because this is too good to be true, or rather too true to be true-in-the-theatre. And as with action so with acting: the most deliberately realistic player defeats his own ends.

ACTORS AND SCHOLARS

Now please do not think I am suggesting that Shakespeare can only be acted in a highly mannered and artificial style. That extreme is as dangerous as the other, perhaps more dangerous because more unacceptable in an age that tends towards naturalism. You may remember Fielding's account of how Tom Jones took his servant Partridge to see Garrick as Hamlet. Asked which of the players he had liked best, Partridge answered 'with some appearance of indignation at the question, "The King, without doubt". "Indeed, Mr Partridge", says Mrs Miller, "you are not of the same opinion with the town; for they are all agreed, that Hamlet is acted by the best player who ever was on the stage". "He the best player", cries Partridge, with a contemptuous sneer, "Why, I could act as well as he myself. I am sure if I had seen a ghost, I should have looked in the very same manner, and done just as he did...the king for my money; he speaks all the words distinctly, half as loud again as the other.——Anybody may see he is an actor"'. Fielding of course was ridiculing an old-fashioned, 'ham' style of acting, which was perhaps ultimately derived from the Elizabethans but had become rigid and empty with the passage of time and quite unacceptable to the connoisseurs who found the truth of acting in Garrick's more fluent and naturalistic playing. Yet I suspect that even Garrick would have seemed formal by our standards. Certainly the pictures show him making gestures with arm and hand whose stiffness cannot be entirely attributed to the painter. Today audiences nourished on Gerald du Maurier are even less able to take 'ham' than was Fielding, and stylization must be a good way this side even of Garrick. Yet some degree of stylization there should be in presenting plays that range so widely as the Elizabethan and are able, by the use of violent conventions, to render down to stage illusion a variety of actions quite outside the reach of playwrights working in a staider medium. The more the conventions foreshorten and paraphrase real life, the less they coincide with it, the more stylization is needed in the playing. For example, I hope it will not seem too ungallant if I say that again and again it is the playing of the women's parts that lets down a production of Shakespeare. "Miss So-and-So was really *too* girlish", we say, or "The actress' personality seemed to swamp the part", or often "She was somehow too modern for Portia". What I think is at the back of all such remarks is an instinctive recognition that the parts were written for boys and realistic femininity jars with them.

The point I am getting at has been much better put by Granville-Barker. He was writing of *Love's Labour's Lost*, but the words are in some degree true of every play of Shakespeare. He says, first:

The whole play, first and last, demands style....All...in accent and motion must be keyed to a sort of ecstasy, to a strange surpassing of this modern work-a-day world....We must have a beauty of speech that will leave us a little indifferent to the sense of the thing spoken. Navarre and his friends and their ladies must show such distinction and grace that we ask no more pleasure (than to be) in their company. Armado and the rest must command us by the very skill with which they remake mankind. ...The actor, in fine, must think of the dialogue in terms of music; of the tune and rhythm of it as at one with the sense—sometimes outbidding the sense—in telling him what to do and how to do it, in telling him, indeed, what to *be*.

This brings me to the head and front of Shakespeare's conventions: his plays are largely written in verse. And here I must tread warily, for of all the criticisms of acting made by scholars none are so immediately and deeply resented by actors as those that relate to the speaking of verse. "Verse-speaking", say the actors, "is a matter of technique, of professional training, of which no amateur outside the theatre can possibly judge. Moreover, the scholar's criterion of verse-speaking is literary, non-theatrical" (I am still quoting the actor); "he demands that verse should be spoken musically, which means in practice a monotonous and undramatic recitation. It is when we wish to be really rude about a fellow actor that we say 'he sings'."

Now I think that in the actor's first charge there is very little substance. Of all the arts, acting is the most public, and the actor must appeal to the judgment of an unprofessional, though informed, audience. An actor's actor is an even more barren thing than a poet's poet or a painter's painter. The second charge is based on a misunderstanding which I fear must be laid at the door of William Poel, who in other ways has had a generally beneficent effect on Shakespearian production. That the plays are now acted more or less complete, and more or less without a break, we owe largely to him. But Poel's method of rehearsal was to give the actors what he called "the tunes"; in other words he laid down the relative pitch at which each successive word was to be spoken, and the actors learned these precise intonations along with the words to which they applied. Dramatic emphasis, pauses, facial expressiveness, anything that interfered with "the music of the verse", were actively discouraged. I should have thought that such a practice would have cast over Poel's productions an air of glassy unreality. Sir Barry Jackson assures me that this was not so. I suspect nevertheless that the attempt of Poel, the amateur, to impose this essentially anti-dramatic method on the theatre has helped to set the actors ever since against anything that savoured of recitation or a musical rendering of the lines. But in fact when we ask that verse should be spoken musically (and the analogy with music really is inescapable) the very last thing we have in mind is a monotonous sing-song. The whole point of verse is the extraordinary range and variety of expression of which it is capable—much greater than in prose. As George Rylands has said, "Blank verse is such a wonderful medium because it can sing and speak; it can sing both high and low; it can speak both slow and fast; it can contract and expand".

What is demanded of a good speaker of verse is the ability to organize this variety, to range from colloquialism to heroics, from complicated argument to the simplest pathos, without ever breaking the bonds that make of each speech, of each play, one form and pattern. To do this he needs not a 'musical' voice, but the intelligence to use it, or what a musician would call the power of phrasing. A beautiful voice may even be a handicap, tempting its owner to emphasize one element of the verse, the sensuous quality of the sound, at the expense of the rest. Certainly some of the best speakers, in my sense, have inferior instruments, and vice versa, just as a singer with a superb voice may be a shockingly bad musician.

Nor is it true, as Poel's practice suggested, that every speech has one particular 'tune' to which it must go, and no liberty of interpretation is possible. Four virtuoso violinists will phrase the same passage in four distinct ways, all convincing. The point is that they will all *phrase* it, give it balance and musical shape, but each in his own style. Similarly there are as many ways of speaking a Shakespearian speech as there are good actors, and all of them right.

At the same time it is still possible to say that certain ways of speaking a particular speech are definitely wrong. Take Macbeth's soliloquy when, leaving Duncan, his intended victim, at table, he steals away from the banquet to wrestle with his indecision:

> If it were done when 'tis done; then 'twere well
> It were done quickly. If the assassination
> Could trammel up the consequence and catch
> With his surcease success.

The light monosyllables of the opening line, the tumultous overrun of the second, the alliterations of c's and s's, all demand an agitated, hissing, whispering utterance. To deliver the speech rhetorically, to make it 'poetical', is to flatly deny Shakespeare's intention writ large in the very wording of the passage. Or to take an opposite example, there are Hermione's great speeches of self-defence in *The Winter's Tale*, when the King, her husband, brings her to trial:

> Sir, spare your threats:
> The bug which you would fright me with I seek:
> To me can life be no commodity:
> The crown and comfort of my life (your favour)
> I do give lost, for I do feel it gone,
> But know not how it went.

At the Old Vic in 1956 Wendy Hiller delivered this brokenly, with gasps and sobs almost between each word, and so reduced the Queen, "the daughter of the Emperor of Russia", to a hysterical bobby-soxer. For the level simplicity and gravity of Hermione's lines throughout her trial, contrasting so markedly with the contorted idiom of the rest of these early scenes, demand the utmost dignity and nobility of utterance, tense certainly, but with the tenseness of resolution pitched high, not of the jitters. The objection to Miss Hiller's rendering is a double one. In the first place if the passage had, like Macbeth's speech, invited a realistic technique, it could still not have borne such extreme treatment as hers. Verse, by its very nature, must always have some shape and coherence. When Shakespeare wants to convey incoherence, as in Othello's fit, he deliberately abandons the poise and control of verse and writes prose. In the second place this particular speech is one in which Shakespeare's effect is made by non-realistic means.

Now it is the great strength of verse plays in general, of the Elizabethan drama in particular, and of Shakespeare in special, that different categories of effect can exist side by side in the same play, the same scene, the same speech even. *Macbeth* is full of examples. "Is this a dagger that I see before me?" is realistic; "Now o'er the one half world nature seems dead" is impressionistic. In the first half of the speech the actor acts the haunted man, in the second half he acts the haunting. Another excellent example of such a transition occurs in the quarrel scene in *Julius Caesar*. Cassius and Brutus have been arguing about tactics: shall they hold their present strong position or forestall Octavius by marching on to Philippi? The argument, on either side, is vigorous and real, till, suddenly, Brutus broadens it all out with

> There is a tide in the affairs of men,
> Which, taken at the flood, leads on to fortune.

On the surface it is part of the argument; Brutus goes on to point his moral, "on such a full sea are we now afloat". But in fact what the image must convey to the audience is not confidence but foreboding. Brutus' and Cassius' tide, we must feel, is *not* at full, but already inexorably ebbing. The speech has moved over from realism to impressionism.

6-2

In Shakespeare's earlier plays the indirect, non-realistic speeches stand out clearly from the body of the play, like arias from recitative. Even so actors can miss their point. In the 1954 Stratford season you could have heard the Oberon deliver "I know a bank where the wild thyme blows", a piece of scene-painting if ever there was one, as melodramatic plotting; and the Mercutio used the Queen Mab speech, intended to fill the air with uneasy magic, to display the flibberty-gibbetiness of the man. Sometimes a whole character may be cast in the non-realistic mould. The part of Constance in *King John* is full of, is altogether constructed out of, elaborate patterns of language, the balances and contrasts and repetitions of set rhetoric. To superimpose on this formal presentation of tragedy the sobs, the shrieks, the incessantly quivering hands of a real-life hysteric (as did Joan Miller at Stratford in 1957) is to set form against content. You cannot create a part by two incompatible methods of presentation employed simultaneously, and if Shakespeare, in his very writing, has firmly laid down one method, you must go his way. That Miss Miller was, in my opinion, much more successful in the pathos of her final scene was due to the fact that she was there more ready to trust Shakespeare and to allow him to do more of the work for her.

In the later plays the method is more subtle, its application less in black and white. The reason, I think, why no Othello I have ever heard has succeeded with "It is the cause" is that this speech is exactly poised between direct and indirect; a touch too much of realism, a waver too far in the direction of poetry, and it is spoilt. But even in the late plays there are imperative arias, that will not admit of any other treatment. In *Antony and Cleopatra* the scene of Antony's suicide opens with his speech to Eros, "Sometimes we see a cloud that's dragonish". At the Old Vic in 1957 Keith Michell spoke this hesitantly, feeling for the words, seeking to convey by his manner of speech the hero's exhaustion, his renunciation of life and of vitality. This is of course what Shakespeare wants expressed, but not the method of expression he chooses. Antony describes a sky, an evening sky I think, perhaps after storm. The vivid cloudscape presented by his words induces a sense of insubstantiality, of remoteness from earth, of resignation at the sinking of a long day to its close. The picture is a symbol of the final disruption of Antony's career, the dislimning of his own glory, and infuses into the hearer something of Antony's own feelings as he surveys his ending. But the picture must come to us whole and undisturbed, and the actor must at this point give all his powers to describing the clouds and not to describing Antony.

In objecting to Michell's—as to Joan Miller's and Wendy Hiller's—way with the speeches I have quoted, I am not, I repeat, objecting to the naturalistic technique as such, but only to its being overdone; and by this I mean both too great a degree of naturalism in contexts where the technique is, in itself, appropriate, and also its indiscriminate use even where it is not appropriate. Let me illustrate this from the director's handling of a play's action, which parallels, naturally enough, the actor's speaking of the words. It has been very much the modern naturalistic fashion of production to thicken up the detail in the background of the stage picture, injecting vitality and verisimilitude into every third citizen and fourth attendant gentlewoman. There is of course a time for this, and Shakespeare makes it abundantly clear when that time has come; you have only to think of the Roman mob or Jack Cade's rebels. But when for instance he puts a royal retinue on the stage, it has only one purpose, to add dignity to the royalty it follows, and not to present a juicy slice of Elizabethan life. The director who gives us personalities instead of panoply, would-be reality instead of symbol, is guilty of just the same distortion as the actor who bumbasts out a formal speech with psychological invention. On the other hand, the director who allows or persuades his Roman mob to get out of hand is like the actor who lets his speech get out of hand, breaking it down into more realistic detail than a verse-play will bear.

The scholar, then, while leaving the actor to determine precisely how Shakespeare's intentions are to be expressed in modern terms, will ask for two essential conditions to be observed. He will insist that a Shakespeare play, like any other work of art, has one overall shape, style, pattern, essence which any translation into modern terms must preserve; and that within this overall pattern there are contrasts and balances of tone, temper, and even of convention, that must be carefully observed if the structure is to stand. Or, if I may revert to my games metaphor, the Shakespearian rules are both complicated and consistent. From this derives the importance in a Shakespeare production of the director, the umpire whose job it is to see that the players know the rules and observe them. Left to themselves the actors can only provide a disorderly scrimmage. It is not even as if the rules were unchanging, or that experience of one of Shakespeare's plays will fit the actor for any Shakespearian role. There are indeed certain general principles that apply all the way from the *Comedy of Errors* to *The Tempest*, for instance the overriding importance of recognizing and combining variety with unity, of developing infinite light and shade within a consistent all-embracing style. But the style or quality of one play will differ radically from another's. Each has its local rules and by-laws, and to play *Macbeth* in the style of *As You Like It*, or even of *Hamlet*, is to come onto the rugger field equipped for tennis or lacrosse. It is the first duty of a Shakespearian director to see his play whole, discover its peculiar characteristics and appreciate the assumptions on which it is built; and he must then communicate all this to the actors, at least in so far as may enable them to work to common effect, and blend their individual interpretations with those of their fellows.

When a performance fails to catch fire, and we leave the theatre in a dissatisfaction that may be all the more haunting for being vague, it is almost always a failure in total effect that is to blame. Separate scenes, individual performances, may be tested one by one and found at worst adequate, at best superb; but they do not add up to anything, or at least not by that geometrical progression, that compound interest of effectiveness that the theatrical art at its best will generate. This may be because the director has not hit on any one co-ordinating style in which to body forth Shakespeare's single conception; the actors are all at sixes and sevens. As I have said elsewhere, this, I think, was the fault of Peter Brook's Moscow *Hamlet*. Or perhaps he has found what seems to him a modern equivalent for Shakespeare's convention, and it proves inappropriate and inadequate. The 1957 production of *The Two Gentlemen of Verona* at the Old Vic is a case in point. The *décor* and spirit were of the period represented in England by the Regency. So far so good: *Two Gentlemen* is an embodiment of the romantic view of love and adventure, and Shelley and Byron are for us closer and therefore more significant examples of this than, say, Sir Philip Sidney. But this was Regency not as Regency saw itself but as we see it, with more than a touch of the posturing comical about it. The lovers guyed love, the politic duke was more foxy than Ulysses, the brigands were by Gilbert and Sullivan, not by Schiller. Of course the Elizabethans laughed too at the excesses of loverly behaviour, but not at love, at the Miles Gloriosus but never at the profession of arms. Unless these things can be taken seriously, there is surely little point in putting on *The Two Gentlemen* at all. The same criticisms apply to George

Devine's *A Midsummer Night's Dream* at Stratford in 1954. The essence of the *Dream* is surely moonshine and the English countryside; neon lighting and Noah's Ark trees make up an idiom that is totally incompatible with it. Or take a production in which the mis-styling, if it exists, is much more subtle. The sets for the 1957 Stratford production of *As You Like It* have been criticized as being too civilized, too little of a wilderness for the Forest of Arden. At first sight this is nonsense, for this is a pastoral (not a venatorial) play if ever there was one, and Motley's delicious poplar-groves and well-watered meads were perfectly Arcadian. The trouble was that they were too appropriate; they persuaded us that Rosalind really did keep sheep, and that the venison killed by the Duke's retainers was needed to stock a real pot. But *As You Like It* is a fantasy, and if you start to make a logical connection of its goings-on the magic begins to evaporate.

And yet, I must confess, for me any style, even the wrong one, is preferable to Shakespeare with no style at all. I find that the really memorable productions are those most strongly characterized: Edith Evans in an *As You Like It* by Watteau, Peter Brook's iron-barred *Measure for Measure*, the bare and functional, and so truly Elizabethan *Henry V* directed by Byam Shaw in 1950, even that odd but self-consistent distortion of *All's Well That Ends Well* presented at the same theatre by Benthall in 1954. I do not include Gielgud's Japanese *Lear* because that was (saving your reverences) a very hum-drum and non-stylish performance served up, *garni*, in a setting so violently stylized that it had the unforgiveable effect of distracting attention from the play. I quote it to emphasize again, I hope unnecessarily, that 'style' and 'stylization' are not the same thing, and that when I talk of style I do not mean something exterior imposed as a gimmick upon an otherwise normal and inoffensive play. What I do mean is a vision of the play's point and meaning and angle of approach, reflected in every gesture and inflection of the players, interpenetrating action, setting, lighting and music, making of the play a little world of itself which draws the spectator's imagination to be in it though not of it. This is the true stage illusion.

I have taken up much time instructing actor and director in their business. But what of us, the audience? What are our duties? First, I think, humility. By this I do not at all mean that we should be totally uncritical, for some of the worst of recent betrayals of Shakespeare have been fostered by the hysterical enthusiasm of inexperienced audiences. There are indeed occasions when it is the duty of audience and critics to be stern, to declare unequivocally that this is not Shakespeare, but the self-aggrandisement of actor or director feeding upon Shakespeare. But let us not be so pettifoggingly on the watch for minutiae, let us not be hypercritical, demanding perfection where perfection, by definition, cannot be. Despite Ben Jonson, Shakespeare did write "for an age" and, more than that, for the idiosyncrasies of a particular company of actors. The age has disintegrated and the actors are dead. To be faithful to Shakespeare at this remove requires the greatest insight and an infinity of pains and, at the end of it all, the best of productions can be no more than a translation, a compromise in a double or treble sense. It must convert the printed page into terms of the theatre; for Shakespeare's theatrical terms it must find modern equivalents; and in making these adaptations to a different medium and to a new age it must suit them to a wide and varied company of spectators. As Margaret Webster puts it in a wise and truly "stylish" book now available in this country as *Shakespeare Today*:

The modern producer has to be, in some sort, a translator; and he may not translate, as Shakespearian commentators do, for individual readers one by one. He may not count with the single mind, slowly absorbing the power and beauty of the written word with the aid of a fire, a lamp, and a comfortable armchair. He has to produce an integrated piece of theatre, carrying as nearly as possible the full intention of the author, and projecting it instantaneously to several hundred people of the most variously assorted character and receptivity.

If we accept this, an inescapable element in the very nature of the theatrical art, and do not immediately dismiss anything that does not fit our own preconceived idea of perfection, the translation in the theatre can still give us infinitely more of the essential Shakespeare than can the most devoted study of his score.

CLEOPATRA AS ISIS

BY

MICHAEL LLOYD

Cleopatra's most striking qualities closely resemble those of the goddess Isis, and may have been suggested by her. Before I show the sources of Shakespeare's knowledge of the cult of Isis, I must state the view of Cleopatra, and of her relationship with Antony, which suggests such an analogy.

The nature of Cleopatra's love stands in contrast to the Roman view of human relationships with which Antony accords. For Antony, the opposition of business and pleasure imposes a choice:

> The business she hath broached in the state
> Cannot endure my absence. (I, ii, 172–3)

> And though I make this marriage for my peace,
> I' the east my pleasure lies. (II, iii, 39–40)

The words 'business' and 'pleasure' are honest, and they mean no more than they say. It is folly to attempt, as Cleopatra does, to force on Antony's pleasure the interpretation of love. "If it be love indeed, tell me how much" (I, i, 14). The grandiose evasions of his reply do not deceive her. "Excellent falsehood!" is her assessment. It would have been folly had she believed him when he implied the priority of pleasure over business: "Let Rome in Tiber melt....Here is my space." By the end of the act, he has gone to attend to business in Rome.

Part of that business is war; and the contrast of pleasure and war is taken up by the Roman soldier Enobarbus in his reiterated image of the horse (III, vii, 7–9). If the mare went into battle with the horse, the horse would follow its appetite and leave the battle. The prediction proves as true for the Roman soldier as for the beast. It is what Antony does at Actium. It is a transgression of the Roman priority: "Under a compelling occasion let women die" (I, ii, 138). That was Antony's priority in Act I. It may be said to be Caesar's in sacrificing his sister to a political manœuvre.

Such a priority is itself the outcome of the Roman attitude to the affections. Though Antony and Enobarbus find that they ignore them at their ultimate peril, the affections are never experienced with that recognition and fullness which Cleopatra gives them. Relationships entered at their level are lightly left: "Give the gods a thankful sacrifice...when old robes are worn out there are members to make new" (I, ii, 162–6). It is Antony's attitude in turning from Fulvia to Cleopatra, from Cleopatra to Octavia, from Octavia back to Cleopatra. His return to Egypt is sometimes seen as occurring at the dictate of a dominating passion; but it does not. When Antony left Cleopatra, he forgot her. She may console herself with her interpretation of behaviour that is "nor sad nor merry" (I, v, 52). It remains in sharp contrast to her own, and it is not that of a Shakespearian lover. She is in his thoughts only when others remind him of her. Shakespeare shows the sequence of events leading to his return to depend not on passion but on policy. The soothsayer scene shows that if it is to Antony's interest to work in a sphere apart from Caesar's, Egypt offers that sphere. The addition of pleasure (Antony's word) is but an addition, and but pleasure (II, iii, 33–40). The return takes its real impetus from Caesar's initiation of hostilities, and Caesar himself reveals Antony's dominant motive: they

> now are levying
> The kings o'th'earth for war. (III, vi, 67–8)

It is politic of Caesar to proclaim that Cleopatra "hath nodded him to her"; but he betrays his true preoccupation, and Antony's true motive, in the impressive list of kings he goes on to cite as Antony's supporters (III, vi, 65–76).

Antony's exclusive concern with his own interest is incompatible with love as we come to understand it through Cleopatra. He lacks that fidelity which she shows us to be a necessary component. The degree of fidelity he shows to Fulvia and Octavia is not less than he shows to Cleopatra. "A boggler ever" (III, xiii, 110); "our slippery people" (I, ii, 186): Antony's words of others are often true of himself. His long wavering between trust and distrust, fidelity and infidelity is at last recognized by him as a cloudy or watery lack of distinctness (IV, xiv, 2–14). It culminates in the murderous attack he seeks to make on Cleopatra when he supposes (not for the first time) that she has betrayed him (IV, xii, 30–49). Only his belief that she has killed herself for him convinces him finally of her love.

It is against this Roman attitude that the nature of love in Cleopatra must be seen. It is no new thing to point out the martial element in Cleopatra. She will hale a messenger up and down by the hair of his head (II, v, 64). She will threaten her maid (by Isis) with bloody teeth (I, v, 70). She will appear in battle "for a man" (III, vii, 18). This element is wholly devoted to her fulfilment as a lover. To anticipate terms, Bellona is the servant of Venus. That Roman contrast between love and war is in Cleopatra a synthesis. She would fight the messenger as if he were "a Fury crowned with snakes" to reverse the information that her lover has left her. This destructive militancy is turned on Antony himself. She puts her tires on him and wears his sword (II, v, 22–3). She leads the leader (III, vii, 69). Her purpose is to dominate and control him; but if the method is destructive, the purpose is creative. At Actium Cleopatra destroys the Roman Antony for whom love and war (or, in his words, business and pleasure) stood in contrast, to remake him after her own kind. In military respects Shakespeare vindicates her. When next Antony goes to war the soldier and the lover are no longer separate. Cleopatra is the armourer of his heart (IV, iv, 7), and he makes "these wars for Egypt". In them he achieves an unprecedented stature as soldier. Hitherto he had

> ever won
> More in [his] officer than person. (III, i, 16–17)

Shakespeare had belittled him as a practical soldier as early as *Julius Caesar*, v, i, 2–4. The great name he bore as a soldier was but a name, given to what others "effected", a "magical word of war" (III, i, 30–1). In the synthesis of lover and soldier to which Cleopatra forces him, we see him for the first time in an achievement worthy of his reputation.

Cleopatra's love is deepened by her disaster (which includes but is not confined to Antony's death) into an experience which it is the function of the fifth act to state. It is here that her role as faithful wife and mother, the crown of the play, fully evolves. Hints of her jealousy for the name of wife are not lacking early in the play. Her concern for maternity appears as early as the public recognition of her children in the market place. Here again Shakespeare contrasts the Egyptian value with the Roman, when Caesar says that "the unlawful issue" of "their lust" have been named "the kings of kings" (III, vi, 7, 13). We can hardly doubt that this care for her children is Cleopatra's. They are never on Antony's lips. They are on hers again when, to convince Antony of her even greater love for him, she wishes that her children may perish if she does not love him. The demonstration would have no significance were she offering to sacrifice anything less than her dearest. At this point her "brave Egyptians all" are associated with "the memory of my womb", so that the concept of her maternity seems enlarged to include all her subjects, and the concept of queen is merged in that of mother (III, xiii, 158–64).

The theme of mother, with that of wife, is strengthened in the fifth act. In the practical details of the last phase, Antony's request to Caesar is for his own benefit (III, xii, 11–15). What Cleopatra asks is not for herself but "for her heirs" (III, xii, 18). When Antony is dead the former juxtaposition of lover and children remains. He is paramount, and nothing will prevent her from joining him in death, as she had said she would. The children are not more important than this, and formed no impediment when, on finding herself surprised in the monument, she sought without more ado to end herself. Prevented and forced to live, she will scheme for them. She will kneel to Caesar for the gift of "conquered Egypt for my son" (v. ii, 19). She will conceal her treasure for them; or so we may presume. Since they thus preside over her last desperate remedies, it is naïve of us to believe that she kept the treasure to give to Livia and Octavia (v, ii, 168); over-ingenious to conjecture a plot with Seleucus to deceive Caesar into supposing she would not take her life.[1] That intention she does not choose to conceal from him (v, ii, 51, 70). Caesar knows that her children mean more to her than anything save her suicide for Antony, and he threatens her accordingly (v, ii, 127–32). Dolabella, telling her the truth, tells it as it most concerns her: "You with your children will he send before" (v, ii, 201). Since she cannot preserve them she need no longer preserve herself; but in her death the composite figure of wife and mother has fully evolved, and she goes to her 'husband' nursing a child.

II

Out of a militant sexual love emerges wifely and maternal fidelity. The concept receives a succinct formulation in the evocation of Isis at the end of Apuleius's *Golden Asse*:[2]

O blessed Queene of heaven, whether thou be the Dame Ceres which art the originall and motherly nource of all fruitfull things in earth...or whether thou be the celestiall Venus, who in the beginning of the world diddest couple together all kind of things with an ingendered love, by an eternall propagation of humane kind.

The procreative principle is given the name of Ceres or Venus, according to whether its maternal or amorous quality is stressed. The goddess is also invoked as queen of the dead. She replies that she is

the naturall mother of all things, mistresse and governesse of all the Elements, the initiall progeny of worlds...at my will the planets of the ayre, the wholesome winds of the Seas, and the silences of hell be disposed.

Her worshippers call her by different names:

some Juno, other Bellona, other Hecate: and principally...the Ægyptians which are excellent in all kinds of ancient doctrine, and by their proper ceremonies accustome to worship mee, doe call mee Queene Isis (pp. 221–3).

Venus, Bellona, Juno: the names of Isis might be Cleopatra's, and if one cared with her Roman detractors to stress the element of witchcraft, one could add the name of Hecate.

For a critic who sees Cleopatra as exercising a creative more than a destructive influence on Antony, the function of Isis in the novel is not unlike Cleopatra's: "By my meane and benefit thou shalt become a man" (p. 224). Apuleius' influence on Shakespeare has been suggested in the translation of Bottom into an ass, but not of Cleopatra into a goddess. Yet there is much in the fable of Isis that resembles the view of Cleopatra outlined above: more, indeed, than Apuleius gives. "The true wife, the tender mother, the beneficent queen of nature", Frazer calls her. She abandoned all in her great grief to seek out the body of her dead husband Osiris, yet stopped on the way to suckle a child. This, and much more in the Isis legend, tempts us to suppose that Shakespeare may have had access to a fuller account of her cult than Apuleius gives.

Plutarch's account of Isis and Osiris was published in Philemon Holland's translation of the *Moralia* in 1603, and a reading of Holland's text encourages the view that Shakespeare had read it, and was echoing it in parts of the play. The first set of close verbal echoes clusters round the concept of motion. In the cult of Isis, motion has a metaphysical significance which may underlie the soothsayer's profession that he sees the future in his "motion" (II, iii, 14). For the Egyptians, we read in Holland, "have by reprochfull names noted such things as impeach hinder and staye the course of natural things, binding them so, as they cannot go forward" (p. 1311). Isis is, on the contrary, the goddess "of intelligence and motion together", and her name means "a motion animate and wise".

With the concept of motion is coupled that of sexual activity in the interpretation of the fig leaf. The "fig leafe signifieth the imbibition and motion of all things: and besides, it seemeth naturally to resemble the member of generation" (p. 1301). It is doubtless of the latter that Charmian is thinking when she cries, "O excellent! I love long life better than figs" (I, ii, 31). The Egyptian association of generation and motion underlies her subsequent appeal to the goddess Isis concerning Alexas:

O, let him marry a woman that cannot go, sweet Isis, I beseech thee! and let her die too, and give him a worse! and let worse follow worse, till the worst of all follow him laughing to his grave, fifty-fold a cuckold! Good Isis, hear me this prayer (I, ii, 62–7).

The word 'go' in this passage has been variously glossed; but it is clearly intended to stress that association of motion with sexual activity to be found in the interpretation of the fig leaf, and in the following story:

the Aegyptians devise of *Jupiter* this fiction, that both his legs being so growen together in one, that he could not goe at all, for very shame he kept in a desert wildernesse: but *Isis*, by cutting and dividing the same parts of his body, brought him to his sound and upright going againe. Which fable giveth us covertly to understand, that the understanding and reason of God in it selfe going invisibly, and after an unseene maner, proceedeth to generation by the meanes of motion (p. 1312).

To 'goe' is Holland's word. In Charmian's mouth it has superficially the religious significance of motion presided over by the goddess to whom she appeals. Doubtless it is also resonant with that sexual application implied at the end of the quotation: "proceedeth to generation by the meanes of motion". To 'go' thus also shares the meaning of its Latin counterpart in the word 'coitus'.[3] It is this meaning which leads Charmian by a similar associated meaning to the word 'die', which she proceeds to employ in its more common usage.

More than one theme touched on with levity between the soothsayer and the maids is remembered and transformed in the last act of the play. It may be so with the cult of Isis, for that also, frivolously introduced by Charmian, seems to be remembered in an exalted form in v, ii. Warburton thought that Cleopatra's renunciation of the moon (v, ii, 239–40) referred to Isis; and indeed Holland tells us that "Isis is nothing else but the Moone" (p. 1308). He also explains that when she died, her soul became the dog-star. Though we should not expect Charmian to address Cleopatra precisely thus, her "O eastern star!" (v, ii, 307) as she watches Cleopatra die, may recall the transfiguration of Isis.

Such echoes do not appear to occur evenly through the play. They are bunched together. Their appropriateness in I, ii and v, ii is clear. These are scenes in which Egyptian values predominate over Roman. Another cluster may be prompted by Cleopatra's supposed defection over Thidias, and since Antony speaks the tone is ironic. After this event, Antony's "terrene moon" (already noticed by commentators) is eclipsed (III, xiii, 153–4). His "good stars", formerly his "guides", have shot into hell (145–7). The aptness to Cleopatra's supposed desertion and to the mockery of her masquerade as a goddess, is clear. She has ceased to be Cleopatra-Isis. "Moon and stars!" (95) is Antony's first contemptuous rejection of that divinity which Plutarch tells us (in the Lives)[4] Cleopatra claimed. It is followed by a question which, with the eclipse of the moon and the fall of the stars, implies the loss of her identity as Cleopatra-Isis: "What's her name Since she was Cleopatra?"

It is a disillusioned recognition; for, earlier, Antony was willing to play the game of conferring on her the divinity of Isis. When before Actium he calls her his Thetis (III, vii, 60), Dover Wilson assumes that Shakespeare is confusing Thetis with "Tethys, greatest of sea deities, wife of Oceanus, mother of the Nile and other rivers". In that case Antony was intended to give Cleopatra one of the names of Isis, for "they say, that Osiris is the Ocean, and Isis, Tethys, as one would say, the nourse that suckleth and feedeth the whole world" (p. 1301). If Actium shows us the values of Isis claiming an Antony they will destroy and remake, this hint is followed up and the process shown in little by replacing the Roman image of the horse with that of the cow, symbol of Isis:

> Yon ribaudred nag of Egypt—
> Whom leprosy o'ertake! i'th'midst o'th'fight,
> When vantage like a pair of twins appeared,
> Both as the same, or rather ours the elder—
> The breese upon her, like a cow in June!—
> Hoists sails and flies.

(III, x, 10–15).

The tone of the reference need not surprise us. Enobarbus can see Cleopatra only in relation to his own prediction of horse and mare which Antony has fulfilled. To him she is in consequence a nag debauched, and the cow, symbol of her goddess, is evoked in the same temper. It is not the first time that Enobarbus speaks with contempt of the values of Isis; but their evocation alone at this crisis is important.

There is further, in Holland, precedent for Cleopatra's assumption of masculine domination. Apuleius puts it in martial terms by making Isis Bellona. Plutarch says: "and so they name the Moone, Mother of the world; saying, that she is a double nature, male and female" (p. 1304). This is because the moon contains an element of Osiris. Cleopatra likewise has taken to herself an element of Antony's virility symbolized in the sword (II, v, 23 and IV, xiv, 23).

There is clearer indication of Plutarch in Shakespeare's play than of Apuleius. That is perhaps because the two sources are different in kind. One is a full and circumstantial account of a cult, the other is a poetic evocation. Isis is the same figure in both, with a common emphasis on that wifely and maternal devotion in which Cleopatra resembles her. It was from Plutarch that Shakespeare remembered those details of the cult that at times pressed through into his writing. It is Apuleius for whom Isis is Bellona, and that goddess of marriage and childbirth whose name is twice on Cleopatra's lips, Juno (III, xi, 28; IV, xv, 34). Cleopatra is to retain her sovereignty in death, so that

> Dido and her Aeneas shall want troops,
> And all the haunt be ours. (IV, xiv, 53–4)

In this also she resembles the Isis of Apuleius: "At my will the planets of the ayre, the wholesome winds of the Sea, and the silences of hell be disposed" (p. 223). There is one potent word in which all three portraits join; and that is "nurse". In Apuleius Isis is "the originall and motherly nource of all fruitfull things in earth" (p. 221). In Plutarch she is "the nourse that suckleth and feedeth the whole world" (p. 1301). This Shakespeare seems to remember in the fulfilment of Cleopatra's death:

> Peace, peace!
> Dost thou not see my baby at my breast,
> That sucks the nurse asleep? (V, ii, 307–9)

III

Cleopatra was the first to see herself as Isis:

Now for Cleopatra, she did not only wear at that time (but at all other times else when she came abroad) the apparel of the goddess Isis, and so gave audience unto all her subjects as a new Isis.

Shakespeare took up this hint from Plutarch's *Lives* (p. 202). He found in the same source a similar identification of Antony with Bacchus. When Cleopatra first met Antony, it was said "that the goddess Venus was come to play with the god Bacchus" (p. 175). In the *Lives* it is not Hercules but Bacchus who departs from the falling Antony (p. 220). Of this identification also Shakespeare made use in heightening and formulating certain elements in Antony's portrait. There is no need to list the references to wine in the play. Most of them are on Antony's lips (e.g. II, vii, 106; III, xi, 73; xiii, 191; IV, ii, 21, 45; viii, 34, etc.). As the water party "ripens towards" an "Alexandrian feast", it is Antony who overrules the Roman reluctance of Caesar, and exhorts them to a Bacchic dance with the praise of wine, and presides over these "Egyptian Bacchanals" whose climax is the song to Bacchus (II, vii, 95–117).

Bacchus and Hercules are both akin to Antony in the *Lives*, and this kinship Shakespeare develops. Plutarch further shows its implications in the Isis essay: "the generative and nutritive Spirit, is *Bacchus*; but that which striketh and divideth, is *Hercules*" (p. 1304). What is relevant here is that Bacchus is himself akin to Osiris in that essay. Bacchus is "the lord and ruler of the moist nature" (p. 1301); Osiris is "all vertue and power that produceth moisture and water, taking it to be the materiall cause of generation, and the nature generative of seed" (p. 1300). Shakespeare uses the associations of Cleopatra with Isis, of Antony with Bacchus and Hercules. We should expect to find something of the relationship between Antony and Osiris if Shakespeare considered it relevant to the portrait; but he clearly did not. Though Antony may be shown as Bacchus, and Bacchus and Osiris are in one interpretation identical, Osiris commands a field of association (chiefly that which he shares with Isis) which cannot be annexed to Antony. It may be touched on at one point. Since "they both holde and affirme, *Nilus* to be the effluence of *Osiris*" (p. 1302), there may be some hint of identification with Osiris when Antony protests his love "By the fire That quickens Nilus' slime" (I, iii, 68–9). Otherwise it is the failure to develop an analogy which is striking. In view of the many obvious potential resemblances, it must be concluded that Shakespeare deliberately denied to Antony that quality of devoted love which would have been associated with Osiris, and which he chose to keep as the peculiar attribute of Cleopatra-Isis.

I conclude that Shakespeare was acquainted with the cult of Isis from Plutarch's essay, and from Apuleius. They are echoed in his portrait of Cleopatra and her values, but denied to Antony. If we see Antony's tragedy as the centrepiece of the play, its structure is faulty. The fifth act falls, on the contrary, into place as the necessary final stage in the evolution of the play's values, if we see as its subject the statement of the divine humanity which is common to Isis and Cleopatra.

NOTES

1. J. Dover Wilson, New Cambridge Edn., p. xxxv. Line references in this article are to this edition.

2. Translated W. Adlington, 1566. References to Chiltern Edition, 1946.

3. Dryden adds support to this gloss of the word 'go' in a song from *Marriage à la Mode*. He was surely remembering this passage when the words 'go, 'die', and 'Alexis' meet thus:

> Now, my dear, now let us go;
> Now die, my Alexis, and I will die too! (IV, iv)

4. Translated Sir T. North, 1579. References to *Shakespeare's Plutarch*, ed. Skeat, 1875.

SHAKESPEARE'S FRIENDS: HATHAWAYS AND BURMANS AT SHOTTERY[1]

BY

C. J. SISSON

The identity and the status of Shakespeare's wife appear to be in some measure open to question. E. K. Chambers, in his authoritative *William Shakespeare*, is guarded upon her identity: "Anne's parentage is not quite clear."[2] He accepts it only as probable that she was Agnes, daughter of Richard Hathaway of Shottery, among other Hathaways open to consideration. As for her status, there is a marked tendency, especially among the more imaginative writers upon Shakespeare's life, to represent Anne as the yokel daughter of a peasant father, and the marriage as a *mésalliance* for the son of a prominent Stratford burgess. We may well value any further evidence from the records of the time which may help to clarify these questions and to place the marriage in a true perspective. Some such evidence may now be presented, drawn from the records of the Court of Chancery and from Court Rolls of the Manor of Old Stratford.

The Chancery records in question consist mainly of depositions which, after the fashion of Chancery depositions, offer a vivid picture of events and persons of deep interest to the Stratford of 1584, in Shakespeare's twentieth year. Whatever adds to our knowledge of the world of men in which he had personal contacts has an especial interest for us. The witnesses here were men from Stratford, Shottery and Wootton Wawen, among them some friends of Shakespeare's youth, whose evidence is much concerned with Richard Hathaway of Shottery.

I. A CHANCERY COMMISSION AT STRATFORD IN JANUARY 1584

The story that emerges illustrates the operation of procedure by Commission in Chancery, whereby magistrates were appointed by the Court to inquire into a suit in the district of its origin, to take evidence there, to seek agreement between the parties, and to report to the Court in London. In this instance, the unruly passions generated at Stratford by local rivalries, with consequent violence, forced Sir Thomas Lucy of Charlecote, the presiding magistrate, to close his inquiry abruptly, to abandon his Commission, and to refer the matter back to the Court.

It is characteristic of the workings of Chancery, with its constant desire to function as a Court of conciliation, that after inquiry into this riotous interference with one of its Commissions it persisted in attempts to arrive at a local decision by agreement before renewed Commissions. And the end of the story furnishes strong evidence that the Court was no respecter of persons, and was not swayed in its judgments by the prestige of even such a litigant as Ambrose Earl of Warwick, seeking to assert his power in the heart of his own country. We should be ill-advised indeed to be guided by Selden's deep prejudice against Courts of Equity.[3]

Certainly the Court might well have lost its patience upon report of the outcome of the sitting at Stratford on 12 January 1584 of its Commissioners, as an outrage to the dignity of the Court. Sir Thomas Lucy and his fellow-Commissioners were the guests for this purpose of John Smith, the Chamberlain of the Borough, at his house in Stratford. They sat at dinner in Smith's own chamber above, while below, in the common dining-parlour, he provided dinner for the witnesses called for the hearing and for servants of the parties to the dispute to be heard after dinner. One of the parties, Francis Smyth of Wootton Wawen, dined with the Commissioners. The other, the Earl of Warwick, did not attend, but was represented by John Goodman and Mr Fenton, his servants.

After dinner, Francis Smyth came down to the dining-parlour below, and moved among the throng of witnesses and servants there, and his converse with some of the witnesses called to the hearing gave great offence to the Earl's servants who overheard it. Smyth upbraided, and appeared even to threaten, some of the witnesses, especially Roger Burman and Richard Burman of Shottery, and their kinsman Stephen Burman of Stratford. They had, it seemed, supported the Earl against Smyth when the issue of the suit came before the Manor Court of Old Stratford.

"Masters," he said, "You made presentment of my eleven butts of land at Bordon Hill. Take heed, pray God your presentment be true, for if it be not you are like to answer to it." And again, "I marvel you would so rashly so do, considering the land hath been my ancestors' and mine inheritance time out of memory of man. It is no matter if you have done well, so it is; if not you may perhaps hear of it."

These speeches of Smyth's, faithfully reported by the Burmans and others, were overheard by Goodman and Fenton, who had also come into the parlour. Not unreasonably, they accused Smyth of interference with witnesses, and the ensuing dialogue, with its accompanying actions, may best be recorded in dramatic form:

Goodman. Mr Smyth, you do not like a gentleman.
Smyth. Why?
Goodman. For you do my lord great injury.
Smyth. Why, wherein?
Goodman. Marry, you go about to allure my lord's witnesses, and talk with them in corners.
Smyth. I do not.
Goodman. You do.
Smyth. I tell you truly I do not.
Goodman. But thou dost (*advancing upon him*) Thou shalt not.
Smyth. I tell thee thou dost say untruly (*thrusting him away with his hand*).
Goodman. What, dost thou lay thy hands on me? If thou dost lay thy hands on me I will lay my dagger on thy pate (*putting his hand to his dagger and offering to draw it*).

The rising curve of heat in these exchanges is marked in the nice gradations of the change from *you* to *thou*, from mere denial to giving the lie, from words to action, and so to a threatened recourse to weapons. At this stage Fenton and Smyth's gentleman Richard Dale came between Smyth and Goodman to part them, and Smyth immediately went upstairs to complain to Sir Thomas Lucy of his usage by Goodman, whose anger, and Fenton's, now turned upon Dale. Dale, about to follow his master upstairs, lingered to pick up his sword and Smyth's cloak-bag, and found both men in his way:

Fenton. (*grasping Dale by the doublet*) Ah sirrah! What dost thou here? Thou art a knave of all knaves! Away knave! Out of this place!

Goodman. What, villain, wilt thou not go? Go, or I will lay my dagger on thy pate (*putting his hand to his dagger.*)

(*Fenton gives Dale a blow on the side of the head, thrusts him partly through the door and claps the door to upon one of his legs.*)

Dale. I pray you, let me take my other leg with me! (*struggles with Fenton to open the door and free his leg, and goes upstairs.*)

Upon this rueful exit-line he made his way upstairs and met Sir Thomas Lucy looking out in anger at the door of his chamber, who bade him call up Goodman and Fenton. Dale, in great fear and trembling, would by no means go down again to these violent men. Lucy sent one of his own servants. And Dale sent Robert, a humbler servant of Smyth, to pick up all swords lying in the parlour and bring them up, lest sword-play should follow upon words.

It was evident to Sir Thomas Lucy and to his fellow-Commissioners that there was no hope of executing this Commission satisfactorily in such an atmosphere of turmoil, and that the grave question of interference with witnesses and of rioting and violence, amounting to contempt of Court, must be referred to the Court itself in London, along with the original issue of the ownership of the lands in Shottery fields. They reported accordingly in these terms, and the next stage of the inquiry took place in London, with the consequent demand for the presence there in the following April of all witnesses called to the hearing at Stratford, with the exception of Roger Burman of Shottery, an old man of eighty years of age.

2. A SUIT IN CHANCERY

The events so far chronicled are recorded and authenticated in depositions in the Court of Chancery taken at the Chapel of the Rolls in London before the Examiner, Matthew Carew.[4] The dialogue is quoted *verbatim* from the same source.

It would have been difficult indeed for Stratford folk in 1584, and ludicrous for Lucy and the Earl of Warwick, to conceive a later age when the records of this debate would be prized for their references to obscure Shottery yeomen, to Richard Hathaway, Shakespeare's father-in-law, Foulke Sandells and the Burmans, friends of Shakespeare and of his wife Anne. But we are moving here among intimates of the poet's youth, and in the first years of his marriage and of the birth of his children.

Some of them were tenants of the Earl of Warwick as Lord of the Manor of Old Stratford, and some of Francis Smyth of Wootton Wawen. And the Earl was desirous of asserting his rights against Francis Smyth in respect of certain lands on Bordon Hill as part of the Manor. The land is described more closely by Richard Burman of Shottery as

xj butts of arable land that lye in the fields of Shottery abbutting vpon the moore there westwards.

To this end Warwick referred the matter to the Manor Court through its steward, Sheldon, and his assistant Thomas Nashe. The Jury of the Manor, upon inquiry, presented that the land was indeed part of the Lord's farm of the Manor. Among the jurors were Richard Hathaway *alias* Gardener, Roger Burman, Richard Burman, and Foulke Sandells. No record of this meeting of the Court is preserved among the few and scattered Court Rolls surviving, but a full account of its inquiry is given in the Chancery depositions of two of the jurors. The Court met, according to their evidence given in April/May 1584, "about a year and a half ago". This points clearly to the Michaelmas Court of 1582, held as usual on the Friday after Michaelmas Day (which in 1582 was Friday, 6 October) about the time of Shakespeare's marriage to Anne Hathaway. Francis Smyth maintained, however, that the land had been for several generations the property of his family, and refused to accept the verdict of the Manor Court.

The Earl, armed with the presentment of the jurors, sought to enforce it by proceeding against Smyth in the Court of Chancery. There he could hope for success, in the absence of documentary proof, by reliance on oral evidence from local sources best informed upon the past history of the land in question. The inquest at the Manor Court might perhaps be envisaged as an encouraging rehearsal for subsequent proceedings in Chancery. The *Bill of Complaint* was lodged in Hilary Term 1583. After the usual bickerings upon the sufficiency of Smyth's *Answer*, the Court ordered Smyth on 7 June to join with Warwick in assent to a Commission to take evidence and to report its conclusions to the Court in Michaelmas Term following. When, later on, this Commission was renewed after initial failure, the Commissioners nominated by Warwick were Sir Thomas Lucy and Edward Boughton, and by Smyth Sir Edward Mounteagle and Andrew Ognell. It is probable that these were also the original Commissioners who met in Stratford, after the usual delays, in January 1584,[5] with the exception of Mounteagle, as Stratford and Chancery records indicate.

The Commissioners met in John Smith's house.[6] "Mr Smith's house", to which there are several references in Stratford records, was situated at the corner of Bull Lane and Old Town, on the site now occupied by the Croft School. It was obviously a house and property of some importance,[7] and John Smith was the third generation of his family, following his father William and his grandfather Richard as the Corporation's tenant at the advantageous rent of fifteen shillings a year. It is true that he paid a 'fine' upon entry. The Corporation might seem to have treated its tenancies as if it was dealing with copyhold lands in a manor, with hereditary claims to tenure. But it is also clear that 'Mr Smith's house' served the Corporation's needs for a house of dignity and space when distinguished visitors were entertained, as upon this visit of Sir Thomas Lucy to hold his inquiry at the behest of the Court of Chancery.

John Smith was a vintner, and concerned with the provision for the material entertainment of distinguished visitors. The quarts of sack, the pottles of claret, the quarterns of sugar, necessary to the comfort of Sir Thomas Lucy at Mr Smith's house, came from Mr Smith's tavern in the High Street. The items were duly reported by Mr Smith in his capacity as Chamberlain among the annual accounts of Corporation expenditure for preceding years, presented on 11 January 1583/4 and on 20 January 1584/5, to Alderman John Shakespeare and the other City Fathers of Stratford.

The witnesses in Chancery, whose depositions were taken between 27 April and 1 May 1584, all speak of the Commission's having been held 'of late' as contrasted with the 'year and a half' since the Manor Court was held. This points to a period of within two or three months at most, that is January or February 1583/4. A series of entries in the Chamberlain's Accounts for 11 January 1583/4 and 20 January 1584/5, covering respectively the periods Michaelmas 1582–Michaelmas 1583 and Michaelmas 1583–Michaelmas 1584, appear to have reference to this occasion.[8]

The Mr Fenton referred to there is described by Shottery witnesses in Chancery as 'one of the

Earl of Warwick's gentlemen'.[9] Mr Turvile is clearly another of the Earl's officers, apparently half as important as Mr Fenton, to judge from the amounts of their respective gifts in money from the Corporation. Two distinct sessions of inquiry appear to be reflected in these accounts. The first was carried out by Fenton alone at some time in the year Michaelmas 1582 to Michaelmas 1583, and it may seem reasonable to suggest this survey as an immediate sequel to the Manor Court of October 1582. The second involved a visit by Sir Thomas Lucy on 12 January 1583/4, and a visit by Fenton and Turvile on 23 January following, when they spent the night at the Bear Inn, having surveyed afresh the Shottery lands.

It is beyond question that Lucy's visit on 12 January 1583/4 was to Mr Smith's house to hold the Commission, and that the survey of 23 January arose out of that abortive meeting and was combined with arranging with the Shottery yeomen concerned for their visit to London to give evidence in Chancery.[10] This would allow reasonable time for them to make their preparations and to journey to London for their examination between 27 April and 1 May.

Francis Smyth was a personage of note in Stratford.[11] His father, Sir John Smith, a Baron of the Exchequer under Henry VIII, had married Anne, the heiress of John Harewell, Lord of the Manor of Lucies, to which she had added the Manor of Wootton Wawen by purchase from Lord John Grey. Francis succeeded to both upon her death in 1562, as also to her land held in Chapel Street in Stratford and to his father's long-standing tenancy of the Mill in Old Stratford and other lands in Shottery, held by lease from Hugh Latimer, bishop of Worcester from October 1535 to July 1539. To these possessions he had added the Manor of Ashby Folville in Leicestershire by his marriage in 1537 to Mary, daughter and heiress of John Morton. At the time of Warwick's suit against him in 1584 he was sixty-one years of age.

There was no question about his Catholic sympathies, though he was prudent enough to avoid the penalties for recusancy by the requisite occasional conformity. He had married his son George to Anne Gifford, daughter of Ursula Throckmorton of Coughton Court and of Sir Thomas Gifford, and this alliance with two powerful Catholic families was cemented when his great-granddaughter Mary married Sir Robert Throckmorton. One of his grandsons entered the Catholic priesthood. It can hardly be doubted that religious party divisions helped to exacerbate, if not indeed to originate, Warwick's attack upon Smyth, in which no quarter was given, as the records show. The Commissioners nominated by the parties reflect this religious cleavage, Sir Thomas Lucy for Warwick, and Sir Edward Mounteagle for Smyth. If Lucy's invitation to Smyth to dine with him and the other Commissioners suggests a desire to assert his neutrality in the quarrel, the extraordinary munificence of the Corporation to Warwick's officers Fenton and Turvile shows Stratford's anxiety to placate the Earl, in this welter of local interests.

Mr Smith's house, on the day of the inquiry, swarmed with the Stratford equivalent of Capulets and Montagues, the gentlemen and retainers on either side bent on quarrelling. Lucy came to the only possible decision. He reported to the Court in London the breakdown of the inquiry, the misdemeanours of the parties present, and the evidence as far as it had been taken, for the Court to take further action.

Before the month was out, on 31 January, the Court of Chancery heard the case afresh with Lucy's report before it. Smyth sought and obtained permission to present and to examine witnesses whose evidence was not heard by Lucy at Stratford when he closed his inquiry prematurely. It was decided that they should be heard on the issue of the land, and that evidence should be taken at the same time on the misdemeanours reported by Lucy. It is for this reason that we have the evidence of Shakespeare's friends Richard Burman and Foulke Sandells on the Shottery lands surviving in Chancery records. These two were examined on 28 April. Warwick raised objections to their evidence on a technical point, and when overruled sought permission to bring further evidence himself to impeach the credit of Burman as a witness. Burman's evidence on the issue was indeed disastrous to Warwick's case.

The evidence given upon the disturbances in John Smith's house bears all the signs of accuracy and truth. On the whole, the account of the affair given by Stephen Burman of Stratford and Richard Burman of Shottery tallies with that given by Smythe's three retainers, John Howes, aged fifty-eight, John Knight, aged sixty-three, and Richard Dale, aged forty.[12] The essential point made by all is that there was no conspiracy or secrecy in Smyth's discussion of the case with the Burmans while awaiting their examination by Lucy. It was openly done in the hearing of all present, and his words, as cited by the witnesses, did not necessarily imply threats. But no attempt was made to conceal the fact of his intervention. The general effect of the evidence on this point is to establish faults on both sides, imprudence on the part of Smyth, and resultant violence on the part of Warwick's officers, who plainly had some excuse for their anger.

The evidence given by Richard Burman and Foulke Sandells, both of Shottery and both members of the Jury of the Manor Court, throws light upon the verdict of that Court upon which the Earl relied. It is indeed an answer to the main question upon which Smyth pressed them in John Smith's dining-parlour, whether the verdict of the Jury was given from their own knowledge or no. Richard Burman, a man of sixty years of age, had never heard of the land being brought into question before the inquest of the Manor Court. He had known it to be occupied by tenants holding from Smyth and his family, by Reynolds from Smyth's father, by Swallow from Smyth's mother and after her death from Smyth himself, and now by Wood-ward from Smyth, as part of Shottery Farm.[13] The Jury, according to Richard's evidence, relied entirely upon the testimony of two of its members, Richard Hathaway *alias* Gardener and Roger Burman, of whom only Roger, now aged over eighty, was still alive. Roger, as Richard recalled the matter, said that he had heard his elders report the land to be of the Manor, and Hathaway had heard his father say so. Foulke Sandells, a younger man, had relied upon Hathaway's positive assertion, and to a less degree upon a merely negative report from Roger that he had never heard it denied that the lands belonged to the Manor Farm. No other proof, they agreed, was adduced for the verdict arrived at by the Jury. In fact, it appears clear that the decisive evidence that guided the Jury was that of Richard Hathaway, who in turn had relied upon his father's report. And Hathaway could not now be examined. He had died a year before the Manor Court met in October 1582.[14] It may seem a very tenuous chain of evidence as sole justification for the verdict of the Jury in Warwick's favour. And it suggests that Hathaway's influence was potent in local affairs at Shottery.

It is not without significance that 'Hewlands', the house occupied by the Hathaway family, was owned by the Earl of Warwick. Smyth, however, was the owner of the house known as 'Burmans'.[15] Some of the Burman family were consequently his tenants, as Hathaway was Warwick's tenant. These tenancies were not involved in the matter at issue, and remained unaffected by the suit. To this extent, the Hathaways were Warwick's men, and some of the

Burmans Smyth's men. Both Richard Burman and Foulke Sandells refer to Hathaway and Roger Burman as tenants of the Earl, and it is a fact that the evidence of these two tenants of his carried the decision of the Manor for the Earl. Richard Burman was notably guarded in his Chancery evidence, and it was he whom Smyth upbraided, and in familiar terms, in the Chamberlain's house. It is clear that Richard was Smyth's tenant at 'Burmans', and that Warwick's advisers feared the weight of his evidence when the suit came to trial. It is further relevant to the rival influences at work that the Burmans, like the Smyths, were of Catholic sympathies, in contrast to Warwick and his friends.

Upon the completion of depositions in London, the final hearing was ordered in June 1584, and twice deferred by Smyth and his counsel. It was at last heard on 2 July, when the Court decreed a further Commission to sit at Stratford on 24 September, with the same Commissioners as before, save that for Smyth his kinsman Edward Brudenell replaced Andrew Ognell. The sitting of the Commission was deferred to 17 October, and even then Smyth failed to appear, though Warwick came in person, and Lucy came from Worcestershire especially to attend. Warwick thereupon reported to the Court, claiming costs. On 7 November the Court awarded him £10 costs against Smyth for these unavailing attendances. The case was heard again before the Court in London, with this report before it, and the Court renewed the Commission, with power to Warwick's Commissioners to decide the issue alone, if Smyth again failed to appear. On 12 February 1585 the parties agreed in Court upon a final meeting of the Commission to determine the case on these terms, to meet in the Stratford Guildhall on 5 April. Everything seems to point to a marked reluctance of Smyth to present his case before the Commissioners, and to the determination of Warwick and his advisers to pursue it to the end.

The end of an interminable series of Chancery decrees and Orders is reached on 17 June 1585, with a Final Decree reported at great length as a conclusion to the case.[16] The Commissioners have met, all four of them, and have agreed upon an award with the consent of all parties concerned, who also desire the Court of Chancery to give effect to the award as if it were a decree of the Court arrived at upon a solemn hearing of the case in open Court. And the Court so decrees. The Lord Chancellor signs the decree accordingly, and Henry Walrond, Smyth's attorney, enrolls it in the Rolls of Chancery as valid for ever and binding upon the parties and their heirs. Unfortunately, the contents of the award are not rehearsed in the Decree. They are said to be contained in an indenture tripartite deposited in Chancery.[17] The records of Stratford Corporation make it clear that the final meeting took place, as ordered by the Court, at Stratford. An undated entry in the Chamberlain's Accounts for 1585–6 records payments totalling three shillings and a penny for a pottle of wine, a pottle of sack, and half a pound of sugar "for my lord of Warwick hys commyssyonours".[18] The Commission met before 21 April 1585, the date of the next entry, and presumably in fact on 5 April, in the Guildhall.

We may be assured that Smyth, perhaps to his surprise, was satisfied. The evidence given in Chancery was plainly in his favour, as against the verdict of the Manor Court under the influence of the Lord of the Manor and his tenants. It was he, moreover, who saw to it that the decree was enrolled, for final validity and record in law, as the party favoured by the decree. A certain sturdiness in his own tenants, Richard Burman and Foulke Sandells, overcoming fear of the great magnate whose shadow overlay their little world, surely swung the Commissioners and the Court to that normal justice which reigns in Elizabethan Chancery, even to the disadvantage of great men, as a thousand cases testify. It is, finally, well to recall that Warwick was then becoming immersed in great affairs of State, in the preparations for the trial of Mary Queen of Scots, in which he participated in 1586.

3. SHAKESPEARE'S MARRIAGE AND THE HATHAWAYS AND BURMANS OF SHOTTERY

It emerges as a side-issue that some friends of Shakespeare's youth, and among them some ancestors of a Warwickshire family of indestructible continuity and reputation, were involved in this controversy over a parcel of Shottery land. The meeting of the Manor Court out of which it sprang was held about the time of Shakespeare's marriage to the daughter of one of the jurors, a second juror being his surety for the wedding, and a third juror the next-door neighbour of his bride. It is certain that Shakespeare would know all about this legal battle, with its repercussions in the Stratford of which his father was a notable citizen and an Alderman. We may reasonably see some reminiscence of these repercussions in his choice of the name Fenton for the young gentleman in *The Merry Wives of Windsor* who carries it away with Mistress Anne Page.

It may be hoped, further, that all lingering doubts may be dissolved as to the identity of Shakespeare's wife. These records reflect the close and intimate relations between Richard Burman, Foulke Sandells, and Richard Hathaway of Shottery, to set alongside Sandells' well-known association with Shakespeare as his surety. It is further to be noted that Hathaway was familiarly known among these Shottery folk as Hathaway *alias* Gardener, that he was clearly a prominent, perhaps the leading, personality among the members of the Manor Jury, and that he was a man of substance in their community.

The ancientry in Shottery of the families of Hathaway and Burman is amply testified in a fragmentary collection of Court Rolls of the Manor of Old Stratford preserved in the Birthplace Museum. In them the Burmans appear as copyholders from 1481 onwards, and the Hathaways, under the name of Gardener, from 1498 onwards.

On 5 October 1498 Robert Gardener is named as a Shottery copyholder, and again as a juror, along with John Gardener, in 1506. On 4 October 1546 John Hathaway is a juror, and again in 1547 and 1548. The Chancery documents make it clear that Richard Hathaway *alias* Gardener was a leading juror in 1581. If his daughter Anne was twenty-five years of age in 1582, he was a householder with a family by 1557. It might seem reasonable to suggest a pedigree for him of four generations at Shottery, with a great-grandfather Robert, a grandfather John, and a father John who began to use the name of Hathaway in preference to that of Gardener. It is to be noted that his intimates Richard Burman and Foulke Sandells, after one reference to him in their Chancery evidence as "Ry Hathway alias Gardener" call him simply "Gardener".[19]

The pedigree of the numerous Burman family is much more complex and difficult to establish, even after careful study of two books devoted by members of the family to its history in Warwickshire, both distinguished by serious exploration of the evidence of historical records and archives.[20] It may be of value to attempt to settle the main line of descent in the tenants of the house and land in Shottery known as 'Burmans', who rented them from Francis Smyth and his ancestors the Harewells, and who by virtue of this tenancy were members of the Jury of the Manor of Old Stratford. It is difficult even to fix the beginning of that tenancy in what came to be the settled abode of the head of the family in Shottery. The Court Roll of 1463 makes no mention of a Burman. Dugdale, however, cites evidence of the tenancy of "John Boreman", ending in 1467, of a house and land, formerly occupied by William Saunders, and now conveyed in chief by the Bishop of Worcester to William Harewell.[21] In 1481 Richard Burman appears and is fined for bad husbandry of his land. In 1482 the fine is increased from 2d. to 3s. 4d. for non-payment. It may seem reasonable to consider John Burman as coming into the tenancy of 'Burmans' in 1445, succeeded by his son Richard Burman in 1467. Later Court Rolls record a Richard Burman as a Juror in 1506, and as Constable in 1546, when both Richard Burman and John Burman, as again in 1547 and in 1548, were Jurors along with John Hathaway. The will of Richard Burman of 20 February 1529 makes bequests to a son Roger, and is witnessed by a Richard Burman.[22]

The Richard Burman who gave evidence in Chancery is clearly the tenant of Francis Smyth and the occupier of 'Burmans', upon whose testimony Smyth had relied. Aged sixty in 1584, he was therefore born in 1523–4. The Roger Burman who attended the meeting in Mr Smith's house is stated to have been eighty years of age in 1582, and was therefore born in 1501–2. He was a tenant of both the Earl and of Smyth. He died in 1591. The Stephen Burman who gave evidence was born in 1537–8.

It seems probable that the line of succession at 'Burmans' moved from John Boreman (d. 1467), to Richard Burman I (d. 1539), to Richard Burman II (d. 1558), and to Richard Burman III (b. 1524). Roger Burman (b. 1502, d. 1591) was the third son of Richard I. Stephen (b. 1538, d. 1607) may possibly have been the son of John, the second son of Richard I, and thus grandson of Richard I, and cousin to Richard III. He was certainly the father of Richard IV (b. 1575, d. 1630).[23] He is described as "of the Parishe of Stretford vpon Avon" when he gave evidence and signed his name as a practised writer. And he occurs frequently in Stratford records. He was not a juror of the Manor, as was Richard III, the tenant of 'Burmans' in 1581–5. Nor was he apparently Smyth's tenant at Shottery.

But whatever complexities and doubts affect the Burman pedigree in Elizabethan England, there can be no question of their close links with the Hathaway family and with Shottery, and consequently of their place as part of the village community which was the focus of the young Shakespeare's life when he came there to find a wife. Richard Burman, the Master of 'Burmans' next door to Hathaway's 'Hewlands', Foulke Sandells, Stephen Burman, and old Roger Burman, knew the young man well, knew his bride, and knew her father as one whose word counted for much in village councils as a man of long-standing authority. There is no ground whatever for the common conception of a *mésalliance* between Shakespeare and a portionless bride from Shottery. Indeed, we may well be led to consider whether the settlement of Hathaway's affairs upon his death was not one cause of delay in a marriage which had long been determined upon, and which had been already declared by the common and valid ceremony of contract, accompanied by bonds from both families to provide for the young couple. The lamentable condition of John Shakespeare's affairs would further complicate such arrangements. There is a further pointer in the close association of Foulke Sandells with the marriage in 1582 as surety. He was a Shottery man, a friend of Hathaway, and, as we now know from these records, he was then of the age of thirty-one, and a man of substance who can describe himself as 'Yeoman'. It was he whom Hathaway chose to be the supervisor of his will in 1581, and the completion of this marriage was surely part of his duties in the settlement of the affairs of the dead man. Hathaway was buried on 7 September 1581. His will was proved on 9 July 1582, and probate was followed by negotiations for a licence for the marriage later in the year, the bonds for which were signed on 28 November.

APPENDIX

Depositions of Foulke Sandells and
Richard Burman upon the land

ffoulke Sandell of Shottrye w^tin the Parishe of Stretforde vpon Avon in the Countie of Warwik yeomã of the age of xxxiij yeres or therabouts sworne and ex^d the xxix^{tie} daye of Aprill in the yere aforesaid &c   To the first Int. that he doth not knowe the right hoñable therll of Warwik who by report is now plaintiffe   But he doth verie well know   ffraunces Smith esquier that is now defend^t And knoweth also the xj butts of arable land meñcõned in this Int. now in question betwene the said Erll and the defend^t

To the 2 that he was pñt about A yere and A half past at A co^rte holden for the said Erll in his mano^r or lordship of old Stretford in the same Countie of Warwik by one Mr Sheldon and one Mr Nashe wch of them was Stuard then he canot certenlye depose at wch co^rte he this depo^t was emongs others ympanelled vpon the Iurye then to inquere of the matters then gyven them in chardge

To the 3. that emongs the thinges that were gyven the said Iurye in charge at the said Co^rte one was that they shuld inquier whether the foresaid xj butts of land were parcell of the lordes fferme of Ould stretford or not   And saith that vpon the Report of one hathwaye ãls* Gardener the said Erlls teññt vpon his othe that the said xj butts of lande were parcell of the lords fferme of old stretford he this depo^t and the said Iurye did pñt the same to be the lords land & parcell of the said fferme at A co^rte holden w^tin the said Mano^r about a yere as he remẽbreth after the said gardener being then dead

To the 4. that for his part he had no certen knowledge as of his owne weth^r the said xj butts of land were the lords land but onlye by the report and affirmacõn of the said Gardener vpon his othe nether was ther any other proof or evidence showed to the said Iurye but the said report of gardener Saving he saith that one Roger Burman an old man another of the said Erlls teññts & of the def^t also and that (as he saith) had duelled w^tin the said lordship by the space of fourescore yeres or verye nere did also then affirme vpon his othe that he in all his tyme did not heare the cõtrarye And otherwise or more to these Interr he saith he cãnot depose

[Mark as signature.]

Rycharde Burman of Shotrey w^tin the Parishe of Stratford vpon avon in the Countie of warr   husband-man of the age of lx yere or therabouts sworne and ex^d the daye and yere aforesaid &c

To the first Int. that he doth know bothe the right hoñable Therll of warwike now compl and ffraunces Smith esquier the now defend^t And knoweth also the xj butts of arable land that lye in the fieldes of Shottrey aforesaid abutting vpon the moore there westwarde now in controũcye betwene the said parties

* 'hathwaye ãls' interlined.

To the 2. that he was pñt at a Coᵗe holden about A yere & A half past for the said Erll wᵗⁱn the Manoʳ or lordshippe of ould Stratforde and at that Corte was one Sheldon Stuard assisted & accompanyed wᵗ one Tho. Nashe, And saith that he this deporᵗ was ympanelled emongs others of the Iurye then to inquyer of such matters as were gyven them in charge at the same and to pñt the same

To the 3. that it was A parcell of the charge gyven to the said Iurye at that Coᵗe to inquyer whether the foresaid xj butts of land were parcell of the ferme grounde of ould Stratforde or not And saithe that by the report of one Ry hathway aĩs Gardener decessed and of one Roger Burman yet lyving & one of the same Iurye that the said xj butts of land were the said Erlls as parcell and belonging to the said fferme of old Stretford he this depoᵗ wᵗ the said Iury vpon the same report did pñt the same to be the said Erlls as parcell of the said fferme.

To the 4. that of his own certen knowledge he neũ knew that the said xj butts of lande did belong to the said fferme for to his Remembrãce he never heard it iñ question before that tyme ffor before that it was vsed to be occupyed and manured by one Mʳ Swallow that was fermoʳ of Shottrey ferme vnder the defts mother while she lieved and vnder the defendᵗ him self and before that by one Reynolds vnder the defts ffather And at the tyme of ther pñtement in the occupacõn of one Woodward by the graunt of the deft And saith that the said Iurye had no other Evidence that he did heare or vnderstand to prove the said lands to be the said Erles as parcell of his lordship or Manoʳ of olde Stratford but the report of the said Roger Burman and Gardener ijᵒ of the said Erlls teñnts Whereof one said he heard his elders say so, and the other sayd he heard his father say the same whoose sayinges vpon ther Othe at the same Corte were accepted for sufficient Evidence for the lorde and therupon pñted accordingly by the said Iurye And this is all that he can saye to the said Int.

[Mark as signature.]

NOTES

1. This article has been prepared with the assistance of a Research Grant from the University of London for the provision of photostats of documents.

2. I, 18.

3. *Table Talk*, ed. Arber (1868), p. 46.

4. P.R.O. C24/170/Smyth *v.* Warwick. Supplementary information is given in a series of voluminous Decrees and Orders in Chancery, C33/65, 67, 69, 70.

5. I have been unable to find any record of the sittings of the Commission among 'Country Depositions' at the P.R.O. Nor, unfortunately, have I found any Pleadings in the Suit Warwick *v.* Smyth, from which we might have learned a fuller history of the land in question. The Bill evidently rested upon a 'terrier' or survey of Warwick's lands in Shottery, as appears from a Decree of 7 June 1583, and Smyth's defence rested upon a lease from the Bishop of Worcester between 1535 and 1539.

6. John Smith, one of the five sons of William Smith, haberdasher of Henley Street, married Margaret Sadler on 17 November 1572. In 1575 he was elected Taster, in 1577 Constable, and was sworn as Burgess or Councillor on 15 January 1578. On 5 October 1582 he was elected Chamberlain, with Richard Court, Alderman on 18 August 1596, Bailiff on 6 October 1598, and Principal Alderman on 3 September 1600. His career was complicated by his recusancy and his partisanship in local disputes and rivalries. On 12 August 1601 he was dismissed from the Council, and died in the following November.

7. Described in *Minutes and Accounts*, III, 105, in a survey of 1582.

8. *Minutes and Accounts*, III, 118, 136, 149.

9. Cf. *Minutes and Accounts*, III, 148 n. 6. This note is clearly in error in suggesting that Fenton represented the Corporation, and there is no doubt that Francis Smyth was the party opposed to Warwick here.

10. It is disconcerting to find that 12 January in that year fell on a Sunday. But I see no good reason for assuming both that the normal method of dating was departed from here and also that a series of items were omitted from the 1582–3 accounts and brought on here as arrears, in order to date them in January 1582–3, when the 12th fell on a Saturday. xij may possibly be an error in copying for xj. But, after all, the Privy Council sometimes met on a Sunday.

11. He is not to be confused with Alderman Francis Smyth and his family, of Stratford-upon-Avon, who figure largely in Corporation records. His pedigree appears in *Visitation of Warwickshire, 1619*, pp. 70–1, cf. *V.C.H. Warwickshire, passim*.

12. It may be some indication of their status that Dale and Knight sign their names like practised writers, whereas Howes can only make an elaborate mark. Stephen, the younger Burman, writes his name, whereas Richard, aged sixty, and Foulke Sandells, aged thirty-three, make marks only.

13. Lady Anne Smyth, widow of Sir John Smyth, died in 1562. Burman's evidence makes it certain that the Francis Smyth concerned was the old man, son of Sir John and Lady Anne, and not his grandson Francis Smyth the Second. He survived until 1605.

14. It is nevertheless stated that his evidence was given 'upon oath'. This was clearly given at an earlier Court, upon a preliminary inquiry. Foulke Sandells in his evidence refers to such an earlier meeting, held a year before the Court which passed the verdict, i.e. in 1581.

15. *Minutes and Accounts*, IV, 113. Survey of 6 October 1590.

16. C33/70, f. 600.

17. I have not succeeded in finding it.

18. *Minutes and Accounts*, III, 163.

19. Sandells, indeed, first refers to him in his evidence simply as "Gardener". "Hathaway alias Gardener" was an afterthought in correction.

20. Sir John Burman, *The Burman Family of Warwickshire* (1916). John Burman, *The Burman Chronicle* (1940).

21. Dugdale, *Antiquities of Warwickshire* (1730 ed.), p. 683. William Saunders was Vicar of Wootton Wawen from 1436 to 1445. William Harewell died in 1501, and was Smyth's maternal great-grandfather.

22. John Burman, *The Burman Chronicle*, p. 14.

23. This account of the Burman descent varies from that proposed by Mr Burman. In considering the evidence of wills, it is important to realize that the testator cannot bequeath his copyhold tenancies of house or land under a Manor, which are governed by customary law. A son therefore, not being a beneficiary under the will but being nevertheless the successor to such tenures, may well be a witness to his father's will.

PLATE V

A. The complete painting

B. A detail

UNASCRIBED PAINTING AT DROTTNINGHOLM THEATRE MUSEUM, SHOWING A BOOTH STAGE
About 1660, probably Flemish

PLATE VI

Iteration.

From eager Acting Sin, comes Iteration,
Or frequent Custome of Sins perpetration;
Which, like great Flesh-Flies liting on rare-Flesh,
Though oft beat-off, (if not kild) come afresh:
Hence, Belzebub is termd Prince of Flesh-fflies,
Cause Sin, still Acts, vntill (by Grace) It Dies.

A. A BUTCHER (*The Ages of Sin, or Sinnes Birth & groweth*)

A Cokes

A Seruant by his Master send abroad
or with a Message, or some vsefull loade,
And stayes to gase on strangers differing
Sigtes parrets nowelties is a right Cokes,

B. A COKES (*A Pake of Knaves*)

The Damēe

Damēes a rouring knawe that weares good clothes,
If his credit serue his prayer are his oathes;
Hees stout where sure he cannot be out braud,
And sweares by God, but hardly will be saiud.

C. THE DAMEE (*A Pake of Knaves*)

Sweetlipps

Sweet lipps is one that when his Masters meate
Is Serud in to the table, will first eate,
And spight, of all reproofe he will be still
His Masters taster gainst his Masters will.

D. SWEETLIPPS (*A Pake of Knaves*)

ILLUSTRATIONS OF SOCIAL LIFE II:
A BUTCHER AND SOME SOCIAL PESTS[1]

BY

F. P. WILSON

The Huntington Library possesses a remarkable collection of seven small books of engravings of the mid-seventeenth century, some of which illustrate various aspects of social life. When in the Bridgewater Library, the seven were bound together in one volume, the items having been numbered and sometimes annotated by the man who played the elder brother in *Comus*, probably while still Viscount Brackley and before he became the second Earl in 1649. The volume is now broken up, and the accession numbers are 60708–14.

The illustrations reproduced here (Pl. VI) with the kind permission of the Huntington Library are taken from two of these items, the second and the seventh. The butcher's shop comes from a book of nine moral emblems, the title of which is given in a cartouche above the first engraving: *The Ages of Sin, or Sinnes Birth & groweth. With the Stepps, and Degrees of Sin, from thought to finall Impenitencie.* The Corser Sale-Catalogue (Sotheby's, March 1869, lot 460) assigns the book to *c.* 1656, and Wing (*Short-Title Catalogue*, A761) to 1655, and both indicate that the name of the printseller, Thomas Jenner, is present in the title. This is not so in the British Museum (Bright), Harvard (Huth) and Huntington copies. I suspect an error, which may have arisen because the British Museum copy, acquired in 1845, was at once bound up with *The Path of Life* published by Jenner in 1656, and catalogued as if it were a part of that work. The other six items in the Huntington collection all seem to belong to the years 1640–2, and the little I know of Jacobus van Langeren, who signs the ninth print ('Finall-Impenitency') 'Ja. v. L. fecit', also suggests an earlier date than 1655–6. His name appears in full on the last print in H. A.'s *Partheneia Sacra* (1633), and he engraved the maps and all but one page of the letter-press in *A Direction for the English Traveller* (1635); on the title-page of the second issue of 1645 Jenner has had his name and address engraved in place of those of Mathew Simons. (Mr W. A. Parish of the Huntington Library introduced me to *A Direction*.) Of the butcher considered unemblematically little need be said. He stands before his shop in the cobbled street attempting to protect his meat with a fly-flap, a medieval word and weapon.

The illustrations of 'A Cokes', 'The Damee', and 'Sweetlipps' are chosen from a series well named *A Pake of Knaves*. I know of no other copy. The year may be very near to 1641 when *A pack of patentees* and Sir Peter Wentworth's *A pack of Puritans* appeared. There are twenty engravings in the pack: 'The whettstone', 'The Busye', 'The Sleepe loue', 'The fflye', 'Sweet-lipps', 'The Damee', 'The Graceless', 'The Sawceboxe', 'Surley', 'The nere be good', 'The overdoo', 'Flatterall', 'Noethrift', 'Much-Craft', 'A Prater', 'Swillbottle', 'The nastye', 'A Cokes', 'A mere Scullion', 'All-hidd'; each occupies a page (verso blank) and each has its descriptive quatrain beneath. Any collection of social pests is bound to remind us of the comedies of Jonson; Surly, Overdo, Cokes and the parasite Fly (not to mention Mosca) are indeed names of Jonsonian characters. The 'Damee' is the roisterer and bully known at various times in the seventeenth century as the damme or damme-boy, the roaring boy, the Tityre-tu, the hector, and the scourer. A cokes is a simpleton. And a sweetlips, glossed by the *Oxford English Dictionary* as an epicure or delicate eater, is better defined as a lick-dish.

NOTES

1. The first instalment in this series appeared in *Shakespeare Survey*, 11, pp. 98–9. The four quarter plates are in reduced facsimile. In the originals 'Iteration' measures 6 × 4 inches and the other three engravings 4 × 3 inches.

INTERNATIONAL NOTES

A selection has been made from the reports received from our correspondents, those which present material of a particularly interesting kind being printed in their entirety, or largely so. It should be emphasized that the choice of countries to be thus represented has depended on the nature of the information presented in the reports, not upon either the importance of the countries concerned or upon the character of the reports themselves.

Australia

In each of the Australian capital cities, the major Shakespearian production of 1957 was the Australian Elizabethan Theatre Trust Drama Company's *Hamlet*, with the visiting English actor Paul Rogers in the title role. Production was by Hugh Hunt. Reviews were generally favourable.

Probably none of the large cities was without other productions of Shakespeare during the year. In Sydney, for example, the Independent Theatre gave performances of both *Macbeth* (produced by Owen Weingott, with Leonard Teale, Patricia Hill and David Burnie in the leading roles) and *The Merchant of Venice* (produced by John Alden, with Patricia Hill as Portia, and Owen Weingott as Shylock).

The Australian Broadcasting Commission also offers full radio versions of the principal plays, from time to time, and also a series of talks on the texts set for the public examinations. These talks, normally delivered by scholars from the universities, are built around performances of selected scenes by leading radio actors and actresses.

It seems that the audience for Shakespeare is constantly growing; certainly the Australian reader can no longer think of the Shakespeare play as being only words on the printed page.   H. J. OLIVER

Austria

It is worth noting that three of the four representative theatres outside Vienna—Graz, Innsbruck, and Salzburg—opened their 1957-8 drama season with performances of Shakespearian plays, a fact which proves that producers can still rely upon the popularity of Shakespeare to attract audiences. On the whole, Shakespeare produc-tions in Austria were numerous, were concerned both with tragedies and comedies, and were, above all, not limited to the regular theatres. Quite a number of the performances demanded attention for experiments in production, the use of certain styles of costumes, new types of scenery or the translations used.

The drama season at Salzburg was opened in October with a performance of *The Taming of the Shrew*. The production was unusual in that it used a modernized and stylized version of the Elizabethan stage. Critics unanimously applauded the swift and uninterrupted flow of the action, which was largely responsible for the vividness and effect of the performance. Equally interesting in the same way was the Graz production of *Hamlet*, where an attempt was made to reconstruct the 'Globe' stage in its main features.

All's Well that Ends Well, which had not been played at any one of the leading Vienna theatres since 1828, was put on by the Akademietheater, Vienna, and *As You Like It* saw a much applauded staging at the Burgtheater. Both the Kammerspiele at Graz, Styria, and the Volkstheater, Vienna, gave *Twelfth Night*, the latter production using Biedermeier costumes. It is not surprising that *A Midsummer Night's Dream* was also performed in 1957 since the play has always been a great favourite with the Austrian public. It was given during the Graz festival season in the garden of Graz Castle. The same play was also given by the Stadttheater St. Pölten, Lower Austria.

The theatres of Innsbruck, Tyrol, and Linz, Upper-Austria, chose *The Winter's Tale*. The Innsbruck production was baroque in character, the intervals filled by Purcell music, and the play, which suffered from an utter lack of concentration, lasted almost four hours.

Of all the dramas *Othello* has proved to be the most popular. It was given at the Burgtheater and the Volkstheater, in Vienna, and by a non-professional group of actors at Friesach, Carynthia. *Othello* was first performed in Vienna in 1785, and the 1957 Burgtheater *première* was the 204th performance of the play in that theatre. This production, however, compared unfavourably with that of 1951–3, and the reviews were either lukewarm or condemnatory. It was felt that the play had been transposed into the sphere of ordinary life and that it thus lost the gigantic, the feverish, and the passionate. The *Othello* of the Volkstheater, with its use of hyper-modern scenery, black back- and side-wings and a movable roof of geometrical pattern, was agreed to be much more effective and closer to the spirit of the play.

SIEGFRIED KORNINGER

Belgium

The Koninklijke Nederlandse Schouwburg, Nationaal Toneel, opened its 1957–8 season with a rather disappointing production of *Twelfth Night*. Partly miscast, the performance suffered under a slow academical rhythm, accentuated by settings not allowing the smooth continuity any Shakespearian play demands, and forcing the producer to bring the curtain down for even minute-quick changes. More interesting productions were *Much Ado about Nothing* (Producer: Gaston Vandermeulen), *The Taming of the Shrew* (Producer: Maurits Balfoort), *The Tempest* (Producer: Ben Royaards) and the controversial *Merry Wives of Windsor* (Producer: Maurits Balfoort).

A 'pocket-size' Shakespeare Festival, organized by Het Reizend Volkstheater, the touring company of Het Nationaal Toneel, has been held in the courtyard of Rubens House in Antwerp.

The only offering of Shakespeare in the French-peaking theatre of Belgium came from the Théâtre du Parc—a new adapted version of *Hamlet* by Anne and Roger Bodart. These authors declare that "it is impossible to translate Shakespeare; if one is at all loyal, one must re-invent him. Shakespeare is the first existentialist; he adumbrates the philosophy of the absurd and the world of nausea. Kierkegaard, Heidegger, Sartre and Camus are present in his texts. Shakespeare, however, speaks better, and he has more courage, being more resolute. On the great road of poetry, the real Shakespeare is the one who goes fastest. He surpasses Sartre, Beckett, Caldwell when he is given the possibility of going 'fast'. This accelerated rhythm is what we have tried to give to our *Hamlet*." This production ran for about a dozen performances in Brussels and went on tour as a 'Spectacle du Cycle Classique' for a series of one-night stands in the provinces (Producer: Louis Boxus; Hamlet: Raoul de Manez).

DOM. DE GRUYTER

China

More and more of Shakespeare's plays are being brought before the public, and for its part the public is extending to them a warm welcome. *Romeo and Juliet* proved popular in Pekin last year: now this has been followed by equally successful productions of *Much Ado* and *Twelfth Night*. At the same time active research in the Shakespearian field is being carried out in Chinese colleges and universities.

CHANG CHEN-HSIEN

Czechoslovakia

Othello was the most produced Shakespeare play in 1957 with nine different productions by professional groups. Second in popularity was *A Midsummer Night's Dream* (7), followed by *Much Ado* (6), *As You Like It*, *Merry Wives* (4), *Romeo and Juliet*, *Twelfth Night* (3), *Hamlet*, *Merchant of Venice*, *Taming of the Shrew* (2), and *Antony and Cleopatra*, *Two Gentlemen of Verona*, *Macbeth*, *Richard III* and *Measure for Measure* (1)—fifteen plays in all, twice the number given, for example, in 1951. These forty-three productions with more than 800 performances bear, I think, comparison with the Shakespearian statistics of any other country. Even a visiting Soviet theatre played Shakespeare's *Much Ado* in Brno! The public never seems to become tired of Shakespeare: new editions of his works appear and are sold out. Even the non-theatre-going public is enjoying Shakespeare in the cinema: the English *Romeo and Juliet* and *Richard III*, released recently, and naturally *Hamlet*, the Soviet *Romeo and Juliet* ballet film and *Othello*, which have been seen already in Czechoslovak cinemas, will soon be joined by an original puppet version of *A Midsummer Night's Dream* produced by Jiří Trnka. As for Prague, the National Theatre announces for spring two Shakespearian productions—*King Lear* and *Hamlet*, both in new translations by Erik A. Saudek and Zdeněk Urbánek, respectively. These two productions are regarded as a major event, because it was long before World War II that these plays were last staged on this foremost stage in Czechoslovakia.

BŘETISLAV HODEK

East Africa

The 1958 Shakespeare Birthday was celebrated in East Africa by an early morning ceremony in the Shakespeare Corner of the Kenya National Theatre, when rosemary and roses were placed in the niche beside the one-hundred-years-old Brugiotti bust of the poet. In the evening, a birthday broadcast was given from the Cable and Wireless radio studio which linked up with the speeches being broadcast from the Nairobi St George's Society banquet.

During the Kenya Drama Festival, scenes were performed from *Macbeth* and *Antony and Cleopatra*. The latter was acted by a team from an up-country farming district. Activities connected with the East African Shakespeare Festival which followed included a puppet theatre production of *Macbeth* and full-scale stage performances of *Othello*, at the Kenya National Theatre, attended by 3000 English-speaking schoolchildren of all races, followed by public performances running for two weeks.　　　　　　　　　　　A. J. R. MASTER

Finland

The most important event of the 1957–8 theatre season was clearly the production of *Hamlet* at the National Theatre in Helsinki. It has been customary to begin the autumn season with a comedy; in 1957, partly to mark the British Exhibition arranged on a large scale in Helsinki in September, the season was opened with *Hamlet*, with Dennis Arundell as visiting producer. Simultaneously, the British Council arranged a Shakespeare exhibition in the foyer of the theatre.

Dennis Arundell's production conformed with the views prevailing on *Hamlet* in England today. It was very favourably received by the audiences and the press. Acting took place mainly on an elevated stage, painted dark and connected with the front stage by a flight of steps. No use was made of naturalistic scenery at all. The few changes which were made in the setting were achieved by altering the position of the black drapes at the back and by changing the lighting. Very little of the text was cut out; this was made possible by the fast tempo of acting, which also enabled the producer to achieve remarkable unity of presentation. Hamlet's role was played by Martti Katajisto, a young and gifted actor, who carried out his task with spectacular success. On the whole, this was a memorable production characterized by fast, powerful, and colourful acting against the black monochrome of the setting.

　　　　　　　　　　　RAFAEL KOSKIMIES

France

With Pierre Brassuer and Suzanne Flon in the leading parts, *The Taming of the Shrew* produced by Georges Vitaly at the Athénée, with costumes and settings by the fashionable and sophisticated Leonor Fini, was bound to make a hit. Vitaly stated that the *Shrew* was one of Shakespeare's weakest comedies, yet one of the most effective on the stage. A literal translation, he thought, would sacrifice movement, rhythm and poetry. So he asked the playwright Jacques Audiberti for an adaptation. Audiberti, after militant years in the 'avant-garde', has become a prosperous 'auteur de boulevard'. The producer seemed to have every trump in hand for a lasting success. The trouble began when Audiberti decided to improve upon Shakespeare, laying the main emphasis on Kate and Petruchio, and developing the girl's part. It was shrewd of him to perceive that this love affair begins as a duel and ends as a duet, and that it is better to quarrel before marriage than after. But it was the producer's and the actor's business to suggest it and there was no need to rewrite the play. Besides, Audiberti is well known for his verbal incontinence. While some critics praised his "langue savoureuse et drue", his "graisse rabelaisienne", others found him long-winded and tedious. André Alter, in *Figaro Littéraire*, turned the scales in favour of the old translator, François-Victor Hugo, by quoting parallel passages from that version and from Audiberti's. This mixed reception explains why Vitaly's *Mégère* lasted only a few months, instead of the expected two years' run.

René Dupuy's production of *Pericles*, at the Ambigu, was most imaginative and moving. The play, as it was staged in Leon Ruth's discreet and faithful adaptation, was a pleasant surprise to most critics, who held the text in poor esteem. Gabriel Marcel found he was never bored, even during the first part, however "puerile and unbelievable", and gathered from the whole "an invincible feeling of the mystery of human destiny and condition". And Jean Jacques Gaultier observed that Claudel must have found inspiration in Shakespeare's narrative conception of drama for his *Soulier de Satin*. Use was made of machinery and pageantry, but in a deliberately naïve way, just as Shakespeare used rhymed couplets for Gower's commentaries. In Jacques Noël's mobile settings the unifying theme was the sea. Jacques Calvi's music, unfortunately, was not exempt from technicolour vulgarity. About twenty-five actors took over eighty parts. Nelly Borgeaud, as Marina, was most convincingly pure and the meeting of father and daughter in v, i became intensely pathetic. In spite of its originality and merit, this play did not attract a large audience, and ended in financial loss.

The young company, La Guilde, now has its own theatre in Menilmontant, in a popular district, miles away from the 'boulevard'. A new series of performances of their *King John*, which I praised in last year's notes, was quite a success.

The Théâtre de la Cité in Villeurbanne, near Lyons, was born with the same object of providing good drama, at popular prices, for a new public. Roger Planchon, the young director and producer, is inspired by the examples of Jean Vilar with his Théâtre National Populaire and Berthold Brecht with his Berliner Ensemble. He had begun his career with productions of Shakespeare and Marlowe at the little Théâtre de la Comédie in Lyons and welcomed the opportunity to experiment in the 'epic drama' upon a large stage. He chose the two parts of *Henry IV*. His ambition was to awaken critical reactions in the spectator, and bring him to pass judgment on history and to compare situations of the past with those of the present. Planchon is aware that it is difficult to do this without distorting the poet's meaning: "The language of princes and kings in Shakespeare", he says, "has nothing to do with language as a means of communication; it leads directly to lyricism, poetry and all that is great and sublime. The difficulty for us who aim at critical realism is to suppress this poetical 'aura' which adds greatness to human beings but tends to cast a veil upon them. Our business is to show, not to sublimise—but without taking anything from or extinguishing anything in the poem." This seems to indicate that he has not read deeply enough into Shakespeare's meaning. However the dilemma is characteristic of the new generation. The production received much praise and it is to be hoped that it will be given in Paris.

Shakespeare remains popular with the public of summer festivals. Jean Anouilh's adaptation of *Twelfth Night*, produced by Georges Douking, was shown in Arras, Beaune and Toulon. Maurice Jacquemont directed *Hamlet* at Sarlat, in the translation by Jacques Copeau and Suzanne Bing. Jean Marchat presented *Romeo and Juliet* in Jean Cocteau's 'accelerated' version. And the Comédie Française production of *Coriolanus* was given in Orange. *Richard III* was chosen by Charles Antonetti for the 'stage dramatique' at Louviers, and Jean Lescure's adaptation of *Measure for Measure*, produced in 1956 at Carcassonne by René Jeauneau, was given the next summer in the Château de Tallard. Hubert Gignoux, after doing good work at the Centre Dramatique de l'Ouest, succeeded Michel Saint-Denis as director of the Centre Dramatique de l'Est. His *Hamlet*, originally produced at Rennes, was presented in Strasbourg for the inauguration of the new Théâtre de la Comédie.

This account of Shakespearian performances was prepared with the assistance of Mlle R. M. Moudouès who kindly placed at my disposal the information of the Centre de Documentation of the Société d'Histoire du Théâtre. JEAN JACQUOT

Germany

Shakespeare's popularity on the German stage is undiminished. Strangely enough, the total of new productions of Shakespeare's plays has, for some years, constantly reached the same general figure. In 1956–7 159 new productions were recorded, last year's output, with 157 productions by 105 different theatres, kept within the same margin. Less than a third of all German theatres had no Shakespeare play on their season's programme. Of the histories *Richard III*, *Richard II* and *Henry IV* were performed; the romances had a somewhat greater frequency, *The Tempest*, *The Winter's Tale* and *Cymbeline* being shown on various stages, of which Bochum theatre gave *Cymbeline* in a realistic production that attracted attention. But even so, histories and romances together made up only one-tenth of the more numerous productions of the tragedies and the comedies. *Hamlet* still takes the lead among the tragedies; of its various productions the one by Fritz Kortner at the Schiller Theater Berlin appears to have been one of the most impressive. *King Lear*, too, with Werner Krauss in the title-role, scored a great success at Düsseldorf, Duisburg and Mannheim. An interesting interpretation of *Othello* was given by the theatre of Frankfurt an der Oder, where the hero was represented not so much as the passionate and jealous Moor as a noble person of great integrity and highly developed ethical feeling who cannot believe in a world of disorder. Hans Schalla's production of *Julius Caesar* in Rothe's translation, given at Bochum, dispensed with all crowds on the stage and concentrated on the words and gestures of the main characters. At Stuttgart, the famous actress Elisabeth Flickenschildt left a strong impression as Lady Macbeth.

The Taming of the Shrew with fifteen new productions was the most popular comedy of the season. At its performance at Karl-Marx-Stadt (Chemnitz) Kate was represented as seeing through Petruchio's game and being intelligent and witty enough to join in the mutual play for the sake of the fun, but by no means put down or 'tamed' by her partner. At Munich, *Twelfth Night* in Fritz Kortner's production contained perhaps too many gags and stressed the comic and grotesque rather than the subtle and poetic aspect of this comedy. This, however, seems to be a recurrent feature of many productions of the comedies, which are apt to be turned into farces. At Düsseldorf *The Merchant of Venice* produced by Karl Heinz Stroux with Ernst Deutsch and Joana Maria Gorvin in the main parts was felt to be a very fine achievement.

The German Gramophone Company has recently brought out several records with scenes and passages from Shakespeare's plays spoken by well-known German actors and actresses. *Hamlet, Romeo and Juliet,* and *Troilus and Cressida* were among the first plays thus made accessible to a wider public.

Another recent expression of the spreading of Shakespeare's works among the masses is the publication of a new series of bilingual editions of single plays at a very low price, of which large numbers were sold. The Rowohlt Verlag has so far issued *Hamlet, Romeo and Juliet,* and *Richard III* in the Schlegel-Tieck translation with notes by Levin L. Schücking and introductions by Wolfgang Clemen. The series is to be continued.

In the field of scholarship the *Schriftenreihe der Shakespeare-Gesellschaft* has continued its series by publishing Charlotte Ehrl's remarkable study on language and character in Shakespeare's plays. Other contributions to Shakespearian scholarship published in Germany were Max Luthi's comprehensive criticism on *Shakespeares Dramen*, Karl Brunner's informative book on Shakespeare and W. Clemen's commentary on *Richard III*.

The eightieth birthday of Rudolf Alexander Schröder, the president of the Shakespeare-Gesellschaft, turned out to be an event of major cultural importance. Numerous honours were conferred upon him, including an honorary doctorship of the University of Rome; his home town, Bremen, produced *Romeo and Juliet* in his translation; and Bundespräsident Heuss spoke on the wireless of his merits as a poet, translator and author, the last humanist of universal education in today's Germany.

WOLFGANG CLEMEN
KARL BRINKMANN

Greece

King Lear, translated by Basil Rotas, was produced at the National Theatre, Athens, directed by Alexis Minotis, who also played the title character. At the same theatre *Cymbeline*, translated by Cleandros Karthaios, was given for the first time in Greece. *Twelfth Night*, translated by Basil Rotas, was produced at the Municipal Theatre of Piraeus, directed by Dimitris Rondiris, with a total of 115 performances.

GEORGE THEOTOKAS

Hungary

On the Hungarian stage, productions of Shakespeare's plays have been as frequent and quite as successful as ever. There is a tradition that the National Theatre of Budapest, the leading theatre of the country, should always have at least one play by Shakespeare in its repertory. During the last two or three years *Richard III* and *Othello* have been given there many times, enjoying considerable popularity. In the latter Ferenc Bessenyei's powerful and memorable rendering of the Moor was one of the momentous events of the theatrical season, although the direction and rather operatic decor were not of the same quality. *Romeo and Juliet* had a fairly long run in the Madách Theatre, presented in realistic costume, heavily underscoring the feud of the two noble families. *The Taming of the Shrew* had many performances in the Theatre of the Hungarian Army (a professional company), produced on a curtainless open stage with scene-shifters in Elizabethan costumes. It was a relief to see Petruchio's customary brutality tempered with joviality and charm.

Outside Budapest, *Othello*, as directed in Kecskemét by Antal Németh, deserves special mention both on account of the three-level stage with stylized *décor* and because of the prominence given to the jealousy of Iago, in whose character the elements relating him to the devil of the mysteries were stressed. In Debrecen *Hamlet* had a run of twenty-six performances and gave a gifted young actor (László Mensáros) opportunity to make his mark.

Shakespeare's tragedies and comedies are one of the main assets of the enterprising State Travelling Company (Állami Faluszínház) which goes about the country and presents its repertory only in villages and small towns where there are no theatres of any sort. In the last three years they gave 185 performances (in almost as many places) of *As You Like It*, presented in rich, realistic costumes. This year they are touring the backwoods with *Romeo and Juliet*.

Shakespeare's popularity is not restricted to the stage. The ten thousand copies of his dramatic works in translation, complete in four volumes, were sold out in a few months after their publication in 1955. Of the single-volume editions of some plays mention should be made of the very cheap popular edition of *Hamlet* and *A Midsummer Night's Dream*, published in one volume (in 1957) to commemorate the 75th anniversary of the death of the translator, János Arany, whose renderings of these plays rank with the Hungarian classics. Fifty thousand copies of this edition were sold in a few weeks.

Bilingual editions were published of *The Tempest* (translated by Mihály Babits) and the *Sonnets* (translated by Pál Jusztusz) and a new edition was brought out of the celebrated translation of the sonnets by the eminent poet Lőrinc Szabó.   LADISLAS ORSZÁGH

Israel

One of the outstanding performances of the year and one of the best the Chamber Theatre has ever given was that of *Romeo and Juliet*. Joseph Milo's production of the play was interesting and affective. He himself played Romeo, with Yizhak Shilo as his double. Juliet was taken by Orna Porath, who had a double in Rosina Frenhoff. The Hebrew version was prepared by Raphael Eliaz.

Eliaz's translation has been published in book form by the Hakibbutz Hameuchad Publishing House. Another Shakespearian play published recently is Lea Goldberg's Hebrew version of *As You Like It* (Sifriath Hapoalim Publishing House).   REUBEN AVINOAM

Italy

No prose version of Shakespeare, no matter how close to the text, is able to convey the magic of Shakespeare's lines. A striking instance of this was given in March 1958 in Rome, where, on the 16th of that month, at a *soirée* of the Theatre Club at the Teatro Quirino, Vittorio Gassman and Peggy Ashcroft interpreted, each in his own language, the famous Orchard Scene (II, ii) of *Romeo and Juliet*. Though Shakespeare himself wrote a bilingual scene (in *Henry V*), nothing could have been more awkward than the contrast between Shakespeare's winged verse passionately delivered by Peggy Ashcroft and the flat prose translation by Paola Ojetti, uttered, or rather muttered, by Gassman in such a shy manner as to suggest that he deliberately wanted to efface himself before the great English actress. The most remarkable performance of a Shakespearian play during the year (December 1957) was that of *Measure for Measure* (*Misura per misura*) at the Teatro Stabile della Città di Genova, in the translation of Luigi Squarzina (producer), with Renzo Ricci as the Duke, Enrico M. Salerno as Angelo, Osvaldo Ruggieri as Claudio, Franco Parenti as Lucio, Valeria Valeri as Isabella, and Bianca Galvan as Mariana, scenery by Luigi Broggi, costumes by Annamaria. There was nothing very remarkable in the setting, but the acting, particularly of Salerno and Parenti, was excellent. Giorgio Strehler, who is mostly responsible for the reputation acquired by the 'Piccolo Teatro' of Milan, produced in November 1957 a memorable

Coriolano, in a translation by Gilberto Tofano, who, however, had not hesitated to modernize the diction in order to suit modern taste; the scenery, by Luciano Damiani, stressed the essentials through a rigorous monochrome; the costumes, by Ezio Frigerio, gave perhaps too much emphasis to the primitive character of the warriors by presenting them as nearly naked as possible, almost as David had done in his heroic paintings. Among the actors, Tino Carraro stressed the human side of Coriolanus, Wanda Capodaglio was a stately Volumnia, Antonio Battistella impersonated Menenius in an unforgettable way, and the young Franco Graziosi distinguished himself in the part of Tullus Aufidius; an equally young actress, Relda Ridoni, gave a sensible interpretation of Virgilia. In January 1958 there was in Naples (Galleria Mediterranea) an exhibition of settings and costumes for Shakespeare's dramas ('Mostra di scene e costumi del teatro di Shakespeare') by the scene-painter Vittorio Piscopo.

Cesare Vico Lodovici has added more translations to his planned complete Shakespeare; the *Allegre comari* and a particularly praiseworthy *Misura per misura* appeared in October 1957. Translations of Shakespeare in Italy by far outnumber critical studies of the texts: an attempt in this latter field has been made by the young librarian of the University of Pavia, Silvano Gerevini, with *Il testo del Riccardo III di Shakespeare* (Pavia, Casa Editrice Renzo Cortina, 1957), a scholarly essay on the problem of the quartos and the formation of the folio, whose conclusions are, however, slight.

The most active Shakespearian scholar in Italy is Gabriele Baldini, whose record this year is very impressive; not only has he given translations of *Richard III* (with text opposite, Rome, Signorelli, 1957) and of *Henry VIII* (Milan, Rizzoli, 1957) with introductions and (for *Richard III*) critical apparatus, but in a handbook, originally planned for broadcast (*Le tragedie di Shakespeare*, Edizioni Radio Italiana, collection: Classe unica, 1957), he has done much more than a work of popularization designed for the general public; difficult as it may seem to throw new light on Shakespeare, Baldini has succeeded in making us see many of the plays from a new angle, particularly when, as in the case of *Lear*, he has been able to use his experience as a musical critic; his claim of a musical function for the images of that tragedy deserves to be given serious attention by all students of Shakespeare. MARIO PRAZ

Japan

The most remarkable Shakespearian performance in 1957 was *The Merry Wives of Windsor* by Haiyu-za, or

Actors' Theatre, led by Koreya Senda as Falstaff. This was dedicated to the memory of the late Sugisaku Aoyama, who was an eminent theatrical leader of this century. The production followed as faithfully as possible the plan upon which he himself had produced the play several years ago. The Tokyo Drama Appreciation Society added *The Taming of the Shrew* to their repertory. This was staged by Kindai Gekijo, or Modern Theatre, with an introductory talk on the poet every evening.

Performances in English were given by various university and college drama groups: *Twelfth Night* by Gakushuin University, *The Merchant of Venice* by Japan Woman's University, *The Taming of the Shrew* by Tsuda-juku University, and *Hamlet* by Tokyo Woman's Christian College.

In *Kumonosujo*, or *The Castle of Cobwebs*, Akira Kurosawa, a well-known director, made a unique film following the theme of *Macbeth* with late medieval Japan for a setting. In this connection it may be noted that Bungaka-zu, or Theatre of Letters, presented a play *Akechi Mitsuhide*, by Tsuneari Fukuda, based on the same Shakespearian original. Both the film and the play aroused much interest and discussion. JIRO OZU

The Netherlands

Three Shakespeare performances were given in the course of the theatrical year 1957-8, *Twelfth Night* by the Haagse Comedie (Hague Theatre), produced by Cees Laseur in a translation by Gerard Messelaar, *Hamlet* by the same company, produced by Paul Steenbergen in a translation by Bert Voeten, and *Macbeth* by the Nederlandse Comedie (Netherlands Theatre), produced by Johan de Meester in a translation by Joris Diels. The first two in particular were highly successful and drew large audiences.

In December 1957 there appeared an introduction to Shakespeare, in the 'Ooievaar' series (Nr. 62) by A. G. H. Bachrach of Leiden, entitled *Naar Het Hem Leek* (*As He Liked It*). It is in six letters as by a staunch Shakespeare supporter to a somewhat sceptical friend. The author successively treats *Henry IV*, *Twelfth Night*, *Hamlet* and *The Winter's Tale*. A biographical table and a chronological list of the plays with their main themes complete this lively and well-documented book.

W. VAN MAANEN

Poland

Active work is being carried on in Poland both in the translation of Shakespeare's plays and in the study of his works. A new version of *Troilus and Cressida* (the fourth Polish rendering) by Zofia Siwicka has been issued by the Państwowy Instytut Wydawniczy, while to the National Polish Library series has been added a new version of *King Lear* by Władysław Tarnawski, with an introduction by myself. (This is the eleventh Polish translation of the tragedy.) I myself am preparing a new edition of *The Tempest*.

Considerable interest has been aroused by a book, *Shakespeare and the War of the Theatres: A Reinterpretation* (Poznań, 1957), by a young Shakespearian scholar, Henryk Zbierski—a discussion of the contrast between the open public playhouses and the more exclusive private theatres. The whole problem has been debated at a meeting of the Philological Committee of the Academy of Sciences.

A reflection of this academic interest is the attendance of no fewer than three Polish representatives at the recent Shakespeare Conference at Stratford-upon-Avon. Full accounts of this Conference have appeared in the *Kwartalnik Neofilologiczny*, an organ of the Polish Academy, and in *Dialog*, a theatrical monthly.

STANISŁAW HELSZTYŃSKI

South Africa

Since the publication of F. C. Kolbe's *Shakespeare's Way*, a book that is now receiving belated recognition, there has been a steady output of Shakespearian literary criticism in this country. Most of it appears in such academic, and other, journals of standing as *Theoria*, *Standpunte* and the newly published *English Studies in Africa*; but it is invariably overlooked in the annual surveys of Shakespearian Studies printed in England and America. Thus there has been no notice of 'Prospero's Wisdom' by G. H. Durrant, 'The Meaning of the Graveyard Scene in *Hamlet*' by N. J. Marquard, and 'The Tragedy of *Othello*' by J. I. de Villiers (all in *Theoria*, 1955); or of 'What's in a Name? A Discussion of *Romeo and Juliet*' by G. H. Durrant (*Theoria*, 1956) and 'The Theme of Responsibility in *Julius Caesar*' by N. J. Marquard (*Standpunte*, no. 4, 1955). Presumably these publications do not come into the hands of the reviewers of *Shakespeare Survey* or *Shakespeare Quarterly*; but as the latter journal printed in the number of autumn 1956 A. Suzman's 'Imagery and Symbolism in Richard II' some more notice might have been expected of it.

A notable production of *Julius Caesar* by the University Players, Johannesburg, took place in the autumn of 1957. The production was by John Boulter, a Shakespearian actor and producer of experience; he chose as his open-air setting the steps and towering Corinthian pillars of

the entrance to the main University Building. In spite of the cinemascope vastness of the stage, and the disproportionately intimate size of the auditorium, the play attracted enough notice from the critics to run for a couple of weeks. The producer was original and effective in handling his crowd scenes and great speeches; and was fortunate in finding a Cassius of histrionic ability and good voice. How much the latter owed to John Gielgud's interpretation in the film is a matter of speculation.
A. C. PARTRIDGE

Sweden

The great event of the season was *As You Like It* at the Göteborgs stadsteater, with Inga Tidblad as Rosalind. This celebrated actress is certainly the leading lady among Swedish interpreters of Shakespeare's women, with her Portia, her Juliet, her Beatrice and perhaps above all her graceful Rosalind. Among other actors ought to be mentioned Per Oscarsson as an excellent Touchstone. The scenery was by Carl Johan Ström and the producer, Hans Dahlin, made full use of the resources of the revolving stage. Perhaps at times the rotation seemed a little too rapid, the spoken words running the risk of being outdistanced.

The performances of the Riksteatern, mentioned in the last report, have developed into great successes: *Twelfth Night* was seen by 39,000 persons, *Othello* by 28,000. The *Taming of the Shrew*, given year by year on the open-air stages, has met with its customary success.

With Gustaf Fredén's *William Shakespeare* (Stockholm, 1958) a valuable volume was added to the Swedish literature on Shakespeare, a thorough and well-balanced critical study, based on the results of modern research.
NILS MOLIN

Switzerland

The eagerness with which Shakespeare is studied in our universities, where the dramatist, the poet and his works are the subject of courses of lectures and seminars almost every term, occasionally flowers into some serious piece of research submitted to the Faculty of Arts for a doctor's degree. Two such dissertations were accepted in recent years, one at Zürich in 1953, the other at Bâle in 1955. They have at last been published. Elisabeth Tschopp's *Zur Verteilung von Vers und Prosa in Shakespeares Dramen* (Swiss Studies in English, vol. 41, Francke Verlag, Bern) is a careful attempt at finding out Shakespeare's reasons for turning from verse to prose or prose to verse in five of the comedies, two of the tragedies and three of the historical plays. In his thesis

The Economy of Action and Word in Shakespeare's Plays (Cooper Monographs, vol. 2, Prof. H. Ludeke editor, Francke Verlag, Bern) Arthur Gerstner-Hirzel endeavours to show, by means of what he calls 'gestic analysis', that the text of the plays abounds in indications as to the outward action, the gestures, that must accompany its delivery. This is of course what all Shakespearian actors have always felt, perhaps more or less instinctively. If neither of these two books brings us anything really new, they bear testimony to the determination that exists in our little country to train Shakespearian scholars.

Mention must be made here of the thoughtful survey of Shakespearian scholarship and criticism in the period 1935–55 included in Rudolf Stamm's *Englische Literatur* which is the eleventh volume in the series of 'Wissenschaftliche Forschungsberichte' published by the Francke Verlag, Bern, 1957. There, students and scholars will find more than forty pages devoted to whatever is of real value in criticism during those twenty years. Stamm has presented, analysed and assessed the work of his very numerous colleagues with as much fairness as thoroughness.

Swiss performances of the plays seem to have been fewer than in former years. At the Zürich Schauspielhaus *The Winter's Tale* and *Romeo and Juliet* in German ran for several nights; they were highly creditable productions without, however, any original or novel feature. According to the critic of the leading Bern newspaper, the *Bund*, a production of *Twelfth Night* at the Stadttheater was one of great, even unusual distinction. The setting used the same stylized scenery throughout; though carefully thought out and bold in conception, it does not appear to have really conquered the public. But the costumes tickled the fancy and delighted the eye of everyone. They subserved in a perfect manner the excellent acting of a slim Viola (Rosemarie Schubert), a very human Malvolio, touching as well as ridiculous (Franz Dehler), and a Maria who set the house roaring with laughter (Nelly Rademacher).

In a Geneva suburb, at Carouge, a newly formed company of young, but experienced, actors have just opened a small playhouse and given for their first production a spirited rendering of *Twelfth Night* which ran for a number of nights from 30 January 1958 onwards until every one in Geneva had seen it. Using no scenery whatever, moving against coloured hangings which changed with every scene and served to enhance its particular tone, clad in costumes that, in their sobriety, formed charming harmonies with the background and helped to bring out the character of each, they triumphed by the sheer force, resourcefulness and subtlety of their acting. They had chosen F. M. V. Hugo's translation in preference to more recent ones, and their choice was entirely justified by the event; it proved eminently actable and conveyed to the audiences as much of Shakespeare's poetry as a translation can. It may sound invidious to select for particular praise any one actor in particular where all suited their parts so well, but Louis Gaulis as the Fool and Mylise Roy as Maria would have delighted the poet himself. It is everybody's wish that such a successful start may help to give Shakespeare a permanent place in the theatrical activity of Geneva.

GEORGES BONNARD

Turkey

The National Conservatoire of Ankara produced *A Midsummer Night's Dream* in February 1957. The production was staged by Mrs Yildiz Akcan of the National Theatre of Ankara, who used my version in Turkish verse. In this production Gülgun Kutlu was a gay and most vivid Puck with her sprightly acrobatic faculties. Her moving picture of the "merry wanderer of the night" who would jest to Oberon and make him smile, lurk in a gossip's bowl, and slip from "the bum of the wisest aunt telling tale" overtopped the production. On 16 May the production was carried to the third century B.C. theatre of Asclepion of Pergamum in Western Turkey. *A Midsummer Night's Dream* was the first Shakespearian play ever performed there. The audience enjoyed the play so much that their laughter sometimes drowned the voices of the performers, who had to mime until they were quiet.

Again at the National Conservatoire of Ankara *The Taming of the Shrew* opened in March 1958. The Shrew, in the person of red-haired and green-eyed Tomris Oguzalp, was a fitting match to the Petruchio of tall, brown-haired, handsome, strong and acrobatic Kartal Tibet. The tennis match and see-saw technique of Act II, sc. i where they first meet particularly enchanted the audience. Mrs Akcan was responsible for this, the third production of the play in Turkey.

NUREDDIN SEVIN

U.S.A.

In 1873 Frederick B. Chatterton, on the occasion of a crippling loss on a production of *Antony and Cleopatra*, uttered the now famous "Shakespeare-spells-ruin" remark which still continues to plague the professional Broadway theatre. Though fortunes *have* been made on

Shakespeare, the I-told-you-so school had its day in early 1957 when Orson Welles' New York City Center production of *King Lear* closed with a loss of about $60,000. A lukewarm reception by the press, excessive back-stage expenses, and the fact that on-stage injuries to Welles necessitated his acting the title role in a wheelchair most likely were contributing factors.

Classic repertory companies, however, continue to give excellent and successful Shakespeare to thousands of New Yorkers. The perennial Shakespeare-wrights presented a vigorous and effective *Julius Caesar*, and a company from the American Shakespeare Festival Company of Connecticut presented *Measure for Measure* and *The Taming of the Shrew* at the off-Broadway Phoenix Theatre for a very successful limited engagement. In its second season, The New York City Shakespeare Festival presented *Romeo and Juliet* and *The Two Gentlemen of Verona* to over 150,000 who paid no admission to the outdoor Central Park theatre.

The American Shakespeare Festival Theater and Academy (ASFTA) at Stratford, Connecticut, in its third season scored its greatest triumph. Although Earle Hyman's *Othello* did not meet with universal approval, *The Merchant of Venice* was cited as the company's best production thus far. The inimitable characterization of Morris Carnovsky as Shylock and Katherine Hepburn as Portia were highly praised. Miss Hepburn also starred in *Much Ado* (*décor* of the Spanish south-west) to the Benedick of Alfred Drake (who also received plaudits for his Iago). Over 150,000 saw the plays in a season which had to be extended by a week to meet the great demand for seats. When artistic director John Houseman addressed a group at the American Educational Theater Association meeting in Boston he declared that the "dazzling success" of both Stratfords (Canada and Connecticut) may be accounted for by the hypothesis that "large numbers of people are finding the modern drama lacking in exaltation, poetry, and majesty, and are turning to Shakespeare for those qualities which make a temple of the theater".

Elsewhere in the U.S.A. old festivals continue and new ones are inaugurated. Only one loss is to be recorded —the Antioch Area Theater Shakespeare-under-the-Stars festival. Hofstra College continued with its eighth annual Festival, offering *As You Like It*. The seventeenth Oregon Shakespeare Festival broke its previous record with a 23 per cent increase to 24,338. Of its four plays— *As You Like It*, *The Two Gentlemen of Verona*, *Othello*, and *Pericles*—the first was most popular. The eighth Annual Festival in the Globe replica at San Diego, California, offered *King Lear* and *The Tempest*, the latter being directed by B. Iden Payne. A new Festival was inaugurated at the Phoenix (Arizona) Little Theater with a programme of *Macbeth*, *Julius Caesar*, and *Much Ado*.

To call the roll of college- and university-sponsored Shakespeare would far exceed our space limitation. Special mention, however, may be made of the facts that the new Kansas University Theater opened with *1 Henry IV* and that the new Phi Beta Kappa Hall at William and Mary College, heralded as the "best equipped non-professional theater in the world", opened with *Romeo and Juliet*. Other notable productions were guest director Robert Speaight's *Midsummer Night's Dream* at St Mary's College, Notre Dame, and George B. Dowell's *Winter's Tale* in Botticelli-inspired costume at Vassar College. A musical version of *Twelfth Night* was offered at the University of Tulsa in Oklahoma. At Ithaca College in New York a modern dress *Merry Wives* was presented. The Bob Jones University (Greenville, South Carolina) Shakespeare tradition, too, is noteworthy. Since 1929 Bob Jones, Jun., has produced eighteen different plays, the 1957 offering being *Julius Caesar*. These Classic Players perform with but one or two intermissions on an apron stage on which scene changes occur sometimes during 'blackouts', at other times in full view of the audience—frequently with the aid of a revolving turntable or moving wagons. Original orchestral music bridges the mood from scene to scene.

LOUIS MARDER

U.S.S.R.

Hamlet nowadays is performed more frequently than any other of Shakespeare's plays in the U.S.S.R. N. Okhlopkov's production is still running at the Moscow Mayakovski Theatre, and during the 1957–8 season Moscow audiences were presented with a new production of the tragedy at the Vakhtangov Theatre, the title-role being played by M. Astangov, one of the most gifted and skilful Soviet actors of today, and for this part he had been preparing himself for twenty years. The most significant aspect in his interpretation is the exploration of the depths of Hamlet's mind and his subtle irony. Among other successful productions of the tragedy that by the Perm Drama Theatre, directed by A. Mikhailov, should be mentioned.

At the same time, during recent years a tendency has been developing among Soviet directors to produce some plays of Shakespeare which are less known to theatrical audiences. Recently, M. Kedrov, the director of the Moscow Art Theatre, produced *The Winter's Tale*, and the graduates of the Theatre Institute staged *Cymbeline*, a play which very rarely appears on the Soviet stage. The Soviet tradition of producing Shakespeare's tragedies was considerably enriched by the daring and very interesting performance of *Antony and Cleopatra* at the Tallin Drama Theatre, with the leading Estonian actors Aino Talvi as Cleopatra and Kaarel Karm as Anthony, as well as by *Richard III* in the Tbilisi Theatre, with Godsiashwili in the title role.

An original interpretation of *The Merry Wives of Windsor* was presented by Y. Savadski, director of the Moscow Mossoviet Theatre. In order to maintain the spirit of revelry and gaiety throughout the entire performance, a kind of merry fair was organized during the intervals, in which both the actors and the audience took part. This innovation was a great success, but the producer's rather free attitude to the text of the comedy has provoked some disagreement.

Shakespeare is strengthening his position in ballet and in opera. In 1958 the well-known Georgian dancer V. Tchabukiani was awarded a Lenin Prize for his performance of the title role in the ballet version of *Othello*. In Moscow, together with the famous *Romeo and Juliet* starring Galina Ulanova, a comic ballet of *The Merry Wives of Windsor* is being performed. Recently a first night of the new Shebalin opera *The Taming of the Shrew* scored a great success at the Bolshoi Theatre.

The All-Russia Theatre Society has started preparations for the coming 400th anniversary of Shakespeare's birth. Among other activities some regional Shakespeare conferences are being organized. The first of them will take place in Perm at the beginning of the 1958–9 season; its aim is to discuss the Shakespearian performances of the theatres of Siberia and the Ural district.

Outstanding among Soviet studies of Shakespeare is the new complete edition of the poet's works edited with commentaries by A. Smirnov and A. Anikst. The first two volumes containing the early histories and comedies have already appeared.

Y. SHVEDOV

SHAKESPEARE PRODUCTIONS IN THE UNITED KINGDOM: 1957

A LIST COMPILED FROM ITS RECORDS BY THE
SHAKESPEARE MEMORIAL LIBRARY, BIRMINGHAM

JANUARY

21   *Othello*: Arena Theatre, at Newcastle-upon-Tyne. *Producer:* JOHN ENGLISH.

22   *The Two Gentlemen of Verona*: The Old Vic Company, at the Old Vic Theatre, London. *Producer:* MICHAEL LANGHAM.

22   *Twelfth Night*: The Playhouse, Nottingham. *Producer:* J. HARRISON.

28   *The Comedy of Errors*: Oldham Repertory Theatre Club at The Coliseum, Oldham. *Producer:* HARRY LOMAX.

28   *As You Like It*: West of England Theatre Company at the Queens Hall, Barnstaple. (Afterwards on tour in the West of England and Wales, under the auspices of the Arts Council.) *Producer:* JOYCE WORSLEY.

FEBRUARY

4   *Twelfth Night*: Civic Theatre, Chesterfield. *Producer:* G. MAXWELL JACKSON.

12   *Henry V*: Birmingham Repertory Theatre. *Producer:* DOUGLAS SEALE.

12   *Henry V*: Library Theatre, Manchester. *Producer:* DAVID SCASE.

15   *The Comedy of Errors*: The Norwich Players, The Maddermarket Theatre, Norwich. *Producer:* FRANK HARWOOD.

MARCH

5   *Macbeth*: The Marlowe Theatre, Canterbury. *Director:* CLIFFORD WILLIAMS.

5   *Antony and Cleopatra*: The Old Vic Company, at the Old Vic Theatre, London. (Later at Baalbek Festival, Lebanon.) *Producer:* ROBERT HELPMANN.

11   *As You Like it*: The Marlowe Society, at the Arts Theatre, Cambridge. (Later at Leiden, Holland.) Producer and actors are anonymous.

11   *Julius Caesar*: Guildford Repertory Theatre. *Producer:* BRYAN BAILEY.

12   *The Merchant of Venice*: Northampton Repertory Theatre. *Producer:* LIONEL HAMILTON.

25   *King Lear*: Oldham Repertory Theatre Club, at The Coliseum, Oldham. *Producer:* HARRY LOMAX.

29   *Henry V*: Sloane School, Chelsea. *Producer:* GUY BOAS.

APRIL

2   *As You Like It*: Shakespeare Memorial Theatre, Stratford-upon-Avon. *Producer:* GLEN BYAM SHAW.

16   *King John*: Shakespeare Memorial Theatre. Stratford-upon-Avon. *Producer:* DOUGLAS SEALE.

22   *Henry IV, Part II*: The Youth Theatre, at Toynbee Hall Theatre, London. *Producer:* MICHAEL CROFT.

APRIL

23   *Titus Andronicus:* The Old Vic Company, at the Old Vic Theatre, London. *Producer:* WALTER HUDD.

23   *The Comedy of Errors:* The Old Vic Company, at the Old Vic Theatre, London. *Producer:* WALTER HUDD.

MAY

1   *As You Like It:* Dundee Repertory Company. *Producer:* RAYMOND WESTWELL.

7   *The Taming of the Shrew:* The Playhouse, Liverpool. *Producer:* WILLARD STOKER.

14   *A Midsummer Night's Dream:* Bristol Old Vic Company, at the Theatre Royal, Bristol. *Producer:* JOHN MOODY.

28   *Julius Caesar:* Shakespeare Memorial Theatre, Stratford-upon-Avon. *Producer:* GLEN BYAM SHAW.

29   *Richard III:* The Old Vic Company, at the Old Vic Theatre, London. *Producer:* DOUGLAS SEALE.

JUNE

19   *Henry V:* Oxford University Dramatic Society, at Magdalen Grove, Magdalen College, Oxford. *Producer:* PETER DEWS.

JULY

1   *The Merry Wives of Windsor:* Birmingham University Guild Theatre Group at The University, Birmingham. *Producers:* FIONA ANDERSON and ROGER JEROME.

1   *Titus Andronicus:* The Shakespeare Memorial Theatre Company, Stratford-upon-Avon, at the Stoll Theatre, London, previously on tour on the Continent. *Producer:* PETER BROOK.

2   *Cymbeline:* Shakespeare Memorial Theatre, Stratford-upon-Avon. *Producer:* PETER HALL.

6   *The Merchant of Venice:* The Curtain Theatre, Rochdale. *Producer:* ARTHUR LORD.

8   *Henry IV, Part I:* Shrewsbury Castle, for the Shrewsbury Summer Festival. (Open air production.) *Producer:* not given.

AUGUST

13   *The Tempest:* Shakespeare Memorial Theatre, Stratford-upon-Avon. *Producer:* PETER BROOK.

SEPTEMBER

3   *Macbeth:* Theatre Workshop at the Theatre Royal, Stratford, London, previously at the Zurich International Festival and Moscow. *Producer:* JOAN LITTLEWOOD.

18   *Hamlet:* Old Vic Theatre Company, at the Old Vic Theatre, London (afterwards on tour in France and the U.S.A.). *Producer:* MICHAEL BENTHALL.

29   *Twelfth Night:* Bristol Old Vic Theatre Company, at the Theatre Royal, Bristol. *Producer:* JOHN MOODY.

OCTOBER

1   *Macbeth:* The David Lewis New Theatre Company, Liverpool. *Producer:* THOMAS G. READ.

14   *Twelfth Night:* The Citizens Theatre, Glasgow. *Producer:* PETER DUGUID.

16   *Henry VI, Parts I and II:* The Old Vic Company, at the Old Vic Theatre, London. *Producer:* DOUGLAS SEALE.

17   *Henry VI, Part III:* The Old Vic Company, at the Old Vic Theatre, London. *Producer:* DOUGLAS SEALE.

SHAKESPEARE PRODUCTIONS IN THE UNITED KINGDOM

NOVEMBER

4   *Hamlet:* Perth Repertory Theatre Company. *Producer:* DAVID STEUART.

4   *The Merchant of Venice:* Wimbledon Theatre Players at the Wimbledon Theatre. *Producer:* JOHN MCKELVEY.

11   *Henry IV, Part I:* Ipswich Theatre. *Producer:* PETER COE.

12   *Twelfth Night:* Library Theatre, Manchester. *Producer:* DAVID SCASE.

18   *Richard II:* Guildford Repertory Theatre. *Producer:* ROBERT MARSDEN.

19   *Measure for Measure:* The Old Vic Company, at the Old Vic Theatre, London. *Producer:* MARGARET WEBSTER.

25   *A Midsummer Night's Dream:* Salisbury Arts Theatre at The Playhouse, Salisbury. *Producer:* FREDERICK PEISLEY.

DECEMBER

2   *Hamlet:* Theatre Royal, Lincoln. Producer not known.

23   *A Midsummer Night's Dream:* The Old Vic Company, at the Old Vic Theatre, London. *Producer:* MICHAEL BENTHALL.

THE WHIRLIGIG OF TIME:
A REVIEW OF RECENT PRODUCTIONS

BY

ROY WALKER

It took the Old Vic nine years up to 1923 to stage all Shakespeare's plays. To produce all the Folio plays in the five seasons 1953–8 was a strenuous undertaking. Nine plays remained for the final season, reduced to eight productions by combining the first two Parts of *Henry VI*, but standards inevitably suffered. Nevertheless, the five-year plan had drawn one-and-a-quarter million people to Shakespeare, there had been a successful visit to New York and, later in 1958, the Old Vic Company was to set out on a six-months tour of North America. The Waterloo Road stage was then to be freed from Shakespeare's monopoly, though it remains to be seen whether Schiller and others will draw sufficient audiences.

As remarked in last year's article, the order of the five-year plan was haphazard, but at least it concluded with a production of *Henry VIII* which brought back Dame Edith Evans to the Old Vic after ten years' absence and Sir John Gielgud after eighteen. The Shakespearian authorship of *Henry VIII* has long been under suspicion. It has been banished from the company of the Histories.[1] It has been burlesqued, to the extent of tossing the royal infant into the audience to bring down the curtain on a storm of cheers and cries of rage.[2] It has come in useful to compliment three modern monarchs on their coronations. It is generally regarded as an episodic and uneven play, to be supported by elaborate stage spectacle and star performers who will make something of its two or three good scenes. Michael Benthall's production, with Sir John Gielgud as Wolsey, Dame Edith Evans as Queen Katharine and Harry Andrews as the King, handsomely dressed by Loudon Sainthill, did not suggest that the director held any other view, but it was in some ways the best of recent years. Before describing this production it may be worth while briefly to inquire whether what is becoming firm stage tradition and scholarly dogma is unassailable.

Is *Henry VIII* really so remote from the other Histories? Since the English stage has not, so far as we know, acted all ten Histories in succession and in order of the events with which they deal, the question cannot be put to the theatrical test. If it was, might we not feel that *Henry VIII* stands apart from the *Henry VI–Richard III* tetralogy somewhat as *King John* does from *Richard II–Henry V*? Are they, in any degree, planned as prologue and epilogue to the main series? Themes announced in the 'prologue' play and resumed in the main series are certainly resolved in the 'epilogue'. *King John* shows a league of English and French kings broken by a powerful cardinal and John's title to be considered a sort of forerunner of the Reformation discredited by his final submission to Rome. *Henry VIII* opens with a word-picture of another league between an English and a French king in France, there looms through it the scarlet figure of another cardinal bent on breaking the league, and this play ends the long Shakespearian story of wars with France and trouble with the Roman church, which includes Agincourt and the intrigues of Cardinal Beaufort in the following reign. Is Shakespeare's theme finally resolved until he has brought it almost to his own date with a vision of the substance of the Tudor peace foreshadowed in the Tudor marriage at the end of *Richard III*? Is it not of the essence of Shakespeare's multiple drama that peace is not assured until the reconciliation of Church and State is complete?

Henry VIII can, in fact, be seen as the drama of the Reformation itself. The King is deliberately distanced in his central temporal position, a solid-standing figure who sums up in himself, to some extent, the qualities of the kings who went before him on Shakespeare's stage. But the churchmen are on the stage at first and last and Wolsey quits it before Cranmer enters for the first time. This transformation of the figure of the Church, from a proud puppet-master of kings to a humble servant of his royal lord, and from pride brought down to prophecy raised up, with all that is implied of the relative values of temporal and spiritual reward and punishment, should give the play at least a certain unity.

Michael Benthall's production omitted the prologue and the epilogue. The one, beginning "I come no more to make you laugh" might sound like an unkind reflection on the antics in the last Old Vic and Stratford productions of *Henry VIII* by Tyrone Guthrie.[3] The other, beginning "'Tis ten to one this play can never please" might seem too near the truth for comfort. Previous productions divided the play into two halves, with the interval coming after Katharine's trial. This one divided it into three parts, the intervals coming after the falls of Buckingham and Wolsey. The play gained considerably from this articulation, which brought out the succession of nemesis-actions not dissimilar to the series R. G. Moulton noted in *Richard III*.[4] With some cutting and rearrangement in the last act, and the two ten-minute intervals, the play took three hours to perform.

Action was not much delayed for changes of scene, which were lightly indicated by variations on a permanent setting. But to effect these changes the stage was frequently blacked out for a few seconds, a method little better than the now out-of-date one of lowering the curtain. The high proscenium doors were draped with rich ornamental hangings edged in gilt. For indoor scenes the centre of the stage was closed with a curtain bearing the royal monogram. For outdoor scenes a clear view was left to the cyclorama. For the trial scene the back was filled with a screen of slender pillars which, with similar side-pieces, suggested that the palace was becoming a prison for the unfortunate Queen. Heavy decorated curtains were dropped in, leaving a smaller central opening, to provide a more intimate setting for Katharine at Kimbolton than was available on the wide-open permanent settings by Tanya Moiseiwitsch in Tyrone Guthrie's productions of the play.

Norfolk made little of the splendid word-picture of the Field of the Cloth of Gold, but there was a vigorous, blustering Buckingham (Jack Gwillim). Wolsey's first appearance was the cue for a particularly inept piece of stage-management. Norfolk saw him approaching, off-stage left, whereupon the central curtain rose on cue before the entrance and when the procession had passed through it was lowered again. Wolsey, an impressive figure in the traditional flowing scarlet robe, walked under a canopy borne by four attendants in scapulas and surplices, preceded by two halberdiers and an official bearing the purse on a cushion, and followed by three more clerics in black, two of whom bore tall silver crucifixes, and a nobleman, also in black. Wolsey's pause and turn on the two centre steps and his menacing glance in Buckingham's direction were played with the full authority of Gielgud's grand manner; the proud and dangerous character was instantly established. Buckingham, noisy and threatening until his arrest, then fell effectively quiet, so that we sensed nothing in his life would become him like the leaving of it.

After a brief black-out the King, to whom Harry Andrews brought just the necessary vigorous shrewdness, was discovered on one of two central thrones, before a curtain of dull gold, deep in discussion with the cardinal. The grouping and movement continued to strike out the dramatic action in bold simple lines. As the Queen pleaded with her husband, Wolsey fell away downstage and remained watchfully and majestically poised, clutching a crimson testament, as she brought her complaint against him. Henry was soon convinced and his rebuke to Wolsey was angry and peremptory. The sense was well created that he was open to the influence of the good woman his wife. But when the King's attention became fixed on what Buckingham's surveyor was saying, Wolsey, now seated on a stool a step below the throne, engaged in a silent struggle for control of the King with the Queen, throned on his other side. At the climax, Henry plunged downstage to seize the surveyor and push him to the floor. He left the stage reaching for Wolsey's supporting arm, unmindful now of Katharine.

A cut of nearly fifty lines at the beginning of the next scene lost the discussion of French fashions and took us quickly on to York House. It was soon apparent that Anne Bullen (Jill Dixon) was a cool and calculating little minx. She showed no surprise when the King unmasked or bashfulness at being vigorously embraced by him. Wolsey, pausing to observe the encounter, seemed more amused than alarmed. The next scene introduced not only the two Gentlemen but also the Lord Chamberlain (Paul Daneman), who was able to tell them what had passed at Buckingham's trial. Buckingham, in black, was now calm and dignified, but the farewell and forgiveness were somewhat underplayed, particularly as the climax of the first 'act' in this production. The final tableau left him outlined against the cyclorama, with the axes menacing his head. As he passed on, the axes moved after him and the interval curtain fell, the final dialogue between the Gentlemen omitted.

The second 'act' opened with another clumsy piece of stage-management of the central curtain. The King, kneeling in silent prayer, rose and took his seat on the throne-chair, and the curtain which had been held back was allowed to fall into place. The whole curtain rose to reveal him to the Gentlemen, whom he waved away on the entrance of Wolsey with Campeius (Derek Godfrey). A black-out separated this scene from that between Anne and the Old Lady (Rosalind Atkinson) and another black-out preceded the trial scene. The King, who had changed from his first act crimson costume to a striking one of mustard yellow richly ornamented in gold, sat on a throne before one of the proscenium doors, and Wolsey occupied a throne on the opposite side of the stage, Campeius seated near him. Movement was clearly designed to repeat the pattern of Wolsey's intervention between the King and Queen, as in the first scene between these three. After kneeling to the King, who was clearly moved by her appeal, Katharine returned to the centre of the stage and heard the cardinals at first with her back turned to the audience. She turned to address Wolsey, who rose and, as he continued, crossed to come between her and the King.

Hereabouts there was emphasis on the words 'patient' and 'patience'[5] and in the next scene Patience was placed to Katharine's right (nearest to stage centre) as the Queen sat with her other women working at a large tapestry on her knees. As Patience is not named until the Kimbolton scene later, the full effect of what the producer intended was not apparent to anyone unfamiliar with the play. But this still, silent figure (Margaret Courtenay) in dark grey velvet, confronting the cardinals across her seated mistress, nevertheless effectively suggested that the real duel was between them and her, the Queen's good angel.

The 'act' closed with the scene of Wolsey's fall. Early in the interview Henry threw himself into his throne. As Wolsey approached him, protesting loyalty, and made to slide on to the stool he had occupied before, the King banged down his foot on it, a studied insult that shook the cardinal's composure. Wolsey's fall from power into a state of grace was a rending struggle in which Gielgud rose to something near the heights of his memorable Angelo.[6] The victory of 'patience' was noble but the Cardinal, utterly spent, slumped on to Cromwell's shoulder. The 'act' closed on this slow exit, the actor seeming almost diminished in stature by his ordeal.

It was the Chamberlain, again, who joined the two Gentlemen in the scene of the coronation procession, and he described the events in the Abbey before the procession passed across the back of the stage, with Anne crowned and carrying the orb and sceptre, walking beneath a canopy borne by four of what seemed more like Wolsey's entourage, in scapulas and white surplices over crimson robes, than "four barons of the Cinque-ports". But at least the procession was shown, as it was not in Tyrone Guthrie's Old Vic and Stratford productions. It was all the more important that we should be allowed to see Katharine's vision, in which the garlands held over her head figure a higher coronation for this queen. This is omitted in most modern productions, and Michael Benthall also left it to our imagination, though we heard distant voices singing 'Hallelujah' above the music. Edith Evans beautifully suggested something transcendent as she rendered in her own inimitable way the direction "holdeth up her hands to heaven". In flowing white robe with a long scarf of light grey wound loosely about her head and shoulders, she recalled the figure of Katharine as William Blake imagined it, in the water-colour drawing found in a copy of the Second Folio now in the British Museum.[7] (Some play-goers may also have been reminded of her performance of the Countess in Christopher Fry's *The Dark is Light Enough*, at the end of which she passed peacefully away in her chair.) Here the figure of Patience achieved its full symbolic and gently human value, as she knelt beside her mistress' chair, her long, high-shouldered sleeves folding like the wings of a compassionate dark angel; and Griffith (Derek Francis) was as much a figure of charity. Katharine's slow exit, her arm round Patience for support, had a silent eloquence that made one see the poet's purpose in personifying Patience as a lady in waiting.

The producer remodelled the rest of the play to bring it swiftly to a close. The entrance of the Old Lady with the news of the royal birth was delayed. The King's interview with Cranmer (David Dodimead) was shortened and nothing was said of the royal ring. The King left the stage at "the good man weeps!" and Cranmer was assailed there and then by his enemies, not kept waiting at door next morning. The King re-entered behind the group, as Gardiner (David Waller) ordered the Guard to see Cranmer safe in the Tower, and Henry's command to him to embrace his enemy was no sooner obeyed than the Old Lady entered with tidings of the birth of Elizabeth. This re-ordering worked well enough in its own way, though Shakespeare knew what he was about in making the new birth precede the delivery of Cranmer from his tormentors. The porter scene was cut so that we passed at once to the palace for the christening. When Cranmer gave the child the name Elizabeth, the Old Lady, struck with the modern parallel,

turned to the audience and cried "Elizabeth!!!", burying her face in her hands, quite over-
come with joy. She knelt, holding the child, while Cranmer delivered his oration, and the
King seized it in his own arms before the curtain fell to thrice repeated cries of "God Bless
Elizabeth".

Guthrie once treated Cranmer as "a comical old ninny"[8] with "shattering effect on the play
as a whole". On any fair reading, particularly the sort of valuation suggested earlier in this
article, the rise of Cranmer and the final prophecy should be as moving as the fall of Wolsey.
The Cardinal is the better acting role and famous actors have usually preferred it. In a production where Gielgud was Wolsey, and a capable but undistinguished member of the repertory
company was Cranmer, it was hardly possible that we would not be reminded of those other
Shakespearian lines about what happens when a well-graced actor leaves the stage. As already
noted, Wolsey does so before Cranmer appears, and it was suggested that the poetic effect is of
transfiguration of the figure of the Church, a sort of personification of the Reformation itself.
Had Gielgud doubled Wolsey and Cranmer the whole pattern of the play might have been
illuminated. Certainly *Henry VIII* will never escape anticlimax, if not the suspicion of a
patched-up patriotic ending, until it finds a Cranmer worthy to succeed its Wolsey.

A controversial but not unfruitful essay might be attempted on Shakespeare's use of two
triangles of forces, or pairs of scales. In both patterns the protagonist is the apex of the triangle,
or the point of the balance. In one pattern the point of the triangle is foremost and the conflicting
forces converge upon and meet in it. This is the typical pattern of the four great tragedies that
take their titles from the name of a protagonist who is set between personifications of good and
evil. In the other pattern, the point of the triangle or the balance is distanced from us, the conflicting forces clash directly in the foreground. This is a pattern to be found in some of the
Histories and Comedies. The risk here is that the significance of the remote central figure will
be underrated or overlooked in the dramatic conflict in the foreground. Shakespeare could have
meant to put us on the right track in titling his Antonio play *The Merchant of Venice* rather than
'The Lady of Belmont against the Jew of Venice', or *Henry VI* instead of 'Margaret of Anjou
against the House of York'; even *Julius Caesar* is a more illuminating title for that Roman
tragedy than 'Brutus against Antony'. These passive or withdrawn protagonists, who sometimes have short or unspectacular parts, do not attract star actors, and they are 'still centres'
of different kinds. They may seem to be mere helpless spectators of the conflicts into which they
are drawn, like Antonio and Henry VI, or they may be unmoved movers like Caesar and
Henry VIII; but in most cases they ultimately represent the highest spiritual value, or bring about
the true reconciliation of conflicting opposites, in the drama.

Even if this sketch of dramatic patterns is persuasive in so summary a statement, *Twelfth Night*
may hardly seem a case in point. It has not a 'personal' title, and it hardly seems to have a
central character, prominent or retired, unless we follow, as most star actors and modern productions do, the theatrical logic of opportunity that led to the comedy's being called, as early as
1623, 'Malvolio'. It has, of course, the two elements usual in a Shakespeare comedy, a romantic
plot and a comic plot, usually played for contrast and counterpoint rather than brought to any
final resolution and harmony. In the programme note to Peter Hall's production at Stratford
in 1958, Ivor Brown speaks of the comic plot as 'secondary' but that hardly does justice to what

may have been the producer's intention in keeping Malvolio in his place. Yet to select any one of the endearingly familiar characters as central and to balance the comic and romantic plots accordingly may seem, at best, an arbitrary attempt at novelty. Something of the sort, however, was what Hall seemed to be attempting. In making Feste the centre of the whirligig of time that brings in its revenges he had, at any rate, the authority of the New Cambridge edition. "We must hold," declared Q,[9] "and insist on holding Feste, Master of the Revels, to be the master-mind and controller of *Twelfth Night*, its comic spirit and president...." In the absence of a full supporting argument the assertion may seem arbitrary. A parallel to stimulate imagination in this direction might be found in the comparison of the bitter-sweet figure of Feste alone on the stage at the end, when the three couples go off, with that of the Merchant at the end of the earlier comedy when three other couples go off leaving alone the man to whom they owe, in some degree, their wedded happiness. There is also the fact that the title of *Twelfth Night* may be more indicative than it seems to us, who have lost any sense of twelfth night as a red-letter day in the calendar, the time of the Saturnalia which was also once the true date of Christmas. As John Stow[10] tells us,

In the feast of Christmas, there was in the king's house, wheresoever he was lodged, a lord of misrule, or master of merry disports; and the like had ye in the house of every noble man of honour, or good worship, were he spiritual or temporal.

Is there more to that ubiquitous comic-sad spirit of Feste, a fool who lives by the church and masquerades as a veritable Abbot of Unreason, in this saturnalian comic romance of the snobbish steward who aspires to be his mistress' master and the faithful servant who becomes her master's mistress, than was apparent to Pepys[11] when he wrote it off as "not related at all to the name or day" (and as "a silly play") and to such moderns as J. Q. Adams[12] when they agree with him, on the first point at any rate? The merit of Peter Hall's production, tentative rather than definitive, aspiring rather than assured, was that it gave new life to such a question. Perhaps Feste, whose song of the wind and the rain is heard next on the lips of Lear's Fool, has grown in the succession of Shakespeare's jesters, from the Touchstone who matches the motley of court and country to something more like the sadly wise Old Clown of such a modern Christian artist as Rouault?

Peter Hall's focus on Feste met the audience entering the theatre, on the drop-curtain painted by Lila de Nobili, who designed his 1957 Stratford production of *Cymbeline*. The central feature was a silvery aureoled figure in clown's costume descending into a dark world in which the faces of other characters seen in shadow were touched with the radiance. With his ass's ears he might well have been a disguised Mercury whose winged cap enabled him to go into whatever part of the universe he pleased with the greatest celerity. As music sounded a front spot focused on this coolly glowing figure, which dissolved as lights came up behind to make the curtain transparent. There a small group of musicians harmonized the music which is the food of love and, on the forestage, a group of gentlemen stood motionless in silhouette. The tableau of the drop had been transposed from the vertical to the horizontal, but nothing went well for love until Feste (Cyril Luckham) appeared. As soon as his quicksilver wit proved his young and feather-brained Olivia (Geraldine McEwan) a fool, this mature Feste[13] gave us a shrewd hint that this was not altogether fool. "There is no slander in an allowed fool" and "Now Mercury endue thee with leasing, for thou speakest well of fools" responds the wise fool whom Mercury's winged cap fits.

From the romantic mistress to the comic kinsman; at the end of the first 'act' Feste found out the bully-boy Sir Toby (Patrick Wymark) and the fool absolute, Sir Andrew (Richard Johnson) for the drinking-scene, set not in a wine-cellar but in a glowing Warwickshire walled garden where these laughing cavaliers were rebuked by Malvolio (Mark Dignam)—"the devil a puritan that he is"—kill-joy of comic and romantic plots. As has been observed,[14] Maria's plan to 'let the fool make a third' in the gulling of this peacock is contradicted later, in the letter scene, when Fabian unaccountably deputizes for Feste. This production minimized the inconsistency by letting Feste feign sleep, head on arm, at a table. As the others went out he raised his head and stared thoughtfully after them. The stage darkened rapidly on this picture, wood-pigeons cooing amorously in the distance, for the 'act' interval. That at least left the emphasis on Feste, but what could he have been thinking so seriously about, unless it was why Fabian had been allowed to usurp his place later in the play? The present writer wonders if this was not the actors' doing at some time before 1623. Might not an actor of Malvolio object that besides having more than his share of the comedy, and songs besides, Feste was stealing his best scene by business behind the box-tree? All Fabian's lines and entrances are somewhat suspect,[15] and the problem is not solved, as in this production, by introducing him with Olivia in I, v.

The second 'act' began with the Duke's "Give me some music..." acceptably echoing the opening of the first. Feste's sad song seemed to woo Orsino to accept the death of a hopeless love that new and true love might be born, he is lost unless the melancholy god make his doublet of changeable taffeta. After the letter scene, from which Feste was so unaccountably absent, Viola met the fellow "wise enough to play the fool", whose keen eyes seemed to penetrate her disguise. But then Feste was, as usual, missing from the mock duel. Surely he, and not Fabian, was to be Viola's second, well assured this cock would not fight? Was not that the point of Feste's shock when, taking Sebastian for his sister in the next scene, he finds the young man now has mettle enough? This scene, ending with Olivia suddenly smitten with Sebastian, closed the second 'act' and the brief final 'act' began with an abbreviated version of Feste's visitation of Malvolio, in rapid succession as Sir Topas and as himself, the dungeon being a cellar in the garden.

The play ended as it began, with music, all the romantic and comic characters, except Malvolio, dancing together in a golden distance behind a gauze curtain in love's now triumphant harmony, with Feste, the goer-between of the worlds of romance and comedy, and perhaps also of the gods and human kind, seated on the fore-stage in gathering dusk, sadly remembering how the world began. Now it was their light that just touched his figure, forlorn at the thought that there was no more for him to do in this world. Even a god who plays the wise fool may be left lonely at the dance of human love.

The producer had made the romantic plot more consistently light comedy by treating Olivia as a feather-brained little goose; he had kept the comics well on the subtle side of farce, and so made it possible for his Mercury to modulate between the two worlds of the play and make them one. His choice of Cavalier costume gave the maximum thematic contrast with Malvolio's Puritan habit,[16] served the opposition of amours and austerity, and brought out what is most English in Shakespeare's Never-Never Land of Illyria. It also eased the problem of the identical

PLATE VII

A. KATHARINE'S VISION
Engraving by William Blake
(British Museum)

B. KATHARINE'S VISION
Henry VIII, the Old Vic, 1958. Produced by
Michael Benthall, designed by Loudon Sainthill

C. WOLSEY, KATHARINE AND PATIENCE
Old Vic production

PLATE VIII

A. The figure of Feste

B. Sebastian and Viola

C. Olivia, Malvolio and Feste

'TWELFTH NIGHT', SHAKESPEARE MEMORIAL THEATRE, 1958
Produced by Peter Hall, Designed by Lila de Nobili

twins[17] with a hair-style equally suitable to boy and girl. He had, in Dorothy Tutin, a Viola of irresistible freshness and charm. The rest of a Stratford company for once not star-studded was of its own fairly high standard with none outstanding. This was a *Twelfth Night* that did not altogether succeed, but a production that continually threw fresh light on a comedy about which most of us have long ceased to think freshly, which we too easily accept as a cherished but somewhat shapeless romantic-comic routine.

NOTES

1. "It is worth noting that it (*Henry VIII*) cannot be fitted into the scheme of the earlier histories, and is not discussed in Tillyard's *Shakespeare's History Plays* (1944), or in Lily B. Campbell's *Shakespeare's 'Histories'* (San Marino, California, 1948)."—R. A. Foakes, Arden ed. *King Henry VIII* (1957), p. xlii, n.

2. Terence Gray's production of *Henry VIII* at the Festival Theatre, Cambridge, in 1931. The finale, which out-Heroded Herod, is fully described by Norman Marshall, *The Other Theatre* (1947), pp. 66–7.

3. Guthrie produced *Henry VIII* at Sadler's Wells in 1933, with Charles Laughton, who had recently appeared in the film, *The Private Life of Henry VIII*. His 1949 Stratford production is described by M. St Clare Byrne in *Shakespeare Survey*, 3 (1950), pp. 120–9 and, as "an orgy of irresponsible invention", by Norman Marshall, *The Producer and the Play* (1957), pp. 196–7. The production was repeated at Stratford in 1950 with changes in the cast. Guthrie's 1953 Old Vic production is described by the late T. C. Kemp in *Shakespeare Survey*, 7 (1954), pp. 124–5, as following the lines of his earlier Stratford production; and, more adversely, by Roy Walker, 'Theatre Royal' in *The Twentieth Century* (June 1953).

4. R. G. Moulton, *Shakespeare as a Dramatic Artist* (1885), pp. 107–24. J. Dover Wilson, ed. *Richard III* (1954), pp. xl–xliii, approvingly summarizes Moulton's argument.

5. 'Patience' occurs twelve times in *Henry VIII*, more often than in any play of Shakespeare's except *Othello* (13). It is confined to (or spoken of) only Buckingham, Wolsey, Katharine (and her personified Patience) and Cranmer. It is mainly associated with Katharine and Cranmer, touching Buckingham and Wolsey only once each; they do not use it themselves, though Wolsey exhorts the Queen to "be patient yet" and has the—prophetic—reply "I will when you are humble". Katharine uses it positively once (III, i, 137) after adversity; Cranmer twice (V, ii, 19; V, iii, 66) in adversity. This purposive pattern seems to warrant the Old Vic producer's attempt to give thematic treatment to 'patience' in this play. For Patience in the Old Vic 1958 production see Pl. VIIc.

6. In Peter Brook's 1950 Stratford production of *Measure for Measure*, described by Richard David in *Shakespeare Survey*, 4 (1951), pp. 135–8.

7. Reproduced in *The Times* (9 Dec. 1954) and Pl. VIIA. For the Old Vic 1958 Katharine see Pl. VIIB.

8. Norman Marshall, *The Producer and the Play* (1957), p. 197.

9. A. Quiller-Couch (and J. Dover Wilson), ed. *Twelfth Night* (1930, 1949), p. xxvi. See also L. G. Salingar, 'The Design of *Twelfth Night*' in *Shakespeare Quarterly*, IX (Spring 1958): "...saturnalian spirit invades the whole play" (p. 118). "There are discordant strains, then, in the harmony of *Twelfth Night*...As far as any actor can resolve them, this task falls on Feste...it is precisely on this finely-poised balance of his that the whole play comes to rest" (pp. 135–6).

10. John Stow, *The Survey of London*, Everyman Library ed. (1912, etc.), p. 89. He is describing customs in pre-Elizabethan London.

11. Pepys' comment on the performance he saw on 'Twelfth Day' 1663 is quoted by Harold Child in his stage-history of the play in the New Cambridge edition, pp. 173–4.

12. "Possibly it was in honor of this grand occasion [the Twelfth Night revel of 1600] that Shakespeare rechristened the comedy with the otherwise irrelevant title *Twelfth Night*." (A footnote cites Pepys in support of this description of the title.)—J. Q. Adams, *A Life of William Shakespeare* (n.d.), p. 292.

13. Ngaio Marsh, 'A Note on a Production of *Twelfth Night*', in *Shakespeare Survey*, 8, p. 72, argues for a young Olivia. Allardyce Nicoll told the writer that he recalls seeing a comic Olivia in a production by the Habima

Players. Granville-Barker, in his 1912 Savoy Theatre production of *Twelfth Night* "gave the part [of Feste] to an actor no longer young".—Norman Marshall, *The Producer and the Play* (1957), p. 160. The actor, Hayden Coffin, was fifty in 1912. For the 1958 Stratford Feste, see Pl. VIII A.

14. J. Dover Wilson, New Cambridge ed. *Twelfth Night*, pp. 93–4.

15. They can mostly be plausibly distributed, or returned, to Feste, Sir Andrew and Maria. The opening of the final scene, v, i, is particularly suspect. Why introduce the business of the letter only to leave it aside for some 300 lines, during which Fabian neither speaks nor is spoken to and may or may not be on stage? Was not Maria, rather than Fabian, meant to say "myself and Toby set this device against Malvolio here", v, i, 367–8?

16. See Plate VIII c.

17. See Plate VIII B. The writer has seen powdered wigs used with even greater effect, and at closer quarters, in an enchanting production on Twelfth Night 1954 in the spacious late-eighteenth century Old Dining Room of Attingham Park, Shropshire, a property belonging to the National Trust.

THE YEAR'S CONTRIBUTIONS TO
SHAKESPEARIAN STUDY

1. CRITICAL STUDIES

reviewed by CLIFFORD LEECH

The burden of Shakespeare criticism has become so grievous that no one today can undertake a general study of the dramatist in the confident belief that he has read, and remembered, everything of value that has already been written concerning his theme. He will be likely, therefore, to come to a point of disregard, trying to see the works by his own light, aided only by those writers who have exercised a special influence upon him. This might not be altogether a bad thing if there were not also in our time a strong desire to systematize a writer's outlook, to find in him a code or firmly held attitude that we can take for our own. Thus in general studies there is a powerful urge to devise a pattern agreeable to the critic and, with some neglect of other current views, to assert its dominance in Shakespeare. The danger is less great in studies of individual plays: there it is possible, though not easy, to familiarize oneself with a large part of what has already been written, and this should discourage one from arriving too quickly at a conclusion that claims definitive rank. Moreover, the fact that the critic is restricting himself to a single play limits the extent of his claim. It is modester and safer to interpret a play than to present 'Shakespeare' in a nutshell.

These remarks are prompted by the high degree of success achieved by a study of *Othello* by Robert B. Heilman[1] and by a study of *Richard III* by Wolfgang Clemen.[2] In method these books are far apart: Heilman uses something of the 'spatial' approach, considering in particular the attitudes induced by the figures of Othello and Iago, observing Shakespeare's employment of images and character-contrasts, and suggesting the *Weltanschauung* that emerges; Clemen goes through his play scene by scene, comments on almost every detail of every speech, relates the play in general and in its particulars to its sources and to the drama of its time, and is anxious to make us aware too of the 'timeless' element that coexists with the 'Elizabethan'. The books are alike, however, in their abundant documentation: one feels that almost nothing written on his play has escaped the notice of either critic, and indeed the end-notes in Heilman's book are so extensive that his reader may feel often distracted from following the argument. They are alike, too, in their judicious weighing of evidence: they have, certainly and with Heilman strongly, a point of view, but it is one that has been weighed most deliberately.

Perhaps the most notable thing that Clemen has demonstrated is that the style of *Richard III* is more varied, more subtly related to the details of character and situation, than is commonly recognized, and he has, too, considered the function of each scene, noting for example where a section of the play serves a purpose quite other than the furthering of the plot. The method of scene-by-scene comment is a sign of the writer's caution, but it has to be admitted that this makes it more difficult for the reader to come to a full perception of the play as here presented. Heil-

---

[1] *Magic in the Web: Action and Language in Othello* (Lexington: University of Kentucky Press, 1956).
[2] *Kommentar zu Shakespeares Richard III: Interpretation eines Dramas* (Göttingen: Vandenhoeck und Ruprecht, 1957).

man's method, though indeed more hazardous, takes us at once into the critic's confidence, and the majority of readers will find this more attractive. There is perhaps, in the first half of the book, a too persistent hunting of the image, and on occasion the shade of Bradley-of-the-notes is not absent. But the analysis of Othello's character—seen as compounded of weakness and 'nobility', as never reaching fully adult stature and as thus bringing the play into some relationship with more modern variants of tragedy—is profoundly illuminating. (L. L. Schücking[1] has recently taken exception to a current tendency to denigrate this character, but appears to ride too easily over the evidence of unripeness.) Heilman insists on the individuality of the play's characters which goes along with their archetypal properties, and this is only one illustration of his ability to see the particulars of the play from more than one viewpoint. There is a valuable demonstration of the imperfections of Othello's 'justice' in the cashiering of Cassio, and a very full study of the final scene, on which Heilman carries conviction when he says that "The shock is that of a murder by rite, of an exotic depravity in which the selfless spiritual concern and the wholly selfish violence are confounded". Certainly this book cannot be neglected by any future critic of the play.

Briefer contributions on *Othello* have come from Albert Gerard,[2] who studies in particular the limitations of Othello's mind and his love, and is among those who affirm the hero's damnation (a matter shrewdly disregarded by Heilman), Henry J. Webb,[3] who suggests that Shakespeare originally intended Othello to be a plain blunt soldier, actually 'rude' of speech, but decided that this type-figure would not suit his purposes, and Walter Nash,[4] who notes a special frequency of paired adjectives, nouns and verbs in Othello's speech and in Iago's when he appears to be imitating Othello. On *Richard III*, J. Dover Wilson[5] has quoted medical evidence as a basis for suggesting that Richard, by eating his strawberries, may have deliberately induced an urticarial rash in order to accuse Jane Shore and thus strike at Hastings.

It will be convenient now to consider the books and articles on the comedies, histories and tragedies. John Russell Brown[6] has devoted a book to the comedies, and begins with the sound observation that it is difficult to explain the enduring hold of these plays if the substance of their thought is as trifling as critical comment often suggests. We may, however, find it more difficult to follow him when he emphasizes three ideas as basic in the plays—"love's wealth", "love's truth", and "love's order". The first of these does usefully draw attention to the recurrent use of commercial imagery, but the others (presumably carrying the meaning that true love helps one to see clearly and makes things fall into a healthful pattern) do not seem to cast much illumination. When Brown gets away from his scheme, he is perceptive of the complexities of things: he writes excellently on *The Merchant of Venice*, and comments sensibly though summarily on the Dark Comedies. Some of his footnotes show the ultra-Bradleian

[1] 'Der neue Othello (F. R. Leavis' Othello-Deutung)', *Studies in English Language and Literature Presented to Professor Dr Karl Brunner on the Occasion of his Seventieth Birthday* (Vienna–Stuttgart, 1957), pp. 191–9.

[2] '"Egregiously an Ass": The Dark Side of the Moor. A view of Othello's Mind', *Shakespeare Survey*, 10 (1957), 98–106.

[3] '"Rude am I in my Speech"', *English Studies*, XXXIX (April 1958), 67–72.

[4] 'Paired Words in *Othello*: Shakespeare's Use of a Stylistic Device', *ibid.* pp. 62–7.

[5] 'A Note on 'Richard III': The Bishop of Ely's Strawberries', *Modern Language Review*, LII (October 1957), 563–4.

[6] *Shakespeare and his Comedies* (Methuen, 1957).

tendency (to deduce the smaller fact that the dramatist has not imparted to us) noted in connection with Heilman's book. Clearly, however, Brown writes with the enthusiasm that can be productive.

An interesting short study of *A Midsummer Night's Dream* has come from Paul A. Olson,[1] who considers the play in relation to love-allegory in Spenser, Lyly and other contemporaries of Shakespeare. This is diligently and convincingly done, especially in its demonstration of the contrast between the Theseus–Hippolita and Oberon–Titania relationships. Yet there is something odd in the tone of the writing. Olson admits that Shakespeare is not over-serious with his young lovers and recognizes their predicament as "comic", yet he can refer to "the pattern of fall and redemption which they experience" and can say of the play as a whole that "Shakespeare's purpose is to bring to life certain truths about wedlock": surely Shakespeare merely used these 'truths' as part of a dramatic pattern appropriate to a wedding festivity. The critic of the comedies must try not to be too full of high sentence. On the same play Peter F. Fisher[2] has noted the four worlds of the characters, assigned a label to each, and observed that they are brought together in the last act. Miss Dorothy C. Hockey[3] has found "a unity of plot-device" in *Much Ado* in that much of the action in all three stories depends on 'noting', or rather 'mis-noting' or observing wrongly, and (referring to Kökeritz) suggests that the title gives us an Elizabethan pun on 'noting' and 'nothing'. Articles on *Troilus and Cressida* with certain common features have come from William R. Bowden[4] and E. Davis.[5] Each is a partisan for Hector and Troilus, and Davis for Ulysses as well. Bowden approves Hector's decision to go on with the war, putting 'honour' above 'reason'; Davis avers that to give back Helen would be to act like Cressida. Bowden rightly sees that the play demonstrates the ineffectiveness of reason, but gets into the earthquake zone when, anxious to support the war-party, he declares "true worth is in a sense non-existent until it is recognised"—"in a sense" is rich indeed—and relates this to Troilus' "What is aught, but as 'tis valued?" Davis reaches a height of ingenuity when he suggests that Ulysses took Troilus to spy on Cressida in order to make him an "anger-maddened" and therefore incompetent fighter. Yet Davis can recognize the "rich and varied" quality of the play, and they are both surely right in their sympathetic response to Hector. They overlook, *inter alia*, that—as with Othello—sympathy and full approval do not need to go hand-in-hand. In an article by Hamish F. G. Swanston[6] there is a fuller perception of the play's antitheses, which are over-strenuously related to the oppositions characteristic of baroque art: Swanston sees, however, that there is here no baroque synthesis, which he believes must depend on a Christian concept alien to the play.

A valuable account of the history play in Shakespeare's time has come from Irving Ribner.[7] The field covered stretches from the early sixteenth century to the Civil War. Ribner stresses the political element in Elizabethan 'history', and provides a useful summary of the multiple

[1] 'A Midsummer Night's Dream and the Meaning of Court Marriage', *ELH*, xxiv (June 1957), 95–119.
[2] 'The Argument of *A Midsummer Night's Dream*', *Shakespeare Quarterly*, viii (Summer 1957), 307–10.
[3] 'Notes Notes, Forsooth...', *ibid.* pp. 353–8.
[4] 'The Human Shakespeare and *Troilus and Cressida*', *Shakespeare Quarterly*, viii (Spring 1957), 167–77.
[5] 'Troilus and Cressida', *English Studies in Africa*, i (March 1958), 10–26.
[6] 'The Baroque Element in *Troilus and Cressida*', *Durham University Journal*, n.s. xix (December 1957), 14–23.
[7] *The English History Play in the Age of Shakespeare* (Princeton: Princeton University Press, 1957).

aims of the historiographers. He sees, however, that the Tudor doctrine of passive obedience had its opponents (especially in France and among English exiles), and that this may have exerted an influence on certain history plays, notably in Macduff's response to Malcolm's self-denigration. He observes that in the seventeenth century a stricter notion of historical truth seems to assert itself, and relates this to *Henry VIII*, Jonson's Roman plays, and *Perkin Warbeck*: this could, indeed, have been supported by noting the secondary titles *All is True*, *A Strange Truth*, and the objections apparently raised against Chapman's fictional *Revenge of Bussy*. At times there is some simplification, as when he sees *Tamburlaine* as presenting merely an ideal and an object for emulation (with no reference to Roy W. Battenhouse's perhaps equally one-sided view of the matter), or when he fails to note the stigmatizing of rebellion as 'unnatural' in *Edward II*. He rightly emphasizes, however, the double aspect of the political thought in *Richard II*. Although we are warned that this book deals only with the historical aspects of Shakespeare's histories and of *Lear*, *Macbeth* and other plays which contain a historical element, the impression given is that, at least on one level of significance, these plays are straightforward demonstrations of Tudor political ideas; the wider references of both Parts of *Henry IV* and the critical undercurrent in *Henry V* are here not explored. Moreover, the desire to unearth political doctrine in the plays examined leads Ribner to see *Henry VIII* as 'mere disjointed pageantry'. There is certainly valuable matter here for the reader who recognizes that the plays are being seen from a single viewpoint.

J. A. Bryant, Jun.,[1] contributes a judiciously balanced article on *Richard II*. He considers the ritual-aspects of the play, and notes how the ideas of Christ, Adam, Cain, and Abel are associated with Richard and also in some measure with Bolingbroke. Further, he sees in the play links with the Christian mass and with fertility-rituals. The manifold character of these associations should, he points out, prevent the play from being interpreted in terms of a single ritual-framework. Philip Williams[2] supports J. I. M. Stewart's view of Falstaff as Prince Hal's father-substitute, in whom the real father is vicariousy killed: a number of details are engagingly adduced in support, but Williams does not pretend that this is more than a single aspect of the character and the play. While taking pleasure in this article, we may wonder what deep motive prompts the repeated assertion that the rejection of Falstaff is found acceptable, and may feel that the argument needs to be linked with Hal's finding a new father in the Lord Chief Justice at the end of Part II. Bernard Spivack[3] has usefully traced the relationship of Falstaff to morality figures, with a realization that the figure in Shakespeare is a hybrid, partly a morality-type, partly a 'human' character.

This year's most important book on the tragedies has been written by Harold S. Wilson.[4] It is a study of ten plays—Bradley's four, *Romeo and Juliet*, the three Roman plays, *Troilus*, and *Timon*—and an arrangement of them into a system. First there are those plays which belong to the 'Order of Faith', two (*Romeo* and *Hamlet*) which show the working of Providence towards harmony, two (*Othello* and *Macbeth*) which show Providence's just punishment of sin: these two pairs present respectively 'thesis' and 'antithesis'. Then there are plays which belong to the 'Order of Nature', two (*Julius Caesar* and *Coriolanus*) which show their main characters emerging

---

[1] 'The Linked Analogies of *Richard II*', *Sewanee Review*, LXV (Summer 1957), 420–33.
[2] 'The Birth and Death of Falstaff Reconsidered', *Shakespeare Quarterly*, VIII (Summer 1957), 359–65.
[3] 'Falstaff and the Psychomachia', *Shakespeare Quarterly*, VIII (Autumn 1957), 449–59.
[4] *On the Design of Shakespearian Tragedy* (Toronto: University of Toronto Press, 1957).

successfully from a trial conducted according to purely secular values, two (*Troilus* and *Timon*) where these same values are shown as persistently neglected: again the terms 'thesis' and 'antithesis' are used for these two pairs. Finally, a 'synthesis' emerges in *Antony and Cleopatra* and in *Lear*: the value here affirmed is that of human love, a derivative from Christianity but not presented in specifically Christian terms. The thought behind this arrangement is evidently considerable, but we may wonder a little at its disregard of chronology, with the suggestion of Shakespeare going back from time to time to fill in a gap in the scheme. Nevertheless, we are in Wilson's debt for his underlining of the great variety of Shakespearian tragedy: not all of us would go to the point of seeing *Troilus* as belonging here, but it is well to be reminded of the large differences that separate the other plays from one another. And, though not every reader will agree to the placing of *Antony* along with *Lear* in the supreme place, Wilson's argument does fit in with our general sense of a greater amplitude in the experience presented here, a wider range of implication in the thought, than we encounter elsewhere. We may regretfully fail to accept his system, and be aware too of an occasional forcing of the argument, yet feel that he is sensitive to the character of the work he is interpreting.

Franklin M. Dickey[1] has given attention to *Romeo*, *Troilus* and *Antony*, to which he attaches the label "Shakespeare's Love Tragedies". This book is useful in its demonstration of the critical attitude to love taken up frequently in Shakespeare's time, but there is a too easy disregard of the continuance of the Courtly Love tradition, with only bare reference to Lawrence Babb's *The Elizabethan Malady* (1951), where the coexistence of the two opposing attitudes was aptly shown. On *Antony and Cleopatra* Dickey presents a wholesome corrective to the common view of the play as glorifying the love of the two chief characters, and he has a particularly useful observation that, in Elizabethan writings, "the old who love passionately are more to be censured than pitied". Yet even on this play he presents a one-sided case, at no time recognizing the critical character of Shakespeare's picture of the Roman world. If, however, he has only part of the truth on *Antony*, we may feel altogether more sceptical of his view of *Romeo*. This he sees as a demonstration of passion in excess leading inevitably to disaster. He declares at one moment that Romeo's suicide is the "ultimate sin", though quickly, and oddly, he adds that perhaps he might be forgiven. He has to admit, too, that Juliet's love is reasonably conducted, so Romeo, it appears, must bear the full blame in this moral tale. We can learn a good deal from Dickey about Elizabethan writings on the subject of love, but we must be more cautious than he has been in applying his information to the writings of a major poet. He sees *Venus and Adonis*, incidentally, as a highly moral work: perhaps we ought to hope that Gabriel Harvey's "younger sort" were taking a similar view, though we may be puzzled that Shakespeare should promise a "graver labour" to follow it.

Charles Norton Coe[2] has argued that, though Shakespeare may have observed the 'conventions' of the Elizabethan stage, his success in the presentation of villainous characters depends on the degree to which he has achieved verisimilitude—that is, through convincing motivation, complexity and general liveliness. Where this book suffers is in its disregard of the difference in dramatic style between the tragic writings of the early 1590's (*Titus*, *Richard III*) and the more 'realistic' Jacobean tragedy: Coe is simply inclined to blame the one for not being the other.

[1] *Not Wisely But Too Well: Shakespeare's Love Tragedies* (San Marino: The Huntington Library, 1957).
[2] *Shakespeare's Villains* (New York: Bookman Associates, 1957).

Moreover, he does not see that different criteria are necessary when we encounter Goneril and Regan, that the elemental evil in them can have its effect without the normal means for securing plausibility. This oversight is, of course, not uncommon in critical studies restricted to comment on characterization.

A notable brief study of the tragedies as a whole has come from Roy W. Battenhouse.[1] It is a contribution to a symposium in which a number of theologians, philosophers, and professors of English have studied the relation between tragic writing and the Christian faith. The editor, Nathan A. Scott, Jun., has made in his foreword the shrewd observation that the tragic attitude, depending on an "*attentiveness* to the contingencies and sufferings that it is the lot of man to endure", is rarely uniformly maintained by the writers we shall agree to call 'tragic'. This should lead to a demonstration of a tension between Christian and a-Christian impulses within the works studied. Several contributors, however, have shown themselves anxious to stress the Christian element: for Battenhouse, the tragedies of Shakespeare display the working of the Old Adam, and this approach makes the plays into object lessons in which we may be made aware of our need to do better than the hero. Such an approach is thoroughly compatible with good observation of the characters' failings in plays such as *Othello* and *Troilus*, where Shakespeare's sympathy goes along with sharp criticism, but it can make heavy weather of *Romeo and Juliet*.

Briefer studies of the separate tragedies include two articles which comment usefully on *Titus* while illustrating the current academic denigration of this play, consequent perhaps on its recent successful revival in the theatre.[2] R. F. Hill[3] draws attention to the play's eccentricity in its use of stylistic devices, and concludes that it must be either of earlier date than anything else in the Folio or written by more than one author. Eugene M. Waith[4] shows the close dependence on Ovid and the consequent stress on '*admiratio*'. Certainly we do not feel Titus' predicament as we feel that of any later Shakespearian tragic hero, but it is odd to find Waith linking this character with Tamburlaine and Bussy as "almost beyond praise or blame, an object of admiration": we may legitimately wonder if any of the three, especially perhaps Bussy, is as far away from us as that. Miss Carolyn Heilbrun[5] has written a spirited and reasonable defence of Gertrude against Bradley's charge that she has a 'soft animal nature...very dull and very shallow': her weakness, rather, was lust. This article is less convincing in its attempt to acquit Gertrude of the charge of adultery. G. K. Hunter[6] argues that the echoes of Isocrates in Polonius' words to Laertes are commonly used in the period without any kind of ridicule or criticism: nevertheless, he suggests that we come to see the inadequacy of this worldly wisdom in the *Hamlet*-context, as we may similarly see that of the Countess in *All's Well*. Alex Aronson[7] sees the paradox of Hamlet rejecting 'seems' for 'is' yet putting on an antic disposition: he is struggling always for

---

[1] 'Shakespearean Tragedy: A Christian Interpretation', in *The Tragic Vision and the Christian Faith*, edited by Nathan A. Scott, Jun. (New York: Association Press, 1957).

[2] Cf. Richard David's review of the Stratford 1955 *Titus* in *Shakespeare Survey*, 10 (1957).

[3] 'The Composition of *Titus Andronicus*', *Shakespeare Survey*, 10 (1957), 60–70.

[4] 'The Metamorphosis of Violence in *Titus Andronicus*', *ibid.* pp. 39–49.

[5] 'The Character of Hamlet's Mother', *Shakespeare Quarterly*, VIII (Spring 1957), 201–6.

[6] 'Isocrates' Precepts and Polonius' Character', *Shakespeare Quarterly*, VIII (Autumn 1957), 501–6. Hunter is replying to Mrs Josephine Waters Bennett's article, 'Characterization in Polonius' Advice to Laertes', *Shakespeare Quarterly*, IV, 3–9.

[7] 'More Matter, with Less Art: A Study in the Rhetorics of Hamlet', *The Visvabharati Quarterly* (West Bengal).

'nature' yet inhibited from achieving it in word or action. The play's world is 'a verbal civilization', in which Hamlet is reduced ultimately to 'silence'. A highly perceptive article—one of the most notable of the year—has come from William Frost[1] on the opening scene of *Lear*. He notes the large part played by rituals of all kinds in Elizabethan drama and their relation to the essential character of acting, and sees too their limiting effect: ritual lessens individuation of character and induces a feeling of 'mechanization'; a sudden introduction of ritual can make an easy but ultimately disturbing theatrical impression. The heavy ritualization of the first scene of *Lear* is set off by the naturalistic beginning and ending of the scene and, more profoundly, by the mock-rituals and hints of ritual in the rest of the play. Finally Lear and Cordelia are figures altogether apart from ritual, "a pair of jailbirds and losers" who are appropriately forgotten by Albany during the ritualized action of the sub-plot in Act V. The ending here is contrasted with the concluding rituals of *Hamlet*, *Othello* and *Antony and Cleopatra*. An ingenious attempt to explain Cordelia's "singularly graceless and offhand" reply to Lear's demand for the profession of love has been made by Ivor Morris.[2] He argues that it exemplifies a kind of irony found elsewhere in Shakespeare—a taking of the viewpoint of the person addressed and a demonstration of its invalidity. Cordelia is pointing out that love cannot be measured like land. If we ask why this is not made plain in an aside, Morris replies that Shakespeare wanted us to be as surprised as Lear, and that perhaps Cordelia attempted to explain things at I, i, 126. The argument overlooks Cordelia's failure to comment until after Goneril's speech: it seems only the dreadful precedent of "Dearer than eyesight, space, and liberty" that induces the youngest daughter's refusal to take part in the rather shocking game. Briefer notes on this play have come from Mrs Winifred M. T. Nowottny,[3] who draws attention to "Lear's habit of asking questions" and sees the play's movement as towards "revelation through suffering (rather than redemption through suffering)", from F. W. Bradbrook,[4] who finds an echo of Shylock in Cordelia's reference to "my bond", and from Karl Hammerle,[5] who notes echoes of the play in *The Return of the Native*. Richard Flatter[6] has argued that the Hecate-scene in *Macbeth* is indubitably Shakespeare's, as being central to the play and altogether superior in writing to the speech of Hecate in *The Witch*. M. D. W. Jeffreys[7] comments on the composite character of the Weird Sisters in an article which is in places inadequately documented and which seems at one moment to base an argument on a Capell stage-direction. Christopher Gillie[8] argues that Banquo's function must be seen in relation to those of Macbeth, Ross and Macduff: Banquo's "equivocation" is thus presented against a background of a "variety of moral attitudes". R. P. Draper[9] links *Timon* with the Last Plays,

[1] 'Shakespeare's Rituals and the Opening of *King Lear*', *Hudson Review*, x (Winter 1957–8), 577–85.

[2] 'Cordelia and Lear', *Shakespeare Quarterly*, VIII (Spring 1957), 140–58.

[3] 'Lear's Questions', *Shakespeare Survey*, 10 (1957), 90–7.

[4] 'Shylock and King Lear', *Notes and Queries*, CCII (April 1957), 142–3.

[5] 'Transpositionen aus Shakespeares *King Lear* in Thomas Hardys *Return of the Native*', *Studies in English Language and Literature Presented to Professor Dr Karl Brunner*, pp. 58–73.

[6] 'Who wrote the Hecate-scene?', *Shakespeare-Jahrbuch*, XCIII (1957), 196–210.

[7] 'The Weird Sisters in Macbeth', *English Studies in Africa*, I (March 1958), 43–54.

[8] 'Banquo and Edgar—Character or Function?', *Essays in Criticism*, VII (July 1957), 322–4. Gillie is here replying to Leo Kirschbaum's article of the same title, *ibid.* pp. 1–21. F. W. Bateson, *ibid.* pp. 324–5, supporting Kirschbaum, suggests that James I would not have liked to see equivocation in Banquo.

[9] 'Timon of Athens', *Shakespeare Quarterly*, VIII (Spring 1957), 195–200.

but expresses this idea oddly in saying that Alcibiades "seems to foreshadow the regenerative theme". Comments on *Antony and Cleopatra* have come from Maurice Charney[1] and Sylvan Barnet.[2] Charney sees the pattern of Antony's tragedy reflected in images relating to his sword, to lowness and height, and to dissolution: he rightly brings out the phallic as well as the military significance of the sword-imagery. Barnet traces *anagnorisis* and *peripeteia* in the deaths of Antony, Cleopatra and Enobarbus: in such an argument it is odd to find Cleopatra's death called 'triumphant'. With special reference to the scene of Volumnia's pleading, Hermann Heuer[3] compares Shakespeare with Plutarch, Amyot and North, and finds that the dramatist emphasizes the 'unnatural' in Coriolanus's treachery and introduces a note of 'mystery' into the character: no mention is made of possibly satiric overtones in the presentation of Volumnia. Finally on the Roman plays we should note J. C. Maxwell's[4] packed survey of twentieth-century critical writing on the subject, and T. J. B. Spencer's[5] series of brilliant *aperçus* on the relation of Shakespeare's use of the Roman theme to general Renascence views of the ancient world.

Prominent among general studies during the year is L. C. Knights' British Academy Lecture,[6] which links Shakespeare's 'political' thinking to a tradition (powerful in the Middle Ages, but of greater antiquity) according to which the laws of society were based on a sense of oneness with other human beings as individuals. Shakespeare, Knights suggests, was not an illustrator of abstract principles but a man whose 'general' thinking was inextricably bound up with his sense of the human person. The wide range of reference in this lecture, and the sobriety of its tone, do not disguise a sense of urgency in the writing: for this critic Shakespeare remains a part of humane studies. William M. Schutte[7] has given a full commentary on the Shakespeare-passage in Joyce's *Ulysses*, with an indication of the importance of Joyce's knowledge of Shakespeare (for which he was largely dependent on Lee, Brandes and Harris) among the materials of the book. In three lectures relating Shakespeare and Jonson, S. Musgrove[8] emphasizes Jonson's tribute to Shakespeare, suggests that the two poets exercised a reciprocal influence on one another in the writing of *Lear* and *Volpone*, and usefully underlines the 'Elizabethan' aspect of Jonson's fancy. Robert Fricker[9] draws attention to Shakespeare's increasing mastery of visual effect, used sometimes for demonstration of character, sometimes for expression of the play's total idea (as in the banquet-scene in *Macbeth*). R. G. Howarth[10] has published some broadcast talks in which there is robust lopping away of the complex and the ambivalent. John Lawlor[11] has suggested that, despite recent studies of imagery, older suppositions concerning Shakespeare may con-

---

[1] 'Shakespeare's Antony: A Study of Image Themes', *Studies in Philology*, LIV (April 1957), 149–61.

[2] 'Recognition and Reversal in *Antony and Cleopatra*', *Shakespeare Quarterly*, VIII (Summer 1957), 331–4.

[3] 'From Plutarch to Shakespeare', *Shakespeare Survey*, 10 (1957), 50–9.

[4] 'Shakespeare's Roman Plays: 1900–1956', *ibid.* pp. 1–11.

[5] 'Shakespeare and the Elizabethan Romans', *ibid.* pp. 27–38.

[6] *Shakespeare's Politics: With some Reflections on the Nature of Tradition* (Annual Shakespeare Lecture of the British Academy, 1957).

[7] *Joyce and Shakespeare: A Study in the Meaning of Ulysses* (New Haven: Yale University Press, 1957).

[8] *Shakespeare and Jonson: The Macmillan Brown Lectures 1957* (Auckland University College, 1957).

[9] 'Das szenische Bild bei Shakespeare', *Annales Universitatis Saraviensis* (*Philosophie-Lettres*), v (1956), 227–40.

[10] *Shakespeare by Air: Broadcasts to Schools* (Sydney: Angus and Robertson, 1957).

[11] 'Mind and Hand: Some Reflections on the Study of Shakespeare's Imagery', *Shakespeare Quarterly*, VIII (Spring 1957), 179–93.

tinue to exert a limiting influence, and that there is the problem of relating image-study to a consideration of what can be apprehended in the theatre: the first point is not, however, made fully explicit and the second is merely raised. Ernest Schanzer[1] has noted reversions to earlier styles (often for comic effect) and anticipations of later in various Shakespeare plays, and draws attention to some extreme cases where we must assume a later insertion or a survival of an early version. Lorentz Eckhoff[2] finds that Shakespeare gives approval to stoically-minded characters. Horst Oppel[3] traces the increasingly deep exploration of grief in Shakespeare's plays, noting how he differs from his predecessors in putting the stress on the grieving character, and how grief can go along with a growth in wisdom. Reinhold Schneider[4] discusses the idea of authority, human and divine, as presented by Shakespeare.

Two volumes devoted to extracts from Shakespeare criticism should here be noted. Ernst Th. Sehrt[5] has edited a collection of German translations of well-known pieces of English critical writing, extending from Pope's Preface to an extract from E. M. W. Tillyard's *Shakespeare's History Plays*, and F. E. Halliday[6] has brought out a new edition of his *Shakespeare and his Critics*, omitting the original Part I and substantially adding to the excerpts from critics in Part II. With these books may be linked Rudolf Stamm's[7] remarkable survey of contributions to research on English literature from the sixteenth century to the nineteenth, covering the years 1935–55: forty-three pages are given to Shakespeare studies, and these form a useful annotated bibliography. Inevitably Stamm is selective, and he rightly does not disguise his preferences and judgments. Other contributions to the history of Shakespeare criticism have been made by Hanns Braun,[8] noting Lessing's abundant use of Shakespeare's practice in his critical writing; by Sylvan Barnet,[9] criticizing Coleridge's view that Shakespeare's puns are to be justified through their appropriateness to the character speaking; and by P. A. W. Collins,[10] sketching and evaluating Shaw's opinions on Shakespeare. Finally we should note two contributions on the translation of Shakespeare: Edvard Beyer[11] has surveyed the problems facing the translator of Shakespeare into any of the Scandinavian languages, and has found among Norwegian versions a special merit in that of Henrik Rytter; René Pruvost[12] has paid tribute to André Koszul for his attempt to give to a French reader "à peu près la même impression que celle que l'Anglais d'aujourd'hui reçoit en écoutant le texte de l'original".

[1] 'Atavism and Anticipation in Shakespeare's Style', *Essays in Criticism*, VII (July 1957), 242–56.
[2] 'Stoicism in Shakespeare...and elsewhere', *Studies in English Language and Literature Presented to Professor Dr Karl Brunner*, pp. 32–42.
[3] 'Shakespeare und das Leid', *Shakespeare-Jahrbuch*, XCIII (1957), 38–81.
[4] 'Das Bild der Herrschaft in Shakespeares Dramen', *ibid*. pp. 9–37.
[5] *Shakespeare: Englische Essays aus drei Jahrhunderten zum Verständnis seiner Werke* (Stuttgart: Alfred Kröner Verlag, 1958).
[6] *Shakespeare and his Critics* (Duckworth, 1958).
[7] *Englische Literatur* (Bern: A. Francke, 1957).
[8] 'Shakespeare als Nothelfer der Kritik', *Shakespeare-Jahrbuch*, XCIII (1957), 82–8.
[9] 'Coleridge on Puns: A Note to his Shakespeare Criticism', *Journal of English and Germanic Philology*, LVI (October 1957), 602–9.
[10] 'Shaw on Shakespeare', *Shakespeare Quarterly*, VIII (Winter 1957), 1–13.
[11] *Problemer omkring oversettelser av Shakespeares dramatikk* (Bergen: A. S. John Griegs Boktrykkeri, 1956).
[12] 'André Koszul et la Traduction', *Bulletin de la Faculté des Lettres de Strasbourg*, XXXVI (November 1957), 145–54.

2. SHAKESPEARE'S LIFE, TIMES AND STAGE

reviewed by R. A. FOAKES

In what is probably his most entertaining and useful book[1] to date on Shakespeare, F. E. Halliday traces the growth of various attitudes to the dramatist from his eclipse in the Commonwealth period to the adulation of the nineteenth century. There are lively chapters on the squabbles of eighteenth-century editors, on Garrick's Stratford festival and the cult of "Avonian Willy, bard divine", on the Shakespeare Gallery, Bowdler, Collier and the Shakespeare Society, the tercentenary celebrations, and on Fleay and the disintegrators. The whole is cleverly linked together, and makes an amusing guide to bardolatry, as well as providing an introduction to what every student should know about fashions in taste, as these have affected the editing and acting of Shakespeare's plays. Halliday neatly demolishes the claims of Baconians and Oxfordians in his last chapters; two American cryptographers go further, and make a detailed analysis[2] of the supposed ciphers which have been used to 'reveal' Bacon or others as the author of Shakespeare's plays. This is often fascinating, and would be thoroughly entertaining, did not the authors seem to take themselves and the whole business a little too seriously; but it is a notable record of human eccentricity, of talent and energy wasted on dredging rivers, opening tombs, and pursuing a variety of illusory clues. One might think that such onslaughts would bring the Anti-Stratfordians to repent; but they do not cease to put forward with huge solemnity their claims.[3] Perhaps the Friedmans were justified in composing a serious criticism, but one cannot help feeling that Halliday has the best word in describing all this as "matter for a psychologist and a May morning".[4]

Perhaps it is the special perspective gained by working at a distance and in an alien language that makes continental scholars bolder than English ones in finding topical allusions and in pressing their claims. This can be a virtue and a vice; it is both in Henryk Zbierski's *Shakespeare and the 'War of the Theatres'*.[5] His general argument is quite a good one, that the war of the theatres should be seen primarily not as a poetomachia, a quarrel between Jonson and Marston, but in terms of the rivalry between the public and private theatres. It is a pity that he had to rely on outdated books or popular résumés, and had not seen Harbage's *Shakespeare and the Rival Traditions*; in spite of this handicap he presents his case forcefully. But in his desire to find allusions to Jonson and the whole affair in Shakespeare, he accumulates hypotheses as if several established a fact; and in his anxiety to brand Jonson as "enemy number one...of the popular theatre", he forgets that Jonson was writing for the King's Men again by 1604. As a whole the book is tendentious, to say the least.

Gustav Ungerer's well-argued section on 'Shakespeare and Spain' in the latter part of his

---

[1] *The Cult of Shakespeare* (Duckworth, 1957).

[2] William F. and Elizebeth S. Friedman, *The Shakespearean Ciphers Examined* (Cambridge University Press, 1957).

[3] A second edition of William Kent and others, *Edward de Vere 17th Earl of Oxford, the Real Shakespeare* (The Shakespeare Fellowship, 1957), has appeared.

[4] H. A. Shield continues his unexciting exploration of Shakespeare's social connections in 'Links with Shakespeare, xv', *Notes and Queries* (December 1957), pp. 522–3.

[5] Poznań: Państowe Wydawnictwo Naukowe, 1957.

book[1] is, to a lesser degree, open to the same kind of criticism. He has amassed some important information concerning Antonio Pérez and his visits to England, and shows that this extravagant and unstable figure made a great impact on English courtiers as a speaker, letter-writer and politician. He may well be right in thinking that Shakespeare is glancing at Pérez in Don Armado, who certainly seems to parody a number of the oddities for which the Spaniard was noted. But the evidence is hardly strong enough to support his further claim that Shakespeare knew Spanish, had access to the letters of Pérez as these circulated, and satirized their style. His general case is a strong one, however, though he feels it necessary to assume a revision of *Love's Labour's Lost* in 1598 when the allusions to Pérez were, he claims, added.

The major discovery of the year has a bearing on this play; T. W. Baldwin has edited, with facsimiles, two leaves of a bookseller's accounts found in the binding of a book printed in 1637.[2] Both leaves name titles, and on the earlier, dated 1603, is a list of plays which includes *The Merchant of Venice*, *The Taming of a Shrew*, *Love's Labour's Lost* and "loves labor won". It thus reinforces the evidence from Meres's *Palladis Tamia* that Shakespeare wrote a play known as *Love's Labour's Won*; if the other titles in this new list and in Meres are eliminated, then the strongest candidates for identification, assuming it to be a known play, are *Much Ado* and *All's Well*. Baldwin argues strongly that it is an early version of the latter, but there is no real evidence. The many other titles of all kinds of books are of considerable bibliographical interest, and may provide evidence of some hitherto unknown editions, as for instance of Deloney's *Gentle Craft*, which is extant only in an edition of 1637.

Some of the most important work on Shakespeare in recent years has been on his sources, and the extent of his reading. It is appropriate that the first part of Geoffrey Bullough's *Narrative and Dramatic Sources of Shakespeare*[3] should appear concurrently with Kenneth Muir's *Shakespeare's Sources*[4] and the New Arden edition of the plays. It is the first of five promised volumes, which will assemble in good texts the main sources and analogues of Shakespeare's plays and poems, and deals with seven early plays and the two narrative poems. In a judicious introduction to each of these the editor discusses the relevance of the sources to Shakespeare's text, and includes extracts from those he judged it unnecessary to print in full. A very handsomely made and well-planned book is completed by a useful bibliography. Bullough recognizes that a book of this kind is bound to displease some scholars. He has not included everything; he rejects, for instance, Muir's theory that Mouffet's *Of the Silkworms, and their Flies*, was an important source for parts of *A Midsummer Night's Dream*; but he has printed more than could have been hoped for, and this volume contains, among much else, Warner's translation of *Menaechmi*, Gascoigne's *Supposes*, and Brooke's *Romeus and Juliet*. He has not given Latin originals, except of Ovid's *Fasti* for *The Rape of Lucrece*, but translations; in a number of cases these are translations which Shakespeare used, or may have used, and although it would have

[1] *Anglo-Spanish Relations in Tudor Literature* (Bern: A. Francke, 1956).

[2] *Shakespeare's Love's Labor's Won* (Carbondale: Southern Illinois University Press, 1957). It is worth noting one error in transcription: Baldwin reads "1 farest 8d pener", where the facsimile shows "1 foresta(?or) de penu(?a)".

[3] London: Routlege and Kegan Paul; New York: Columbia University Press, 1957. Volume 1 deals with early comedies, up to *The Merchant of Venice*, the narrative poems, and *Romeo and Juliet*.

[4] Reviewed in *Shakespeare Survey*, 11 (1958), 143.

been helpful to have more Latin texts, Bullough is providing an immensely useful and wholly admirable working collection of source-material. He may, in any case, take comfort from the latest view put forward in the perennial controversy over Shakespeare's 'small Latin'; J. Dover Wilson argues strongly[1] that, though the dramatist knew some Latin, he generally turned to English translations for his borrowings. Hereward T. Price[2] cites, as evidence that Shakespeare knew Latin, a signature, probably genuine, in a copy of W. Lambarde's *Archaionomia* in the Folger Library; but this hardly weighs against Dover Wilson's conclusion.

A number of new parallels with Shakespeare have been recorded: the similarities noted by Inga-Stina Ekeblad[3] between *Selimus* and *King Lear*, by J. W. Lever[4] between the prefatory verses in Chapman's Homer and Sonnet LV, and by Kenneth Muir[5] between Henry Swinburne's *Brief Treatise of Testaments* and *Hamlet*, may be significant; but R. L. Eagle[6] strains credulity in tracking analogies between Catullus and Shakespeare. I. B. Cauthen[7] traces the word 'flibberti-gibbet' to *The Castle of Perseverance*, and thinks it is used in *Lear* in a rich sense that was not simply derived from Harsnett. Kenneth Muir[8] has found an interesting link with *Pericles* in Bernal Diaz's *Conquest of New Spain*. In drawing attention to connections between *Trappolin Supposed a Prince*, an English version of a *commedia dell'arte* seen by Aston Cokain in 1632, and *Measure for Measure*, Helen A. Kaufman[9] suggests that a comparison may help to restore balance to criticism of Shakespeare's play by bringing out its real merriment and showing how much less seriously it would have been regarded in the early seventeenth century than now.

Some interesting work has also been done on known sources. Robert Ornstein[10] argues that Shakespeare found in Seneca's Moral Essays a "compelling viewpoint which served as a framework in which to order Plutarch's diffuse materials" for *Julius Caesar*, and which suggested an ironic view of Brutus. Rather less convincingly, Karl F. Thompson[11] would see the death of *Richard II* as a martyrdom in popular terms, in the manner in which it is presented by Foxe. Robert Adger Law[12] seeks rather mechanically to show that the use of sources in *Henry VIII* reflects dual authorship of the play; and Matthew P. McDiarmid[13] suggests that the author of *The Troublesome Reign of King John* borrowed from Matthew Paris, and that the priority of Shakespeare's play cannot be argued from his use of this source. Both of these articles are prompted by recent New Arden editions, as is also Robert Adger Law's note 'On the Date of *King John*',[14] in which he restates the case for placing it in or about 1595. One other comment on dating concerns *Othello*;

[1] 'Shakespeare's "Small Latin"—How Much?', *Shakespeare Survey*, 10 (1957), 12–26.
[2] 'Shakespeare's Classical Scholarship', *Review of English Studies*, n.s. IX (February 1958), 54–5.
[3] '*King Lear* and *Selimus*', *Notes and Queries* (May 1957), pp. 193–4.
[4] 'Chapman and Shakespeare', *Notes and Queries* (March 1958), pp. 99–100.
[5] 'Henry Swinburne and Shakespeare', *Notes and Queries* (July 1957), pp. 285–6.
[6] 'Shakespeare and Catullus', *Notes and Queries* (December 1957), pp. 521–2.
[7] '"The Foule Flibbertigibbet." *King Lear*, III. v. 113, IV. i. 60', *Notes and Queries* (March 1958), pp. 98–9.
[8] 'A Mexican Marina', *English Studies*, XXXIX (April 1958), 74–5.
[9] '*Trappolin Supposed a Prince* and *Measure for Measure*', *Modern Language Quarterly*, XVIII (June 1957), 113–24.
[10] 'Seneca and the Political Drama of *Julius Caesar*', *Journal of English and Germanic Philology*, LVII (January 1958), 51–6.
[11] 'Richard II, Martyr', *Shakespeare Quarterly*, VIII (Spring 1957), 159–66.
[12] 'Holinshed and *Henry the Eighth*', *Texas Studies in English*, XXXVI (1957), 3–11.
[13] 'Concerning *The Troublesome Reign of King John*', *Notes and Queries* (October 1957), pp. 435–8.
[14] *Studies in Philology*, LIV (April 1957), 119–27.

Marvin Rosenberg[1] believes that Queen Anne's taste, as reflected in Jonson's *Masque of Blackness*, may have influenced Shakespeare in his choice of a Moor as his hero for *Othello* in 1605.

Two doctors provide useful explanations of minor difficulties. J. Dover Wilson[2] cites a letter from one who thinks that Richard III's accusation of witchcraft against Hastings, made after he had eaten strawberries, was carefully planned by the king, who knew he could produce an 'urticarial rash' by eating the fruit. The other, Harry Keil, learnedly argues[3] that the

> round little worm
> Prick'd from the lazy finger of a maid

in *Romeo and Juliet* is a reference to the parasite which causes scabies; he supports his case with a wealth of medical and philological material. The troublesome "school of night" passage in *Love's Labour's Lost* has provoked J. H. P. Pafford[4] to offer another emendation, to "shield of night"; and Hilda M. Hulme[5] indicates the full sense of "copy" as *copia*, plenty, in a passage in *The Comedy of Errors*. A more generally interpretative article by Sholom J. Kahn[6] is based upon the differences between the stage-directions in the Quarto and Folio texts of *Lear* regarding Lear's entries; he thinks that these indicate a difference "in the interpretations of two actors" concerning the exact point at which Lear becomes mad. However questionable this view, he acutely perceives that the movement from verse to prose in the king's speeches marks a progression to a climax which an actor should observe.

Shakespeare's theatre receives handsome tribute in Irwin Smith's splendidly produced book,[7] which includes a series of scale drawings of J. C. Adams' reconstruction of the Globe, designed to aid others in making models. It also presents admirably the findings of modern scholarship regarding this theatre, and, among its numerous illustrations, includes a new map of *c.* 1620 which affords further evidence that the Globe was situated to the south of Maiden Lane. Although Smith has read the critics of Adams, and accepts one or two modifications of his theories, he is still an ardent disciple; and he gives further currency to some very dubious assumptions, accepting, for instance, the theory that outdoor scenes took place on the platform, indoor scenes on the inner or upper stages. So in his full analyses of the staging of *Romeo and Juliet* and *2 Henry IV*, he allots long scenes (II, ii of the latter, for example) to one of the rear stages because they appear to be indoor scenes, or in order to comply with what he asserts was a rule of the Elizabethan theatre, that "a change of dramatic place was accompanied and indicated by a change of stage". He allows that the action probably moved from the inner stage to the platform in such scenes, but his claim that it was conventional "for the last actors to move back into the rear-stage" as the scene drew to an end, so restoring the illusion of an indoor scene, cannot be established from the text, and half-destroys his general principle; it is doubtful whether Shakespeare ever sought to create the sort of illusions that Smith and Adams have in mind. But this is a well-written,

---

[1] 'On the Dating of *Othello*', *English Studies*, XXXIX (April 1958), 72–4.

[2] 'A Note on *Richard III*: The Bishop of Ely's Strawberries', *Modern Language Review*, LII (October 1957), 563–4.

[3] 'Scabies and the Queen Mab Passage in *Romeo and Juliet*', *Journal of the History of Ideas*, XVIII (June 1957), 394–410.

[4] '"Schoole of Night" (*Love's Labour's Lost*, IV. iii. 252)', *Notes and Queries* (April 1957), p. 143.

[5] 'On the Meaning of "Copy" (*Comedy of Errors*, V. i. 62)', *Neophilologus*, XXIV (January 1958), 73–4.

[6] '"Enter Lear Mad"', *Shakespeare Quarterly*, VIII (Summer 1957), 311–29.

[7] *Shakespeare's Globe Playhouse, A Modern Reconstruction* (New York: Charles Scribner's Sons, 1956).

sensibly argued book, and if it enters into speculation about the inner and upper stages, so does everyone; Richard Hosley's rejection[1] of Adams's principle regarding exterior and interior scenes seems entirely justified, but it is not so easy to accept his view that the stage-façade of the Globe was exactly like that shown in De Witt's drawing of the Swan theatre, and that the primary use of the upper-stage was for spectators.

William A. Armstrong[2] sheds light on the meaning of 'canopy' in Elizabethan usage, as signifying both a covered chair of state and, more simply, a curtain. The history of the use of classical costume in Shakespeare's plays has been examined by W. M. Merchant.[3] Walter Sorell[4] contributes a genial survey of the kinds of dance which might have been used in Shakespeare's plays; and Jean Jacquot's lavish *Les Fêtes de la Renaissance*[5] includes a suggestive essay by Frederick W. Sternfeld on the symbolic value of music in late plays of Shakespeare that were produced at court. He cites Jean Bodin's *Six Books of the Commonweale*, translated in 1606, which finds in the harmony of music a symbol of harmony in the state, and argues that music is used in this way in *The Winter's Tale* and *The Tempest* especially, where the unions of the young, idealized lovers may be related to the proposed marriages of Prince Henry and Princess Elizabeth. This volume will be of major interest to historians of the stage; it contains essays on Chapman, Dekker, Jonson, on Lord Mayor's shows, and numerous other articles on European masques, pageants and court-plays, chiefly of the period between 1570 and 1630.

The problems of producing Shakespeare in the modern theatre are a major concern of *Shakespeare-Jahrbuch* for 1957, to which a number of distinguished scholars with experience of producing and men of the theatre contribute essays. Several are concerned with the trend towards simplicity in the staging of Shakespeare's plays during this century. Oskar Wälterlin[6] comments from his own experience on the effect this trend has had in giving actors full scope for their art; Robert Speaight[7] writes on the influence of Poel and Granville-Barker. Alan S. Downer[8] considers the virtues and vices of commercial and academic productions in America, and notes how the former tend to remake Shakespeare "according to the demands of modern theatrical convention", the latter to see the plays as museum pieces. Hermann Herrey[9] also stresses the danger of imposing a vision upon Shakespeare; but he argues that the producer's task is to present the plays as living theatre, that the producer must come to terms with the nature of the modern theatre, and try within its conditions to bring out the intrinsic character of each play. His view would find support from Hans R. Linder,[10] who surveys a number of modern productions, and suggests that each theatre, presenting its individual interpretation, can achieve a valid expression of Shakespeare's art; Teo Otto[11] argues along similar lines in contrasting three

---

[1] 'Shakespeare's Use of a Gallery over the Stage', *Shakespeare Survey*, 10 (1957), 77–89.

[2] '"Canopy" in Elizabethan Theatrical Terminology', *Notes and Queries* (October 1957), pp. 433–4.

[3] 'Classical Costume in Shakespearian Productions', *Shakespeare Survey*, 10 (1957), 71–6.

[4] 'Shakespeare and the Dance', *Shakespeare Quarterly*, VIII (Summer 1957), 367–84.

[5] Paris: Éditions du Centre National de la Recherche Scientifique, 1956. Sternfeld's essay occupies pp. 319–33.

[6] 'Randglossen zur Shakespeare-Inszenierung', *Shakespeare-Jahrbuch*, XCIII (1957), 128–40.

[7] 'The Pioneers', *ibid.* pp. 170–4.

[8] 'Shakespeare in the Contemporary American Theater', *ibid.* pp. 154–69.

[9] 'Shakespeare-Interpretation auf der Bühne', *ibid.* pp. 114–25.

[10] 'Shakespeare als Test: Notizen zum heutigen Theater', *ibid.* pp. 89–97.

[11] 'Shakespeare-Aufführungen und Bühnenbild', *ibid.* pp. 141–4.

productions of the last thirty years, and claiming that each generation can find a solution to the perennial problem of comprehending Shakespeare's vision, entering into his world. The idea that works of genius reveal their power in their adaptability to the fashions of each period informs Siegfried Melchinger's essay,[1] in which he welcomes the influence of modern drama on current methods of recreating Shakespeare's plays on the stage. Finally, Nevill Coghill[2] stresses the virtues of spontaneity, scholarship, and fine elocution in university productions in England.

Elsewhere A. S. Knowland[3] emphasizes that a dramatic script "has to be brought to life by the interpreters", and that a producer's guidance is necessary to ensure this. Such a view is a feature of most of the *Shakespeare-Jahrbuch* essays, and it appears also in many of the ever more numerous reviews of current productions. The most valuable of these, as combining a sensitive observation of detail with an intimate concern for the plays performed, are Richard David's review[4] of *Titus Andronicus* and *Othello* at Stratford-upon-Avon, and Muriel St Clare Byrne's account[5] of *The Tempest* at the same theatre. The Old Vic's season is treated enthusiastically by this same reviewer,[6] who is very sympathetic towards its stylized *Two Gentlemen*. The American festivals at Stratford, Connecticut; San Diego, California; Ashland, Oregon; Toronto, and Stratford, Ontario, receive tribute;[7] indeed, Arnold Edinborough thinks the last is now not only in "the big league", but "has no serious rival for the pennant". It is useful to have on record what has been achieved at Antioch College,[8] where all the plays have now been presented during five seasons. Alice Griffin[9] reviews the New York season, and James G. McManaway[10] has an interesting survey of the wide range of experiment in staging, settings and costumes in American productions of 1955-6. Recent film versions of Shakespeare's plays, and German productions, notably of *Coriolanus* and all the dark comedies, are surveyed by Karl Brinkman.[11] Articles of interest to historians of the theatre include O. F. Babler's note[12] on Czechoslovakian versions of *A Midsummer Night's Dream*, W. T. Hasting's account[13] of Shakespearian productions in

[1] 'Shakespeare und das moderne Welttheater', *ibid.* pp. 98-113.

[2] 'University Contributions to Shakespeare Production in England', *ibid.* pp. 175-85.

[3] 'Shakespeare in the Theatre', *Essays in Criticism*, VII (July 1957), 325-30.

[4] 'Drams of Eale', *Shakespeare Survey*, 10 (1957), 126-34.

[5] '*The Tempest* at Stratford-on-Avon', *Theatre Notebook*, XII (Autumn 1957), 25-9.

[6] 'The Shakespeare Season at the Old Vic, 1956-57, and Stratford-upon-Avon, 1957', *Shakespeare Quarterly*, VIII (Autumn 1957), 461-97.

[7] Claire McGlinchee, 'Stratford, Connecticut, Shakespeare Festival, 1957', *Shakespeare Quarterly*, VIII (Autumn 1957), 507-10; Charles Frederick Johnson, 'San Diego National Shakespeare Festival', *ibid.* pp. 531-4; Robert D. Horn, 'Shakespeare at Ashland, Oregon, 1957', *ibid.* pp. 527-30; Earle Grey, 'Shakespeare Festival, Toronto, Canada', *Shakespeare Survey*, 10 (1957), 111-14; Arnold Edinborough, 'Canada's Permanent Elizabethan Theatre', *Shakespeare Quarterly*, VIII (Autumn 1957), 511-14.

[8] Robert G. Shedd, 'Shakespeare at Antioch, 1957: Past Record and Present Achievement', *Shakespeare Quarterly*, VIII (Autumn 1957), 521-5.

[9] 'Shakespeare in New York City, 1956-57', *ibid.* pp. 515-19.

[10] 'Shakespearian Productions in America in 1955-6', *Shakespeare-Jahrbuch*, XCIII (1957), 145-53.

[11] 'Filmbericht' and 'Bühnenbericht 1956/7', *ibid.* pp. 216-27.

[12] 'Shakespeare's *Midsummer Night's Dream* in Czech and Slovakian', *Notes and Queries* (April 1957), 151-3.

[13] 'Shakespeare in Providence', *Shakespeare Quarterly*, VIII (Summer 1957), 335-51.

Providence, Rhode Island, Dov Vardi's review[1] of translations into Hebrew, and Ray B. Browne's commentary[2] on nineteenth-century popular songs based on Shakespeare.

Two general introductory books on Shakespeare deserve notice. In one, Karl Brunner[3] rather drily aims to summarize the results of modern scholarship for the common reader, and is concerned only with facts; he has a note, which is more descriptive than critical, on each of the plays, and treats *Troilus and Cressida* among the tragedies. The other, by A. G. H. Bachrach,[4] is mainly critical, and concentrates especially on *Henry IV*, *Twelfth Night*, *Hamlet*, and *The Winter's Tale*. Horst Oppel has written a long and thorough survey[5] of recent German research on various aspects of Shakespeare's work, relating it to what has been done by British and American scholars. A useful manual[6] for teachers and pupils has been produced by W. A. Illsley, in which critical and theatrical terms are explained, Shakespeare's stage is illustrated, and advice is given on setting and sitting examinations. It is intended mainly for oversea territories, but the author hopes that it will be used in England. If it were not limited by its mechanical critical treatment of the plays in terms of plot and character, and its strange reading list which recommends inferior editions and Stopford Brooke as the best in critical reading, one would share his hopes. If the General Certificate of Education Ordinary Level papers are as confined as this suggests, the more is J. H. Walter's essay[7] to be valued, which stresses the need for teachers to help a child to see a play as a whole, and to keep foremost in mind "its essential unity and the idea of production".

3. TEXTUAL STUDIES

reviewed by JAMES G. McMANAWAY

The place of honour in the field of bibliographical and textual studies must be given to the third volume of W. W. Greg's *Bibliography*,[8] which exceeds all expectations. Devoted primarily to the collections of plays, it gives a formal description of the Pavier-Jaggard nonce collection of 1619 and the four Shakespeare Folios (pp. 1107–21; see also pp. 1249–58), with a succinct account of significant irregularities and of variant issues and reprints. The Appendix reprints wholly or in part booksellers' lists, early play catalogues (indexed), and prefaces to plays; it also describes early private collections and gives publication lists, actor lists, and author lists (the last three indexed). Then in eighteen sections there is a wealth of information about such subjects as authors, dedications and commendations, prologues and epilogues (first lines), adaptations and drolls, court performances, people connected with the theatres such as producers, musicians, and choreographers, title-page mottoes, "Quorum fit mentio", and "Notabilia". This is

---

[1] 'Shakespeare in Hebrew', *Jewish Quarterly*, IV (Spring 1957), 5–8.

[2] 'Shakespeare in the Nineteenth-Century Songsters', *Shakespeare Quarterly*, VIII (Spring 1957), 207–18.

[3] *William Shakespeare* (Tübingen: Max Niemeyer, 1957).

[4] *Naar Het Hem Leek...een Inleiding tot Shakespeare in vijf brieven* (The Hague: Bert Bakker, 1957).

[5] 'Stand und Aufgaben der deutschen Shakespeare-Forschung', *Deutsche Vierteljahrsschrift*, XXXII (1958), 113–71.

[6] *A Shakespeare Manual for Schools* (Cambridge University Press, 1957).

[7] 'Shakespeare in Schools', *Shakespeare Survey*, 10 (1957), 107–10.

[8] Sir Walter W. Greg, *A Bibliography of the English Printed Drama to the Restoration*, vol. III. (London: Oxford University Press for the Bibliographical Society, 1957.)

treasure trove indeed, and there are, besides, more than a score of reproductions of engraved portraits of the playwrights.

The New Shakespeare marches towards completion with the publication of two new titles, *Troilus and Cressida* and *Timon of Athens*. The first,[1] save for C. B. Young's Stage History, is credited exclusively to Alice Walker, whose substantial contributions to our understanding of the textual history and the bibliographical peculiarities of the play made her the logical editor. It is generally agreed that Q is the sole authority for I, i, 1 on to I, ii, 235 (the end of the third page of F) and that thereafter F was printed from a copy of Q that had been corrected by reference to Shakespeare's foul papers. The source of Q was a transcript of these same papers, but whether made by Shakespeare or a scribe is a matter of controversy. Alexander and Sisson, among others, attribute it to the author and so tend to give preference in their texts to the Q readings, where F varies. Chambers thought otherwise, as does Miss Walker, who makes a point of the omission of and confusion in speech tags as signs that the scribe first copied the dialogue and added the speakers' names later. Her position is vulnerable, as is indicated by Greg's explanation of an error in Q at IV, v, 94.[2] F, evidently correctly, reads:

> Halfe stints their strife, before their strokes begin.
> *Vlis.* They are oppos'd already.
> *Aga.* What Troian is that same that lookes so heauy?
> *Vlis.* The yongest Sonne of *Priam*....

Q, incorrectly:

> Halfe stints their strife, before their strokes begin.
> V*lisses*: what Troyan is that same that lookes so heauy?
> *Vlis.* The yongest sonne of *Priam*....

"The compositor", conjectures Greg, "apparently set the prefix for Ulysses but inadvertently omitted his one-line speech, continuing with that of Agamemnon, and the press reader, finding two consecutive speeches assigned to Ulysses, worked the first prefix into the text as a vocative." In one passage, which Greg (p. 346, note 20) has called "perhaps the crucial case", Miss Walker, "contrary to custom", rejects F's "Corrects the ill Aspects of Planets euill" (I, iii, 92) in favour of Q's "Corrects the influence of euill Planets". It is difficult to explain this variant except in terms of editorial revision in the manuscript source of Q. If the editorial pen was that of Shakespeare, equal authority may attach to other readings unique in Q. Miss Walker has exercised some of the liberties she has elsewhere demanded for the modern editor of Shakespeare, especially in the section of text dependent wholly on Q and in many readings left untouched by other editors in which Q and F agree but in which she suspects corruption at the hands of Eld's compositor *A* and Jaggard's *B*. In my opinion, some of these, as at IV, iv, 37, are genuine improvements; a few, such as I, ii, 23, are wrong; and others suggest a desire to produce a smoother and more regular text than perhaps Shakespeare wrote.

The second play, *Timon*,[3] is made especially useful to the general reader by Maxwell's pro-

---

[1] Alice Walker, ed., *Troilus and Cressida* (The New Shakespeare, Cambridge University Press, 1957).

[2] *The Shakespeare First Folio* (Oxford University Press, 1955), p. 349, note A. Greg thinks Shakespeare prepared the transcript, introducing into it some deliberate and perhaps other inadvertent changes.

[3] J. C. Maxwell, ed., *The Life of Timon of Athens* (The New Shakespeare, Cambridge University Press, 1957).

fusion of glossarial and explanatory notes. The play might not have survived had not Jaggard's copyright difficulties about *Troilus* left a vacant space in F. How Shakespeare's foul papers happened to be available to fill the gap is almost beyond speculation, for the play is clearly in an unfinished state[1]. Even so, the text, which occupies leaves gg 1 verso—Hh 6 recto, was not long enough to require the use of the last page of the second quire, which is left blank.

Some of the short lines, mislineations, and prose passages printed in F as verse puzzled earlier editors but can now be recognized as the expedients of compositors (or a compositor) who are trying to fill up space. Maxwell has profited by this knowledge to restore many lines to the form presumably intended by Shakespeare, but he might have done even more without incurring the charge of recklessness. Thus after "He's opposite to humanity" at I, i, 275, he might have rearranged the concluding lines of the scene as blank verse. He is right, I think, in omitting the Senator's "I go sir" at II, i, 33, on the assumption that when preparing fair copy Shakespeare would have cancelled the speech. The same consideration should, in my opinion, have emboldened him to delete the superfluous words at I, ii, 95–7, which in his notes he characterizes as alternatives left standing (or inadequately cancelled) by Shakespeare.

Another edition of major importance is M. R. Ridley's *Othello*.[2] The Introduction and relevant appendices state and maintain the editor's interpretation of the textual evidence adroitly and persuasively and will be consulted for their method by all who deny or wish merely to test the thesis that certain plays in F were printed from corrected copies of quartos. Ridley believes that the Q text of *Othello* was printed from a private transcript of Shakespeare's foul papers made when the play was new and somehow acquired at a later date by Walkley; he thinks the Folio derives from a second transcript of the foul papers, probably prepared for Heminge and Condell, who edited it, incorporating "additions or alterations made by Shakespeare himself, to colour a colourless part, or actors' requests which he accepted". And he conjectures that "if the second transcript was made by the prompter", there would "be almost certainly some memorial contamination". In other words, Q is nearer to what Shakespeare first wrote, and, with the exception of accidental omissions, is the authoritative text. So Ridley returns to the tradition of Johnson and Malone, who also adhered more closely to Q than to F. Much of Ridley's argument is derived from Greg,[3] whose hints about Shakespearian revision he elaborates, and whose qualified dissent from some of Miss Walker's opinions[4] he turns into complete rejection. At the same time, he disagrees with Greg's derivation of F from the prompt-book, because it would have been prepared before there was time for memorial contamination, and because the prompt-book's stage-directions could never have agreed with those in F—he is driven to confess that he can offer no solution to the problem of F's stage-directions. Ridley makes a special plea for caution in substituting modern punctuation for that of copy texts. For readers interested in such matters, the introduction might have included with profit a modicum of bibliographical

---

[1] In his review of this edition, H. J. Oliver expresses his belief that the printer had mixed copy: part foul papers, and part transcript, and mentions the fact that Charlton Hinman has independently come to the conclusion that the manuscript was in two hands—see *Shakespeare Quarterly*, IX, 407.

[2] M. R. Ridley, ed., *Othello* (The New Arden, Methuen, 1958).

[3] *The Shakespeare First Folio*, pp. 408–11.

[4] Alice Walker, 'The 1622 Quarto and the First Folio Texts of *Othello*', *Shakespeare Survey*, 5 (1952), 16–24; *Othello*, in *Textual Problems of the First Folio* (Shakespeare Problems, VII, Cambridge University Press, 1953).

information. I note references to press corrections in Q at I, iii, 64 and IV, i, 77 and to a (?) contemporary MS. reading in the Devonshire–Huntington copy at II, i, 302, but there is no formal consideration of variant formes in Q or F (cf., for example, the problem of "and hell gnaw his bones" at IV, ii, 138 in F). Even more serious is the failure to take into account Miss Walker's demonstration that the progressive modernization by Q and F of –*t* to –*ed* or –'*d* in the past tense and past participle of certain weak verbs is, in Gregs' words, conclusive evidence that F was printed from a corrected copy of Q. Nevertheless, Ridley's textual theories about *Othello* must be given very serious consideration.

After Charlton Hinman's demonstration[1] that Jaggard cast off copy and then printed the First Folio of Shakespeare by formes, rather than *seriatim*, as had hitherto been tacitly assumed, it was natural that investigations would begin in order to discover whether this method was followed in printing books in other formats. One such study by G. W. Williams[2] deals with certain quartos set by a particular compositor in the shop of Thomas Creede between the years 1593 and 1599. Its importance lies in the fact that certain textual and bibliographical problems— as spelling, lineation and the like—can be attacked with greater confidence if the method of composition can be determined. Williams observes that frequently, but not always, it is possible to prove that composition was by formes by means of "(1) the count of type—pieces of a character as they appear in a sheet or a forme, and (2) the presence of substitutions for the character which indicate that the supply of the character has been exhausted in the course of the work".

R. A. Foakes, whose recent edition of *Henry VIII* in the New Arden series rejects the idea of dual authorship, contributes a note[3] about the stints of the two compositors who set the type in the Folio, and from a close examination of the variations in speech-headings for Queen Katharine, Cardinal Wolsey and others he concludes, with Greg,[4] that the copy for Folio *Henry VIII* was a carefully prepared manuscript, written probably in a single hand, and bearing no evidence of prompt use, but he adds that variations in the speech-headings suggest that it was based on foul papers, with the implication that these were from the pen of a single author.

The boundaries of the Shakespeare canon are vigilantly guarded, and properly so, but it may be suspected that the popular reluctance to admit that Shakespeare ever had a collaborator is the chief obstacle to the inclusion of *The Two Noble Kinsmen*, despite its acceptance by Coleridge, Bradley, Chambers, and Greg, to name only a few. Employing the method of E. A. Armstrong,[5] Kenneth Muir[6] finds in the scenes usually attributed to Shakespeare two of the image-clusters (*kite* and *hum*) isolated by Armstrong, and two or three others. One of the more interesting of these involves a reference to the osprey (I, i) in a context of *war, cards, knives, lords, Kings, beds* (=graves), *graves, shadows* and *actions*, that is to be compared to a similar reference in *Coriolanus* (IV, vii), in a context of *war, breaking the neck, sword, lord,* and *sovereignty*, with *tomb, darkened* and *action* in nearby lines. This strong confirmation of the attribution of the play to Shakespeare and Fletcher on the title-page of the Quarto (1634) is given further support by the metrical evidence Muir presents.

---

[1] 'Cast-off Copy for the First Folio of Shakespeare', *Shakespeare Quarterly*, VI (1955), 259–73.
[2] George Walton Williams, 'Setting by Formes in Quarto Printing', *Studies in Bibliography*, XI (1958), 39–53.
[3] 'On the First Folio Text of *Henry VIII*', *Studies in Bibliography*, XI, 55–60.
[4] *The First Folio of Shakespeare*, p. 425.   [5] In *Shakespeare's Imagination* (Lindsay Drummond, 1946).
[6] 'Shakespeare's Hand in *The Two Noble Kinsmen*', *Shakespeare Survey*, 11, pp. 50–9.

10-3

Contrary to the general assumption that *The Two Noble Kinsmen* was printed in 1634 directly from the prompt-book, F. O. Waller[1] maintains convincingly that the indisputable prompt notations in the quarto represent marginal additions, probably by Edward Knight, in the foul sheets of the collaborating authors, though he cites additional evidence that Knight may have made his casual annotations in a literal transcript of the foul sheets prepared anterior to the fair copy that was to become the prompt-book. The article touches on more subjects than can be summarized adequately. In one particular it seems to me to be wrong, that is in its assumption that the actors' parts would be copied out and rehearsals begun before the preparation of the prompt-book. Although one precedent may be cited—a play written for Henslowe—it appears to me unlikely that the King's would have risked the parcelling out of players' parts and the starting of rehearsals before they had in hand a licensed fair copy, ready to be marked as the prompt-book. Waller finds some evidence that the two authors worked independently, scene by scene, from an author's plot, that the Fletcherian portions show a higher finish than those of Shakespeare—as if the latter had been developed little beyond the condition of foul papers—and that Fletcher was the supervising agent, adding occasional lines to the work of his collaborator as he fitted the scenes together.

J. Dover Wilson's invaluable series, 'The New Way with Shakespeare's Texts', continues with a fourth instalment: 'Towards the High road.'[2] This traverses the ground covered by Pollard, McKerrow, and Greg in their exploration of the surviving dramatic manuscripts of Shakespeare's age and of such badly printed 'Good' Quartos as *Romeo* (1599), *Hamlet* (1604-5), and *Much Ado* (1600), and explains how they arrived at the inferences that serve as the basis of modern textual studies. There is no comparable introduction for the general reader or the beginning graduate student to the mysteries of Shakespeare's text, and when the series is concluded, the sections might with advantage be collected into a pamphlet for separate publication.

There have been two welcome additions to the Shakespeare Quarto Facsimiles: *Henry V* (1600) and *Love's Labour's Lost* (1598).[3] Greg's prefatory remarks are, as usual, succinct and authoritative. There has been a change for the worse in the paper in these volumes with the result that the facsimiles are less legible than those issued earlier. In view of the fact that there is no other series of photographic facsimiles of the Shakespeare Quartos, nor likely to be one, I still wish, as I did in reviewing Facsimile no. 1 many years ago, that snippets of the pages of other copies showing press variants might be included at the back of each volume to facilitate bibliographical and textual studies.

Competition in the paper-back field is now providing the public with the least expensive editions of Shakespeare offered at any time since Tonson and Walker battled in the early eighteenth century. The most recent contestant, with four titles to date,[4] is the Laurel Shakespeare under the general editorship of Francis Fergusson. This edition uses the text of Charles J. Sisson and features in each volume a commentary by a prominent actor, producer, or poet.

[1] 'Printer's Copy for *The Two Noble Kinsmen*', *Studies in Bibliography*, XI, 61–84.

[2] *Shakespeare Survey*, 11, pp. 78–88.

[3] Sir Walter Greg, ed. (Oxford at the Clarendon Press, 1957). These are nos. 9 and 10.

[4] *Hamlet* (Laurel Shakespeare, LB 112), commentary by Maurice Evans; *The Taming of the Shrew* (LB 113), commentary by Margaret Webster; *Romeo and Juliet* (LB 114), commentary by W. H. Auden; *Richard III* (LB 115), commentary by Stuart Vaughan (New York, Dell Publishing Co., 1958).

Each volume has an introduction by the general editor and his essay, "Shakespeare and his Theatre", and also a glossary compiled by H. H. Smith. (Should not the first sentence in Section III of "Shakespeare and his Theatre" be modified to take account of the fact that the first Globe was burned to the ground in 1613?)

Additions to the Folger Library General Reader's Shakespeare[1] include *Lear, Merchant, Othello*, and *Hamlet*. These paper-backs have the same practical disposition of notes as the earlier titles and continue to feature a quantity of little known but helpful illustrations from contemporary books and manuscripts. The Pelican Shakespeare has added a title, *Hamlet*,[2] edited by Willard Farnham, with an introduction that merits serious consideration. *King Lear*,[3] edited by Ralph E. C. Houghton, has hard covers, like its predecessors in the New Clarendon series (a typographical error, 1918 for 1948, should be corrected on p. 255).

In a textual study of nineteen pages of text of Qq 3 and 6 of *Richard III* and the corresponding passages of F, Silvano Gerevini[4] evaluates the variants that have resulted from progressive deterioration, collation of Qq with an authoritative manuscript, editorial interference, and the work habits and spelling preferences of F compositors *A* and *B*; he concludes that the copy used in printing F consisted of pages of Q3 and Q6 corrected in manuscript. The pattern of alternation is not simple but might be plotted, he thinks, by rigorous collation of the whole text of the play.

In their preoccupation with problems arising from the nature and authority of dramatic texts and with those that originate in the printing house, twentieth-century editors have tended to neglect philology, content with the *N.E.D.* and the dialect dictionaries. This deficiency is singled out by H. T. Price in his otherwise laudatory review[5] of *New Readings in Shakespeare* by C. J. Sisson. In illustration of what the philologist can contribute to the establishment of text and to its interpretation, Hilda M. Hulme discusses several cruxes and demonstrates that the linguist has yet much to contribute. It is not enough to rely upon the *N.E.D.* and dialect dictionaries. Evidence is available in manuscript sources, unused by lexicographers, that show "a word or sense, in currency a hundred years (sometimes 300 years) (*a*) before the first or (*b*) after the last citation by *N.E.D.*; they show also (*c*) that localizations suggested by *N.E.D.* for the sixteenth, seventeenth and eighteenth centuries are tentative only". Furthermore, Elizabethan pronunciation is important, and it is unsafe to reject a Shakespearian reading solely because no other literary example has been found to warrant the use of the word in the sense required by the context. Let two examples illustrate Miss Hulme's method. In *Romeo and Juliet* II, i, 11–14, Q2 reads

> Speake to my goship *Venus* one faire word,
> One nickname for her purblind sonne and her, (Q1 heire)
> Young *Abraham: Cupid* he that shot so true, (Q1 trim)
> When King *Cophetua* lou'd the begger mayd.

[1] Edited by Louis B. Wright and Virginia L. Freund, New York, The Pocket Library, 1957 and 1958 (nos. PL 57, 60, 61, and 64).
[2] The Pelican Shakespeare (Baltimore, Penguin Books, 1957).
[3] The New Clarendon Shakespeare (Oxford, at the Clarendon Press, 1957).
[4] *Il Testo del Riccardo III* (Pavia, Casa Editrice Renzo Cortina, 1957).
[5] *Modern Philology*, LV (August 1957), 53–5.

Evidence is cited to show that for the linguist *trim* is more meaningful than *true* and that *Abraham*, meaning one who feigns a disability, is to be preferred to *Adam*, the reading of many modern editions. Incidentally, the colon following *Abraham* is frequently encountered in manuscript lists of names. The second example is even more significant. In *Hamlet* III, ii, 61 ff., Q2 reads:

> Nay, doe not thinke I flatter,
> ...why should the poore be flatterd?
> No, let the candied tongue licke absurd pompe,
> And crooke the pregnant hindges of the knee
> Where thrift may follow fauning; (F1 faining)

Miss Hulme argues persuasively that *absurd* means "tasteless", not "ridiculous", and that the context requires acceptance of F's *faining*. Such a modification of the text has far-reaching consequences, altering, as it must, the accepted notions of one of the best-known image clusters. Obviously the day is far distant when Shakespeare's text will be established.

BOOKS RECEIVED

[Inclusion of a book in this list does not preclude its review in a subsequent volume]

ALLEN, DON CAMERON (Editor). *Studies in Honor of T. W. Baldwin* (Urbana: University of Illinois Press, 1958).

BACHRACH, A. G. *Naar Het Hem Leek* (Antwerp: Bakker, 1957).

BALDINI, GABRIELE. *Storia della letteratura Inglese* (Turin: Edizioni Radio Italiana, 1958).

BALDWIN, T. W. *Shakespeare's 'Love's Labour's Won'* (Southern Illinois University Press, 1957).

BERRY, FRANCIS. *Poets' Grammar* (London: Routledge and Kegan Paul, 1958).

BRUNNER, KARL. *William Shakespeare* (Tubingen: Max Niemeyer, 1957).

BULLOUGH, G. *Narrative and Dramatic Sources of Shakespeare; Vol. 1* (London: Routledge and Kegan Paul, 1957).

EHRL, CHARLOTTE. *Sprachstil und Charakter Bei Shakespeare* (Heidelberg: Quelle and Meyer, 1957).

ELLIOTT, G. R. *Dramatic Providence in Macbeth. A Study of Shakespeare's Tragic Theme of Humanity and Grace* (Princeton University Press; London: Oxford University Press, 1958).

FAIRFAX-LUCY, ALICE. *Charlecote and the Lucys. The Chronicle of an English Family* (Oxford University Press, 1958).

GEREVINI, SILVANO. *Il Testo del Riccardo III di Shakespeare* (Pavia: Renzo Cortina, 1957).

HALLIDAY, F. E. *The Cult of Shakespeare* (London: Duckworth, 1957).

ILLSLEY, W. A. *Shakespeare Manual for Schools* (Cambridge University Press, 1957).

JACQUOT, JEAN and ANDRE VEINSTEIN (Editors). *La Mise en scène des œuvres du passé* (Paris: Éditions du Centre National de la Recherche Scientifique, 1957).

KNIGHT, G. WILSON. *The Sovereign Flower* (London: Methuen, 1958).

KNIGHTS, L. C. *Shakespeare's Politics* (Annual British Academy Lecture: Oxford University Press, 1957).

MAAS, PAUL. *Textual Criticism.* Translated from the German by Barbara Flower (Clarendon Press: Oxford University Press, 1957).

MUSGROVE, S. *Shakespeare and Jonson* (Auckland: University College, 1957).

NAGLER, A. M. *Shakespeare's Stage* (New Haven: Yale University Press, 1958).

RIBNER, IRVING. *The English History Play in the Age of Shakespeare* (Princeton University Press, 1957).

ROSATI, SALVATORE. *Il Giro della Ruota; saggio sul King Lear di Shakespeare* (Firenze: Casa Editrice F. le Monnier, 1958).

SHAKESPEARE, WILLIAM

  Complete Works, edited by John Munro, 6 vols. (London: Eyre and Spottiswoode, 1958).

  (New Arden Shakespeare):

    Othello, edited by M. R. Ridley (London: Methuen, 1958).

  (New Cambridge Shakespeare):

    The Life of Timon of Athens, edited by J. Dover Wilson and J. C. Maxwell (Cambridge University Press, 1957).

    Troilus and Cressida, edited by J. Dover Wilson and Alice Walker (Cambridge University Press, 1957).

(Folger Library General Reader's Shakespeare):

A Midsummer Night's Dream, edited by Louis B. Wright and Virginia L. Freund (New York, 1958).

Hamlet, edited by Louis B. Wright and Virginia L. Freund (New York, 1957).

The Merchant of Venice, edited by Louis B. Wright and Virginia L. Freund (New York, 1957).

(The Pelican Shakespeare):

King Lear, edited by A. Harbage (Baltimore; Maryland: Penguin Books, 1958).

Twelfth Night, edited by Charles T. Prouty (Baltimore; Maryland: Penguin Books, 1958).

(The Penguin Shakespeare):

Pericles, edited by G. B. Harrison (London: Penguin Books, 1958).

(Shakespeare Quarto Facsimiles):

No. 11. The True Tragedy of Richard, Duke of York (Henry VI, Part III), 1595, edited by W. W. Greg (Oxford: Clarendon Press, 1958).

SIEGEL, PAUL N. Shakespearean Tragedy and the Elizabethan Compromise (New York: New York University Press, 1957).

SPIVACK, BERNARD. Shakespeare and the Allegory of Evil (Columbia University Press; London: Oxford University Press, 1958).

TILLYARD, E. M. W. The Nature of Comedy and Shakespeare. The English Association Presidential Address, 1958 (Oxford University Press, 1958).

WEST, REBECCA. The Court and the Castle (London: Macmillan, 1958).

WILLIAMS, CHARLES. The Image of the City and other essays. Selected by Anne Ridler (London: Oxford University Press, 1958).

Year's Work in English Studies, Vol. XXXVII, 1956. Edited by Beatrice White and T. S. Dorsch, for The English Association (London: Oxford University Press, 1958).

INDEX

A., H. *Partheneia Sacra* (1633), 107
Adams, J. C., 4, 13, 143–4
Adams, J. Q., 129 n.
Ages of Sin, or Sinnes Birth & groweth, The, 107, 108 n.
Akcan, Yildiz, 117
Akechi Mitsuhide, 115
Alarum for London, 36
Alden, John, 109
Alexander, Peter, 147
Alsloot, van, Dennis, painting of The Triumph of Isabella, 31
Alter, André, 111
Amyot, Jacques, 138
Anderson, Fiona, 120
Andrews, Harry, 122, 124–6
Anikst, A., 118
Anna-Maria, 114
Anne, Queen (wife of James I), 143
Anouilh, Jean
  The Lark, 1
  adaptation of *Twelfth Night*, 112
Antonetti, Charles, 112
Antwerp, festival of 1561, 5
Aoyama, Sugisaku, 115
Apuleius, *Metamorphoses seu de Asino Aureo*, translated W. Adlington, *The Golden Asse* (1566), 90, 91, 93, 94 and n.
Arany, János, 113
Archer, William, 9, 11
Arden of Feversham, 41
Armstrong, E. A., 149
Armstrong, William A., 144
Aronson, Alex, 136
Arundell, Dennis, 111
Ashby Folville Manor, Leicestershire, 99
Ashcroft, Peggy, 114
Astangov, M., 118
Atkinson, Rosalind, 124
Attingham Park, Shropshire, 130 n.
Audiberti, Jacques, French adaptation of *The Taming o the Shrew* (1957), 111
Australia, report on Shakespeare in, 109
Austria, report on Shakespeare in, 109–10
Avinoam, Reuben, 114

Babb, Lawrence, *The Elizabethan Malady* (1951), 135
Babits, Mihály, 114
Babler, O. F., 145
Bachrach, A. G. H., *Naar Het Hem Leek*, 146 and n.
Bailey, Bryan, 119
Baldini, Gabriele, *Le tragedie di Shakespeare*, 114

Baldwin, T. W., *Shakespeare's Love's Labor's Won*, 141 and n.
Bale, John, 21 n.
Balfoort, Maurits, 110
Ballet Comique de la Reine (1581), 21 n.
Balten, Pieter, 32
Barnes, Barnabe, *The Devil's Charter*, 44, 45, 46
Barnet, Sylvan, 138, 139
Barnstaple, interlude at, 19, 21 n.
Bateson, F. W., 137 n.
Battenhouse, Roy W., 134, 136
Battistella, Antonio, 114
Bayreuth, 1
Beaumont, Francis, and Fletcher, John
  A Wife for a Month, 48
  The Little French Lawyer, 48
  The Double Marriage, 48
  Monsieur Thomas, 48
  The Loyal Subject, 48
Beckett, Samuel, 110
  Waiting for Godot, 1, 2, 7
Beijer, Agne, 33
Belgium, report on Shakespeare in, 110
Bennett, Josephine Waters, 136 n.
Benthall, Michael, 120, 121; production of *Henry VIII*, 122–6
Bentley, Gerald E., 65
Bessenyei, Ferenc, 113
Bethell, S. L., *Shakespeare and the Popular Dramatic Tradition* (1944), 57
Beyer, Edvard, *Problemer omkring oversettelser av Shakespeares dramatikk* (1956), 139 and n.
Bing, Suzanne, 112
Blake, William, 125
Boas, Guy, 119
Bodart, Anne and Roger, French adaptation of *Hamlet*, 110
Bodin, Jean, *Six Books of the Commonweale* (1606), 144
Bonnard, Georges, 117
Bordon Hill, *see* Shottery
Borgeaud, Nelly, 111
Boughton, Edward, 98
Boulter, John, 115
Bowden, William R., 133
Bowdler, Thomas, 140
Boxus, Louis, 110
Brackley, Viscount, second Earl of Bridgewater, 107
Bradbrook, F. W., 137
Bradley, A. C., 132, 134, 136, 149
Brandes, Georges, 138
Brasseur, Pierre, 111

INDEX

Braun, Hanns, 139

Brecht, Berthold, 1, 79
  Berliner Ensemble, 112

Breughel, Pieter the younger, 32

Brewer, John S., *Letters and Papers, Foreign and Domestic, of the Reign of Henry VIII* (1862), 20 n., 21 n.

Brinkmann, Karl, 113, 145

Broggi, Luigi, 114

Brome, Richard, *The Antipodes*, 55 n.

Brook, Peter, 78, 85, 86, 120

Brooke, Arthur, *Romeus and Juliet*, 70, 141

Brown, Ivor, 126

Brown, John Russell, *Shakespeare and his Comedies* (1957), 132 and n., 133

Browne, Ray B., 146

Brudenell, Edward, 101

Brugiotti, bust of Shakespeare, 111

Brunner, Karl, 113
  Studies in English Language and Literature Presented to Professor Dr Karl Brunner on the Occasion of his Seventieth Birthday (1957), 132 n.
  William Shakespeare, 146 and n.

Brussels, 32, 33, 34

Bryant, J. A., Jun., 134

Buchell, Arend van, 16, 31

Bullough, Geoffrey, *Narrative and Dramatic Sources of Shakespeare*, 141 and n., 142

Burbage, James, 31

Burman family of Shottery and Stratford, 95–106

Burman, Sir John, *The Burman Family of Warwickshire* (1916), 106 n.

Burman, John, *The Burman Chronicle* (1940), 106 n.

Burnie, David, 109

Byrne, M. St Clare, 129 n., 145

Byron, Lord George, 85

Calderón de la Barca, Pedro, *Life is a Dream*, 6

Callot, Jacques, *Balli di Sfessania*, 32

Calvi, Jacques, 111

Cambridge University, 15
  King's College, 15, 30
  Queens' College, 20 n.

Campbell, Lily B., *Shakespeare's 'Histories'*, 129 n.

Camus, Albert, 110

Capodaglio, Wanda, 114

Carew, Matthew, Examiner in Court of Chancery, 97

Carnovsky, Morris, 117

Carraro, Tino, 114

Cartwright, Thomas, 21 n.

Castle of Perseverance, The, 70 n., 142

Catullus, 142

Cauthen, I. B., 142

Chamberlain, John, 42

'Chambers of Rhetoric', 5

Chambers, Sir E. K., 4, 54, 147, 149
  The Elizabethan Stage (1923), 20 n., 21 n., 55 n.

Chancery, Court of, documents relating to Hathaways and Burmans at Shottery, 95–106

Chapman, George, 144
  See also under Jonson, Ben, *Eastward Ho!*
  Revenge of Bussy D'Ambois, 134
  Translation of Homer, 142

Charney, Maurice, 138

Chatterton, Frederick B., 117

Chekhov, Anton, 79

Chen-Hsien, Chang, 110

Chesterton, G. K., 9

Chettle, Henry, *Hoffman*, 47

Child, Harold, 129 n.

China, report on Shakespeare in, 110

Claudel, Paul, *Soulier de Satin*, 111

Clemen, Wolfgang, 113
  Die Tragödie vor Shakespeare. Ihre Entwicklung im Spiegel der dramatischen Rede (1955), 70 n.
  Kommentar zu Shakespeares Richard III: Interpretation eines Dramas (1957), 131 and n.

Cocteau, Jean, adaptation of *Romeo and Juliet*, 112

Coe, Charles Norton, *Shakespeare's Villains* (1957), 135 and n.

Coe, Peter, 121

Coffin, Hayden, 129 n.

Coghill, Nevill, 145

Cokain, Aston, 142

Coleridge, Samuel Taylor, 139, 149

Collier, John Payne, 140

Collins, P. A. W., 139

Comus, 107

Condell, Henry, 148

Connecticut, American Shakespeare Festival, 117

Copeau, Jacques, 112

Court, Richard, of Stratford-upon-Avon, 105 n.

Courtenay, Margaret, 125

Creede, Thomas, printer, 149

Creizenach, Wilhelm, 11

Croft, Michael, 119

Cruikshank, George, 14

Czechoslovakia, report on Shakespeare in, 110

Dahlin, Hans, 116

Dale, Richard, 96–7, 100

Damiani, Luciano, 114

Daneman, Paul, 124

David, John, 20 n.

David, Richard W., 129 n., 136 n., 145

Davies, Sir John, 16

Davis, E., 133

Day, John, *An Humourous Day's Mirth*, 20

Dead Man's Fortune, The, 48

Dehler, Franz, 116

Dekker, Thomas, 144
  The Roaring Girl, 46 (with Middleton, Thomas)
  Satiromastix, 43, 45
  The Shoemakers' Holiday, 3, 41, 48

INDEX

Delaram, F., portrait of James I, 28
Deloney, Thomas, *The Gentle Craft*, 141
Denmark, 2
Deutsch, Ernst, 113
Devine, George, 86
De Witt, Johannes, Swan Theatre drawing, 9, 11, 16, 25, 28, 29, 31, 32, 34, 35, 41, 42, 45, 46, 53, 144
Dews, Peter, 120
Diaz, Bernal, *Conquest of New Spain*, 142
Dickey, Franklin M., *Not Wisely But Too Well: Shakespeare's Love Tragedies* (1957), 135 and n.
Dignam, Mark, 128
Direction for the English Traveller, A., 107
Dodimead, David, 125
Douking, Georges, 112
Dowell, George B., 118
Downer, Alan S., 144
Drake, Alfred, 117
Draper, John W., 70 n.
Draper, R. P., 137
Drottningholm Theatre Museum, 32
Druids, 8
Dryden, John, *Marriage à la Mode*, 94 n.
Dudley, Ambrose, Earl of Warwick, 20 n., 95–106
Dugdale, Sir Thomas, *Antiquities of Warwickshire*, 105, 106 n.
Duguid, Peter, 120
Du Maurier, Sir Gerald, 81
Dupuy, René, 111
Durand, W. Y., 20 n.
Durrant, G. H., 115

Eagle, R. L., 142
East Africa, report on Shakespeare in, 110–11
Eckhoff, Lorentz, 139
Edinborough, Arnold, 145
Edward IV, 48, 54
Ehrl, Charlotte, *Sprachstil und Charakter bei Shakespeare* (1957), 70 n., 113
Ekeblad, Inga-Stina, 142
Eld, George, printer, 147
Eliaz, Raphael, 114
Elizabeth, Princess (daughter of James I), 144
Elizabeth, Queen, 15, 16, 17, 18
England's Joy, 42
English, John, 119
Equity, Courts of, 95
Evans, Edith, 86, 122, 124–5
Existentialism, 4, 7

Fair Maid of Bristow, The, 36
Fair Maid of the Exchange, The, 51, 52, 54
Farmer, John S., *The Writings of John Bale* (1905), 21 n.
Farnham, Willard, edition of *Hamlet*, 151
Farrar, J. H., 22
Fenton, 96–9

Fergusson, Francis, 150
Feuillerat, Albert, *Documents Relating to the Office of the Revels in the Time of Queen Elizabeth* (1908), 21 n.
Fielding, Henry, *Tom Jones*, 81
Fini, Leonor, 111
Finland, report on Shakespeare in, 111
Fisher, Peter F., 133
Flatter, Richard, 70 n., 137
Fleay, F. G., 140
Fletcher, John,
    The Island Princess, 42
    The Maid in the Mill, 42 (with Rowley, William)
    Sea Voyage, 37
    See also under Beaumont, Francis, and *Two Noble Kinsmen*, 149, 150
Flickenschildt, Elizabeth, 112
Flon, Suzanne, 111
Florio, John, 43
Foakes, R. A., 149
Folk Dance and Song Society, 9
Ford, John, *Perkin Warbeck*, 134
Foxe, John, 142
France, report on Shakespeare in, 111–12
Francis, Derek, 125
Fredén, Gustaf, *William Shakespeare*, 116
Frenhoff, Rosina, 114
Fricker, Robert, 70 n., 138
Friedman, William F., and Elizebeth S., *The Shakespearean Ciphers Examined* (1957), 140 and n.
Frigerio, Ezio, 114
Frost, William, 137
Fry, Christopher, *The Dark is Light Enough*, 125
Fukuda, Tsuneari, 115

Gaederz, Karl, 11
Galvan, Bianca, 114
Gardener, *see* Hathaway, Richard
Garrick, David, 8, 9, 81, 140
Gascoigne, George, *Supposes*, 141
Gassman, Vittorio, 114
Gaulis, Louis, 117
Gaultier, Jean Jacques, 111
Gerard, Albert, 132
Gerevini, Silvano, *Il testo del Riccardo III di Shakespeare*, 114, 151
Germany, report on Shakespeare in, 112–13
Gerstner-Hirzel, Arthur, *The Economy of Action and Word in Shakespeare's Plays* (1957), 70 n., 116
Ghent, Stage of 1539, 5
Gielgud, Sir John, 74, 86, 116, 122–6
Gifford, Anne (daughter of Sir Thomas), 99
Gifford, Mary (great-granddaughter of Sir Thomas), 99
Gifford, Sir Thomas, 99
Gifford, William, 37
Gignoux, Hubert, 112
Gilbert, Sir W. S., 85

INDEX

Gillie, Christopher, 137
Godfrey, Derek, 124
Godfrey, Walter H., 10, 11
Godsiashwili, 118
Goethe, J. W. von, 79, 80
Goldberg, Lea, 114
Goodman, John, 96–7
Gorvin, Joana Maria, 113
Granville-Barker, Harley, 9, 11, 56, 65, 78, 81, 129 n., 144
    Companion to Shakespeare Studies, 11
    Prefaces to Shakespeare, 56, 64, 70 n.
Graves, T. S., 17, 42
    The Court and the London Theatres during the Reign of Elizabeth (1913), 20 n., 21 n.
Gray, Terence, 129 n.
Graziosi, Franco, 114
Greece, report on Shakespeare in, 113
Greene, Robert
    Alphonsus King of Aragon, 19, 35, 55 n.
    James the Fourth, 20
    The Tragical Reign of Selimus, 20
Greg, Sir W. W., 55 n., 148, 149, 150
    Bibliography of the English Printed Drama to the Restoration, Vol. III (1957), 146–7
    The Henslowe Papers (1907), 21 n.
    Malone Society Collections (1923), 20 n.
    Shakespeare Quarto Facsimiles Nos. 9 and 10, 150
Grey, Lord John, 99
Griffin, Alice, 145
Grosart, A. B., *The Complete Poems of Sir John Davies* (1876), 20 n.
Gruyter, Dom de, 110
Guggenheim Memorial Foundation, 46 n.
Guilds, of the Middle Ages, 5
Guthrie, Tyrone, 123, 125, 126
Gwillim, Jack, 123

Hall, Peter, 120; production of *Twelfth Night* (1958), 126–9
Halliday, F. E.
    The Cult of Shakespeare (1957), 140 and n.
    Shakespeare and his Critics (1958), 139 and n.
Hamilton, Lionel, 119
Hammerle, Karl, 137
Harbage, Alfred, 1, 70 n.
    Shakespeare and the Rival Traditions, 140
    Theatre for Shakespeare (1955), 70 n.
Hardwick, 11
Hardy, Thomas, *The Return of the Native*, 137
Harewell, Anne, 99
Harewell, John (Lord of the Manor of Lucies), 99, 102
Harewell, William, 103
Harris, Frank, 138
Harrison, John, 119
Harrison, William, *The Description of Britain*, 20 n.
Harsnett, Samuel, 142

Harvey, Gabriel, 31, 135
Harwood, Frank, 119
Hastings, W. T., 145
Hathaway, Agnes, 95
Hathaway, Anne, 95, 97, 98, 102–6
Hathaway, Richard, of Shottery, 95–106
Heidegger, M., 110
Heilbrun, Carolyn, 136
Heilman, Robert B., *Magic in the Web: Action and Language in Othello* (1956), 131 and n., 132, 133
Helpmann, Robert, 119
Helsztyński, Stanisław, 115
Heminge, John, 148
Henry, Prince (heir of James I), 144
Henslowe, Philip, 18, 19, 21 n., 150
Hepburn, Katherine, 117
Herod, 3
Herrey, Hermann, 144
Heuer, Hermann, 138
Heuss, Bundespräsident, 113
'Hewlands', home of Hathaway family, 100, 103
Heywood, Thomas
    2 If You Know Not Me, 48
    The Golden Age, 51
    The Silver Age, 50, 51
    A Woman Killed with Kindness, 54
Hill, Patricia, 109
Hill, R. F., 136
Hiller, Wendy, 83, 84
Hinman, Charlton, 149
Hobson, Harold, 2
Hockey, Dorothy C., 133
Hodek, Břetislaw, 110
Hodges, C. Walter, 24, 55 n.
    The Globe Restored (1953), 20 n., 21 n., 42
Holinshed, Raphael, 142
Holland, Philemon, 1603 translation of Plutarch's *Moralia*, 91, 92, 93
Hollar, Wenceslas, 22, 29, 30
Hosley, Richard, 55 n., 65, 144
Hotson, Leslie, 1, 18, 21 n., 43
    The First Night of Twelfth Night (1954), 20 n., 21 n.
Houghton, Ralph E. C., edition of *Lear*, 151
Houseman, John, 117
Housman, A. E., *The Shropshire Lad*, 9
Howarth, R. G., *Shakespeare by Air: Broadcasts to Schools* (1957), 138 and n.
Howes, John, 100
Hudd, Walter, 120
Hughes, Thomas, *The Misfortunes of Arthur*, 48
Hugo, François-Victor, 111, 117
Hulme, Hilda M., 143, 151–2
Hungary, report on Shakespeare in, 113–14
Hunt, Hugh, 109
Hunter, G. K., 136
Hyman, Earle, 117

INDEX

Ibsen, Henrik, 79
Illsley, W. A., *A Shakespeare Manual for Schools*, 146 and n.
Israel, report on Shakespeare in, 114
Italy, report on Shakespeare in, 114–15

Jackson, Sir Barry, 80, 82
Jackson, G. Maxwell, 119
Jacquemont, Maurice, 112
Jacquot, Jean, 112
    Les Fêtes de la Renaissance, 144
Jaggard, William, printer, 147, 148, 149
James I, 137 n.
Japan, report on Shakespeare in, 114
Jeauneau, René, 112
Jeffreys, M. D. W., 137
Jenner, Thomas, 107, 108 n.
    The Path of Life (1656), 108 n.
Jerome, Roger, 120
Johnson, Richard, 128
Johnson, Samuel, 148
Jones, Bob, Junior, 118
Jones, Inigo, 13
Jonson, Ben, 17, 86, 134, 140, 143, 144
    Eastward Ho!, 41
    Every Man in his Humour, 54
    Every Man out of his Humour, 36, 38, 46
    The Magnetick Lady, 29
    Masque of Blackness, 143
    The Poetaster, 17
    Sejanus, 36, 41
    Volpone, 44, 48, 138
Joseph, B. L., 70 n.
    Elizabethan Acting, 56, 65
Joyce, James, *Ulysses*, 138
Jusztusz, Pál, 114

Kahn, Sholom J., 143
Karm, Kaarel, 118
Karthaios, Kleandros, 113
Katajisto, Martti, 111
Kaufman, Helen A., 142
Keate, Edith M., *Hampton Court Palace* (1932), 20 n.
Kedrov, M., 118
Keil, Harry, 143
Kelly, William, *Notices Illustrative of the Drama and Other Amusements at Leicester* (1865), 21 n.
Kemp, T. C., 129 n.
Kernodle, George R.,
    From Art to Theatre (1944), 20 n.
Kierkegaard, Søren, 110
Kilkenny, 21 n.
Kirkman, Francis, *The Witts*, 32, 42
Kirschbaum, Leo, 137 n.
Kittredge, G. L., 37
Knight, Edward, 150

Knight, John, 100
Knights, L. C., *Shakespeare's Politics: with some Reflections on the Nature of Tradition* (1957), 138 and n.
Knowland, A. S., 145
Kökeritz, Helge, 133
Kökeritz, Helge, and Prouty, C. T., *Facsimile of the First Folio*, 70 n.
Kolbe, F. C., *Shakespeare's Way*, 115
Konszul, André, 139
Korninger, Siegfried, 110
Kortner, Fritz, 112
Koskimies, Rafael, 111
Krauss, Werner, 112
Kumonosujo (*The Castle of Cobwebs*), 115
Kurosawa, Akira, 115
Kutlu, Gülgun, 117

Lady Rhetoric, 5
Lambard, William, *The Perambulation of Kent*, 28
    Archaionomia, 142
Langaren, Jacobus van, 107
Langham, Michael, 119
Latimer, Hugh, Bishop of Worcester, 99, 105 n.
Laughton, Charles, 129 n.
Law, Robert Adger, 142
Lawlor, John, 138
Lawrence, W. J., 9, 11
    The Physical Conditions of the Elizabethan Public Playhouse (1927), 33
Leavis, F. R., 132 n.
Lee, Sir Henry, *Woodstock*, 48
Lee, Sir Sidney, 138
Lescure, Jean, 112
Lever, J. W., 142
Libraries
    Birmingham Shakespeare Memorial Collection, 119
    Bridgewater, 107
    British Museum, 107, 125
    Cambrai, 32
    Fitzwilliam Museum, 32
    Harvard, 107
    Huntington, 107
Liechtenstein Gallery, 32, 33
Linder, Hans R., 144
Littlewood, Joan, 120
Locrine, 20
Lodovici, Cesare Vico, 114
Lomax, Harry, 119
London, 2, 3, 5, 6, 16, 17, 19, 22
    Bishopsgate, 20 n.
    Gray's Inn, 21 n.
    Guildhall, 19
    Hampton Court, 16; size of the hall, 15
    Inns of Court, 18
    Maiden Lane, 143
London Prodigal, The, 36

INDEX

Lord, Arthur, 120
Love's Labour's Won, 141
Low Countries, the stage of, 4
Luckham, Cyril, 127–8
Lucy, Sir Thomas, of Charlecote, 95–106
Ludeke, H., 116
Luthi, Max, *Shakespeares Dramen*, 113
Lyly, John, 55 n., 133

McDiarmid, Matthew P., 142
McEwan, Geraldine, 127–8
McKelvey, John, 121
McManaway, James G., 145
Maddermarket Theatre, 71, 72, 75
Malone, Edmund, 8, 9, 148
    History of the Stage, 8
Manez, Raoul de, 110
Marcel, Gabriel, 111
Marchat, Jean, 112
Marder, Louis, 118
Marlowe, Christopher, 112
    Doctor Faustus, 37
    Edward II, 134
    Tamburlaine, 2, 3
Marquard, N. J., 115
Marsden, Robert, 121
Marsh, Ngaio, 129 n.
Marshall, Norman
    The Other Theatre (1947), 129 n.
    The Producer and the Play (1957), 129 n.
Marston, John, 140
    See also under Jonson, Ben, *Eastward Ho!*
Mary, Queen of Scots, 102
Mason, John, *The Turk*, 48
Massinger, Philip
    The Guardian, 42
    The Renegado, 42
Master, A. J. R., 111
Maxwell, J. C., 138, 147–8
Mayakovski Theatre, Moscow, 118
Melchinger, Siegfried, 145
Mensaros, Laszlo, 113
Merchant, W. M., 144
Meres, Francis, *Palladis Tamia*, 141
Merry Devil of Edmonton, The, 44
Messalina, title-page engraving, 42
Messel, Oliver, 12
Meulen, A. F. van der, 32, 33
Michell, Keith, 84
Middleton, Thomas, *The Witch*, 137
    see also under Dekker, Thomas, *The Roaring Girl*
Mielziner, Jo., settings of, 7
Mikhailov, A., 118
Miles Gloriosus, 85
Miller, Arthur, *Death of a Salesman*, 7
Miller, Joan, 84

Milo, Joseph, 114
Minotis, Alexis, 113
Moiseiwitsch, Tanya, 123
Molière, 1, 2
    Don Juan, 1, 2
Molin, Nils, 116
Montacute, 11
Moody, John, 120
Morris, Ivor, 137
Morton, John, of Ashby Folville Manor, Leicestershire, 99
Morton, Mary, 99
Moudouès, Mlle R. M., 112
Mouffet, Thomas, *Of the Silkworms, and their Flies*, 141
Moulton, R. G., 123, 129 n.
Mounteagle, Sir Edward, 98–9
Muir, Kenneth, 141, 142, 149
    Shakespeare's Sources, 65, 141 and n.
Müller-Bellinghausen, Anton, 70 n.
Munday, Anthony, 51
    John a Kent and John a Cumber, 19, 50, 51
Murray, John T., *English Dramatic Companies 1558–1642* (1910), 21 n.
Musgrove, S., *Shakespeare and Jonson* (1957), 138 and n.

Nash, Walter, 132
Nashe, Thomas, assistant to steward of Stratford Manor Court, 97
Németh, Antal, 113
Nero, 48
Netherlands, report on Shakespeare in, 115
New English Dictionary, see *Oxford English Dictionary*
Nichols, John, *The Progresses and Public Processions of Queen Elizabeth* (1823), 20 n., 21 n.
Nicoll, Allardyce, 129 n.
Noah, 3
Nobili, Lila de, 127
Noël, Jacques, 111
North, Sir Thomas, 138
    1579 translation of Plutarch's *Lives*, 65, 69, 92, 93, 94 n.
Norwich, 71
    Bishop's Palace, 73
Norwich Players, the, 71, 72, 73
Nowottny, Winifred M. T., 137

Ognell, Andrew, 98, 101
Oguzalp, Tomris, 117
Ojetti, Paola, 114
Okhlopkov, N., 118
Oliver, H. J., 109, 148
Olson, Paul A., 133
Oppel, Horst, 139, 146
Ornstein, Robert, 142
Orszagh, Ladislas, 114
Oscarsson, Per, 116
Otto, Teo, 144–5

INDEX

Ovid, 136
  Fasti, 141
Oxford University
  Christ Church, 21 n.
  Trinity Hall, 16, 19
Oxford English Dictionary, The, 25, 37, 107, 151–2
Ozu, Jiro, 115

Pack of Patentees, A, 107
Pack of Puritans, A, 107
Pafford, J. H. P., 143
Pake of Knaves, A, 107
Parenti, Franco, 114
Paris, 1, 6
Paris, Matthew, 142
Parish, W. A., 107
Partridge, A. C., 116
Payne, B. Iden, 118
Peisley, Frederick, 121
Pérez, Antonio, 141
Philip II, 5
Picasso, Pablo, 12
Piscopo, Vittorio, 114
Planchon, Roger, 112
Plautus, *Aulularia*, 15
Plutarch, 65, 66, 67, 68, 69, 70, 138, 142
  Lives, translated by Sir Thomas North (1579), 92, 93, 94 n.
  Moralia, translated by Philemon Holland (1603), 91, 92
  See also under North, Sir Thomas
Poel, William, 9, 22, 71, 73, 82, 144
Poland, report on Shakespeare in, 115
Porath, Orna, 114
Praz, Mario, 114
Price, Hereward T., 142, 151
Private Life of Henry VIII, 129 n.
Prouty, C. T., 16, 20 n.
  See also under Kökeritz, Helge
Pruvost, René, 139
Purcell, Henry, 109

Quiller-Couch, Sir Arthur, 127

Rademacher, Nelly, 116
Read, Thomas G., 120
Redgrave, Michael, 80
Reinhardt, Max, 79
Revels Office, 16
  Accounts, 17, 18
Revenger's Tragedy, The, 44, 45, 48, 49, 50, 53
Reynolds, —, 100
Reynolds, George F., 65
  The Staging of Elizabethan Plays at the Red Bull Theater (1940), 42
Ribner, Irving, *The English History Play in the Age of Shakespeare* (1957), 133 and n., 134

Ricci, Renzo, 114
Ridley, M. R., 148, 149
Ridoni, Relda, 114
Rogers, Paul, 80, 109
Rondiris, Dimitris, 113
Rosenberg, Marvin, 143
Rotas, Basil, 113
Rothe, Hans, 112
Rouault, 127
Rowe, Nicholas, 4
Rowley, William, *see under* Fletcher, John, *The Maid in the Mill*
Roy, Mylise, 117
Royaards, Ben, 110
Roxana, title-page engraving (1632), 36, 42, 46
Ruggieri, Osvaldo, 114
Russian
  theatre of the 1920's, 8
  revolutionary theatre, 13
Ruth, Leon, 111
Rylands, George, 82
Rytter, Henrik, 139

Sadler, Margaret, of Stratford-upon-Avon, 105 n.
Saint-Denis, Michel, 112
Sainthill, Loudon, 122
Salerno, Enrico M., 114
Salingar, L. G., 129 n.
Sandells, Foulke, 97–106
Sanders, N. J., 55 n.
Saroyan, William, 1
Sartre, Jean-Paul, 110
Saudek, Erik A., 110
Saunders, J. W., 55 n.
Saunders, William, Vicar of Wootton Wawen, 103
Savadski, Y., 118
Scarron, Paul, *Comical Romance*, 32
Scase, David, 119, 121
Schalla, Hans, 112
Schanzer, Ernest, 139
Schiller, J. C. F. von, 85
Schlegel-Tieck translation, 113
Schneider, Reinhold, 139
Schröder, Rudolf Alexander, 113
Schubert, Rosemarie, 116
Schücking, Levin L., 113, 132 and n.
Schutte, William M., *Joyce and Shakespeare: A Study in the Meaning of Ulysses* (1957), 138 and n.
Scott, Nathan A., *The Tragic Vision and the Christian Faith* (1957), 136
Scott, Sir Walter, 9
Seale, Douglas, 119, 120
Second Maiden's Tragedy, The, 42
Sehrt, Ernst Th., *Shakespeare: Englishe Essays aus drei Jahrhunderten zum Verständnis seinen Werke* (1958), 139 and n.

INDEX

Selden, John, *Table Talk*, ed. Arber (1868), 95, 105 n.

Selimus, 142

Semper, Gottfried, 11

Senda, Koreya, 115

Seneca, 142

Sevin, Nureddin, 117

Shakespeare, Hamnet, 75

Shakespeare, John, 98

Shakespeare, William, biographical documents, 95–106

editions

    First Folio, The, 73, 147–52

    Folger Library General Reader's: *Hamlet, Lear, Merchant of Venice, Othello*, 151

    Folio, the Second, 125

    Globe, 70 n.

    Laurel, 150–1

    New Arden: *Henry VIII*, 149; *Othello*, 148–9

    New Cambridge: *Timon of Athens*, 147; *Troilus and Cressida*, 147

    New Clarendon: *Lear*, 151

    Pelican: *Hamlet*, 151

plays

    All's Well that Ends Well, 36, 136, 141; productions: at Shakespeare Memorial Theatre (1954), 86, elsewhere, 109

    Antony and Cleopatra, 36, 37, 47, 59, 65, 70, 88–94, 135, 137, 138; productions: at Old Vic (1957) 84, elsewhere, 110, 111, 117, 118, 119

    As You Like It, 36, 72, 74, 79, 85, 86; productions: at Memorial Theatre (1957), 86, elsewhere, 109, 110, 113, 114, 117, 119, 120

    Comedy of Errors, 85, 143; productions, 119, 120

    Coriolanus, 36, 38, 48, 49, 50, 79, 134; productions, 114, 145

    Cymbeline, productions: at Old Vic (1957) 80, elsewhere, 112, 113, 118, 120, 127

    Hamlet, 2, 36, 46, 47, 62, 73, 75, 78, 85, 134, 136, 137, 142, 146; source in legend, 75; 1604–5 Quarto, 150; Q2 discussed, 152; productions: Memorial Theatre (1956), 1, 4, Brook production (Moscow 1956), 85, elsewhere, 109, 110 (adaptation by Anne and Roger Bodart), 111, 112, 113, 115, 118, 120, 121

    1 Henry IV, 115, 121, 134, 146; productions: Memorial Theatre (1951), 80, elsewhere, 112, 118

    2 Henry IV, 119, 143

    Henry V, 36, 37, 79, 134; productions: at Memorial Theatre (1950), 86, elsewhere, 114, 119, 120

    Henry VI (3 parts), 120, 122, 126

    Henry VIII, 47, 48, 73, 122–6, 129 n., 134, 142, 149; Old Vic production (1958), 122–6; Arden edition, 129 n., 149 and n.

    John, 122, 142; productions: at Memorial Theatre (1957), 84, elsewhere, 112, 119

    Julius Caesar, 36, 70, 83, 89, 126, 134, 142; productions, 112, 115, 117, 118, 119, 120

    Lear, 4, 36, 61, 73, 134, 135, 136, 138, 142, 143; translation, 115; productions: Old Vic (1956), 86, elsewhere, 110, 112, 113, 117, 119

    Love's Labour's Lost, 73, 81, 141, 143

    Macbeth, 4, 36, 40, 50, 77, 82–3, 85, 134, 137, 138; productions, 109, 110, 111, 115, 118, 119, 120

    Measure for Measure, 36, 142; productions: at Shakespeare Memorial Theatre (1950), 86, elsewhere, 110, 114, Connecticut, 117, 121

    Merchant of Venice, 74, 126, 132, 141 and n.; productions, 109, 110, 113, 115, 117, 119, 120, 121

    Merry Wives of Windsor, The, 43, 45, 102; productions, 110, 114, 118, 120

    Midsummer Night's Dream, 73, 74, 133, 141; productions: at Shakespeare Memorial Theatre (1954), 84, 86, elsewhere, 109, 110, 113, 117, 118, 120, 121, Czechoslovakian versions, 145

    Much Ado about Nothing, 63 n., 133, 141; 1600 quarto, 150; productions, 110, 117, 118

    Othello, 36, 38, 78, 131, 132, 134, 136, 137, 142–3, 145; productions, 110, 111, 112, 113, 117, 118, 119

    Pericles, 44, 142; productions, 111, 117

    Richard II, 134; productions, 112, 121

    Richard III, 122, 123, 131, 132, 135; productions, 110, 112, 113, 120; G. Baldini's translation, 114; S. Gerevini's *Il Testo del Riccardo III*, 114, 151

    Romeo and Juliet, 2, 70, 73, 134, 135, 136, 141 n., 143; productions: Memorial Theatre (1954) 84, elsewhere, 110, 113, 114, 115, 116, 117, 118; 1599 Quarto, 150; textual problem of Q2 (II, 1), 151–2

    Taming of the Shrew, The, productions: Connecticut company, 118, others, 109, 110, 111, 112, 113, 115, 118; *Taming of a Shrew, The*, 141

    Tempest, 73, 74, 85, 144, 145; translation, 115; productions, 110, 112, 117

    Timon of Athens, 36, 37, 38, 73, 134, 135, 137

    Titus Andronicus, 135, 136, 145; productions: Brook's, 78, Old Vic, 120

    Troilus and Cressida, 44, 59, 60, 74, 133, 134, 135, 136, 146; translation, 115; production, 113

    Twelfth Night, 36, 63 n., 126–7, 146; productions: Anouilh's adaptation, 112, others, 109, 110, 113, 115, 116, 118, 119, 120–1, at Memorial Theatre (1958), 126–9, 130 n.

    Two Gentlemen of Verona, productions: Old Vic (1957), 85, 145, elsewhere, 110, 117, 119

    Winter's Tale, 83, 144, 146; productions, 109, 112, 115, 116, 118

poems

    Rape of Lucrece, The, 141

    Sonnets, Pal Jusztusz's translation, 114; Lörinc Szabo's translation, 114; Sonnet LV, 142

    Venus and Adonis, 135

Shakespeare-Jahrbuch (1957), 144, 145

Shakespeare Jubilee (1769), 8

Shapiro, I. A., 22

INDEX

Shaw, George Bernard, 139 and n.
Shaw, Glen Byam, 78, 86, 119, 120
Sheldon, 97
Shelley, Percy Bysshe, 85
Shield, H. A., 140 n.
Shilo, Yizhak, 114
Shottery, disputed ownership of lands on Bordon Hill, 1584, 95–106
Shvedov, Y., 118
Sidney, Sir Philip, 85
Simons, Mathew, 107
Sisson, C. J., 21 n., 147, 150–1
   New Readings in Shakespeare, 151
Sitwell family, 12
Skeat, W. W., ed., *Shakespeare's Plutarch* (1875), 94 n.
Smirnov, A., 118
Smith, G. C. Moore, *College Plays Performed in the University of Cambridge* (1923). 20 n.
Smith, H. H., 151
Smith, Irwin, *Shakespeare's Globe Playhouse*, 143
Smith, John, of Stratford, 95–6, 98–106
Smith, Sir John (*temp.* Henry VIII), 99
Smith, Warren D., 38
Smith, William, of Stratford-upon-Avon, 105 n.
Smyth, Francis, of Wootton Wawen, 96–106
Smyth, Francis, Alderman of Stratford-upon-Avon, 106 n.
Smyth, George, of Wootton Wawen, 99
Société d'Histoire du Théâtre, 112
Society for Theatre Research, 55 n.
Sorell, Walter, 144
South Africa, report on Shakespeare in, 115–16
Southern, Richard, 1, 20 n.
   The Open Stage (1953), 36
   The Medieval Theatre in the Round (1957), 70 n.
Spanish, stage, 5
Speaight, Robert, 118, 144
Speed, John, 28
Spencer, T. J. B., 138
Spenser, Edmund, 133
   Thalia, 31
Spivak, Bernard, 134
Squarzina, Luigi, 114
Stamm, Rudolf
   Shakespeare's Word-Scenery (1954), 70 n.
   Englische Literatur (1957), 116, 139 and n.
Stanislavsky, Constantin, 79
Sternfeld, Frederick W., 144
Steuart, David, 121
Stewart, J. I. M., 134
Stoker, Willard, 120
Stonehenge, 8
Stow, John, *Survey of London*, 127, 129 n.
Stratford-upon-Avon, 1, 8, 9, 75
   8th International Shakespeare Conference, 46 n., 75 n., 77

Stratford-upon-Avon
   Bull Lane, 98
   Bear Inn, 99
   Chamberlain's Accounts, 101
   Chapel Street, 99
   Croft School, 98
   Guildhall, 101
   Henley Street, 8
   Manor of Old Stratford, Court Rolls of, 95–106
   Mill in Old Stratford, 99
   Old Town, 98
Stratford, Connecticut, Shakespeare Theatre, 145
Stratford, Ontario, Shakespeare Theatre, 11, 145
Strehler, Giorgio, 114
Stroux, Karl Heinz, 113
Stukely, Dr, 8
Sullivan, Sir Arthur, 85
Surrealism, 12
Sutherland, Graham, 12
Suzman, A., 115
Swallow, —, 100
Swanston, Hamish F. G., 133
Sweden, report on Shakespeare in, 116
Swinburne, Henry, *Brief Treatise of Testaments*, 142
Switzerland, report on Shakespeare in, 116–17
Szabo, Lörinc, 114

Tailor, Robert, *The Hog hath lost his Pearl*, 55 n.
Talvi, Aino, 118
Tanner, Lawrence E., *Westminster School* (1934), 20 n.
Tarlton, Richard, *2 Seven Deadly Sins*, 47
Tchabukiani, V., 118
Teale, Leonard, 109
Theatre, Elizabethan
  companies
    Admiral's men, 18
    Lord Chamberlain's–King's men, 36, 140, 150
  theatres
    Blackfriars, 36
    Boar's Head Inn, 17
    Bull Inn, 20 n.
    Curtain, 16
    Fortune, 22, 23, 24, 27, 28, 46; Contract, 11, 22, 23, 24, 25, 56; Tieck's reconstruction, 11
    Globe, 8, 9, 12, 13, 16, 28, 30, 35, 36, 37, 38, 41, 43, 44, 45, 46, 79, 143, 144
    Hope, 25, 27, 28; contract, 24, 27, 29
    Rose, 16, 18, 19
    Swan, 16, 18, 19, 27, 144; drawing of, *see* de Witt, Johannes
    Theatre, the, 16, 18, 31
Theatres
   Comédie Française, 112
   Drury Lane, 9
   Memorial Theatre, Stratford-upon-Avon, *see under* Shakespeare, William, plays

INDEX

Theatres (*cont.*)
  Old Vic Theatre and Company, 80, 119, 120, 121; productions: of *Winter's Tale* (1956), 83, of *Henry VIII* (1958), 122–6
  Schiller Theatre, Berlin, 112
Théâtre National Populaire, 1, 112
Theotokas, George, 113
Thomas Lord Cromwell, 43, 45, 50
Thompson, E. N. S., *The Controversy between the Puritans and the Stage* (1903), 21 n.
Thompson, Karl F., 142
Thrale, Mrs, 8
Throckmorton, Sir Robert, of Coughton Court, 99
Throckmorton, Ursula, 99
Tibet, Kartal, 117
Tidblad, Inga, 116
Tieck, Ludwig, 11, 12
Tillyard, E. M. W., 129 n.
  Shakespeare's History Plays, 139
Tofano, Gilberto, 114
Tonson, Jacob, 150
Topham Forrest, reconstruction (1921), 22
Tourneur, Cyril, *The Atheist's Tragedy*, 54
Trappolin Supposed a Prince, 142
Trnka, Jiří, 110
Troublesome Reign of King John, The, 142
Tschopp, Elizabeth, *Zur Verteilung von Vers und Prosa in Shakespeares Dramen*, 116
Turkey, report on Shakespeare in, 117
Turvile, 99
Tutin, Dorothy, 129
Two Noble Kinsmen, The, 63 n., 149, 150

Ulanova, Galina, 118
Ungerer, Gustav, *Anglo-Spanish Relations in Tudor Literature*, 140–1, and 141 n.
Urbánek, Zdeněk, 110
U.S.A., report on Shakespeare in, 117–18
U.S.S.R., report on Shakespeare in, 118

Valeri, Valeria, 114
Vandermeulen, Gaston, 110
Van Maanen, W., 115
Vardi, Dov, 146
Vennar, Richard, 42
Venne, van der, 32, 34
Vilar, Jean, 1, 112
Villiers, J. I. de, 115
Vitaly, Georges, 111

Wagner, Richard, 1
Waith, Eugene M., 136
Walker, Alice, 147, 148, 149
  Textual Problems of the First Folio, 148
Walker, Robert, 150
Walker, Roy, 129 n.
Walkley, A. B., 148
Waller, David, 125
Waller, F. O., 150
Walter, J. H., 146
Wälterlin, Oskar, 144
Warner, William, translation of *Menaechmi*, 141
Warning for Fair Women, A, 36, 37, 38, 40, 46, 51, 52
Watkins, Ronald, 70 n.
  On Producing Shakespeare, 60
Webb, Henry J., 132
Webster, John, *The White Devil*, 54
Webster, Margaret, 121
  Shakespeare Today, 86–7
Weingott, Owen, 109
Welles, Orson, 117
Wentworth, Sir Peter, *A Pack of Puritans*, 107
Westwell, Raymond, 120
Whetstone, George, 55 n.
Whistler, Rex, 12
Wilkins, George, *The Miseries of Enforced Marriage*, 36, 40, 41
Williams, Clifford, 119
Williams, G. W., 149
Williams, Philip, 134
Williams, Tennessee
  Cat on a Hot Tin Roof, 1
  Streetcar Named Desire, 7
Wilson, Harold S., *On the Design of Shakespearian Tragedy* (1957), 134 and n., 135
Wilson, John Dover, 92, 94 n., 129 n., 132, 142, 143, 150
Wollaton Hall, 11
Woodward, 100
Worsley, Joyce, 119
Wright, W. A., *see under* Clark, W. G.
Wymark, Patrick, 128

Yeats, W. B., 72
Yorkshire Tragedy, A, 36
Young, C. B., 147

Zbierski, Henryk, *Shakespeare and the 'War of the Theatres'*, 140 and n.